The Purpose of Boys

PARENTING

Nurture the Nature: Understanding and Supporting Your Child's
Unique Core Personality
The Wonder of Children
(previously published as *The Soul of the Child*)
The Wonder of Girls
The Wonder of Boys
A Fine Young Man
The Good Son
What Stories Does My Son Need?
(with Terry Trueman)

PSYCHOLOGY

What Could He Be Thinking?
Love's Journey
Mothers, Sons and Lovers
The Prince and the King

EDUCATION

The Minds of Boys (with Kathy Stevens)
Boys and Girls Learn Differently!: A Guide for Teachers and Parents
(with Patricia Henley and Terry Trueman)
The Boys and Girls Learn Differently Action Guide for Teachers
(with Arlette C. Ballew)
Strategies for Teaching Boys and Girls—Elementary Level:
A Workbook for Educators
Strategies for Teaching Boys and Girls—Secondary Level: A Workbook for Educators
Successful Single Sex Classrooms: A Practical Guide for Teaching Boys and Girls Differently
(with Kathy Stevens and Peggy Daniels)

BUSINESS-CORPORATE

Leadership and the Sexes: Using Gender Science to Create Success in Business
(with Barbara Annis)
The Leading Partners Workbook (with Katherine Coles and Kathy Stevens)

FOR YOUNG ADULTS

Understanding Guys
From Boys to Men

FICTION AND POETRY

The Miracle
An American Mystic
The Odyssey of Telemachus
Emptying
As the Swans Gather

BY THE GURIAN INSTITUTE

It's a Baby Boy! (with Adrian Goldberg and Stacie Bering)
It's a Baby Girl! (with Adrian Goldberg and Stacie Bering)

The Purpose of Boys

HELPING OUR SONS FIND MEANING,
SIGNIFICANCE, AND DIRECTION
IN THEIR LIVES

Michael Gurian

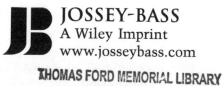

JOSSEY-BASS
A Wiley Imprint
www.josseybass.com

Published by Jossey-Bass
A Wiley Imprint
989 Market Street, San Francisco, CA 94103-1741—www.josseybass.com

Readers should be aware that Internet Web sites offered as citations and/or sources for further information may have changed or disappeared between the time this was written and when it is read. Readers should be aware that some of the anecdotes in this book, including some gathered from media reports, are composites of two or more comments or stories that needed to be shortened for narrative flow. In no cases have meanings been changed, and none involved statistics. In some cases, names have been changed.

Jossey-Bass books and products are available through most bookstores. To contact Jossey-Bass directly call our Customer Care Department within the U.S. at 800-956-7739, outside the U.S. at 317-572-3986, or fax 317-572-4002.

Jossey-Bass also publishes its books in a variety of electronic formats. Some content that appears in print may not be available in electronic books.

Library of Congress Cataloging-in-Publication Data

Gurian, Michael.
    The purpose of boys : helping our sons find meaning, significance, and direction in their lives / Michael Gurian.
        p.   cm.
    Includes bibliographical references and index.
    ISBN 978-0-470-24337-4 (cloth)
    1. Boys—United States.   2. Parent and child—United States.   3. Achievement motivation in boys—United States.   I. Title.
HQ775.G823   2009
155.43'20973—dc22
                                                                        2008045993

Printed in the United States of America
FIRST EDITION
HB Printing   10 9 8 7 6 5 4 3 2 1

CONTENTS

For:

Gail, Gabrielle, and Davita,
my first family

Kathy Stevens, Alan Rinzler,
and everyone in my second family

All the boys, parents, teachers, and others who make up
an ever-expanding third family for all the sons of our world

ACKNOWLEDGMENTS

This book grows from the inspiration and work of many people, both professional and personal. Alan Rinzler, my editor, has joined me for almost two decades in writing efforts that seek to help families and our culture understand our children. He is an editor and also a friend, and I thank him for his devotion to this work.

At Jossey-Bass and John Wiley, Alan is surrounded by a wonderful group of publishers and staff. Many thanks to Debra Hunter, Paul Foster, Jennifer Wenzel, Carol Hartland, Nana K. Twumasi, Andrea Flint, Donna Cohn, and all of you who care so much about families and the cultural changes we are all involved in.

A big thank-you also to Candice Fuhrman, my advocate and agent, who has shepherded this and so many other worthy projects through the publishing process.

Many thanks also to Kathy Stevens, Kelley King, Don Stevens, Daniel Amen, MD, Fran Spielhagen, PhD, Judith Kleinfeld, PhD, Tom Mortenson, PhD, the board of the Boys Project, Lori Ames, Robert Haley, the 100 Black Men Organization of Atlanta, and so many other professionals who care about the purpose of boys.

My deep thanks to the moms, dads, grandparents, and other family members who have shared their wisdom and stories, both through my family therapy practice and through public dialogues.

My thanks also to my brother Phil, whose Web and research talents provide magic from the Internet. He can locate things I couldn't even dream of finding!

My thanks to the Gurian Institute's certified trainers and associates, who have shared their stories with me so that I could share them with you. Our training institute (www.gurianinstitute.com) has had the honor of working in thousands of schools and communities in the United States and abroad because individuals, professionals, and caring institutions have helped us to do so.

This book is the result of twenty-five years of research, both scholarly and wisdom-of-practice, and of listening to what others are doing and thinking about boys. Our sons' lives today represent one of the largest cultural shifts in human history. My thanks to all of you who, through your generous actions, care for the purpose of boys.

Purpose: aim, intention, determination; by design; to put before oneself something to be done or accomplished

—AMERICAN COLLEGE DICTIONARY

The Purpose of Boys

INTRODUCTION: WHAT DO YOU WANT TO BE, SON?

What do you want me to be? I want to be somebody! I just want to be somebody!

—WORDS OF A THIRD-GRADE BOY, REPEATED TO ME BY
SUSAN TRAVERS, HIS TEACHER

MY FATHER-IN-LAW, DEAN REID, NOW GRAY-HAIRED, thin, eighty-five, and a man of few words, was twenty-two, blond-haired, and full of vigor when he flew B-12 bombers over an embattled Europe in 1943. Shot down in Germany, he ejected from his pilot seat, saw that his crew was dead, and limped north toward Norway. Captured by Nazi infantry before he could make it back to freedom, he lived out the rest of World War II in Nazi POW camps near Marburg and Nuremburg.

After his liberation in 1945, he returned to Nebraska, and to his sweetheart, Margaret. During their five decades of marriage, he didn't speak more than a few words to her about his wartime experiences. When I met my wife, Gail, the third child of Margaret and Dean Reid, she told me her father had been shot down in World War II, but "He just doesn't discuss it." Indeed, during the first decade of our marriage, he did not.

But in 1997, when Dean was seventy-four, his mind and heart opened. The film *Saving Private Ryan* affected him deeply, and he decided to show his family, including his wife, children, and grand-children, journals and notes from his time in the war. He recalled how it felt to be the pilot so young, so powerless to save his comrades. He also recalled how committed he felt, when he was liberated from the POW camp and came home, to "being a man."

"A guy had to figure out pretty quick how to become a man, or he wouldn't survive," Dean said. "When I got home, I didn't think too much: I just got to work and raised a family. It's what everyone had fought and died for."

What was it in *Saving Private Ryan* that triggered Dean to look back at his war experiences and share his wisdom? It was many things, he told me, especially what happens at the end of the film, when Captain Miller (Tom Hanks), who has been a mentor to young private Ryan (Matt Damon), dies after a battle on a bridge. His right hand trembling, his eyes closing, Miller whispers to Ryan his last words of wisdom: "Earn this." Ryan hears the whisper amid the storms of noises around him, watches Miller die, then stands up.

The camera watches his young face for a moment, then his face transforms into the face of an elderly man, Private Ryan in his mid-seventies, standing at Captain Miller's grave among the rows of white crosses at Arlington Cemetery. This elder Ryan's children and grand-children are behind him as he turns to his wife, tears in his eyes, and murmurs, "Did I do it? Am I a good man?" His wife is surprised by the question, perhaps because her husband, like Dean, has not spoken of his struggles or the "earn this" during the war, but she responds tenderly, "You did. You are."

If you have not watched this movie and you are raising or educating sons, I hope you will. For Dean Reid and for so many of us, a great deal of what males are striving for in the world, both as boys and men, is glimpsed in the film's final moments. Captain Miller's final words to Private Ryan instruct him to do the very thing that my father-in-law had to do. By saying, "Earn this," the mentor, Miller, is in effect saying to Ryan, "Everyone in this war has died so that you, young man, can live—what will you do with your life? Will you become a good man? Will you live out an important purpose in your life? Manhood is a sacred trust bestowed on you by everyone who has come before and sacrificed all so that you could get your chance to be free. Don't waste it."

Competing Purposes

I was born in 1958, and like so many boys my age, grew up enamored of World War II male heroism. At the same time, as a baby boomer, I came of age in a generation where the male role began one of its most significant shifts in human history. The boys and men of the baby boomer generation experienced a profound change in their self-concept of what is a man, what is an appropriate male role, and how we can, as men, relate to women.

My parents, Jack and Julia Gurian, were five years younger than Gail's parents, Dean and Margaret. My parents helped define my vision of boyhood and manhood by taking my brother, sister, and me on peace marches. My father had served as an instructor in the Air Force between the Second World War and the Korean War, before I was born. But now that they had children, both of my parents (as university professors and later cultural officers in the American Foreign Service), spent their youthful energy fighting against the Vietnam War. Unlike Dean's coming of age fighting the evil of Nazi fascism in aerial battles (and internment), my parents came of age protesting a war they considered immoral, and volunteering through state social service agencies to help returning troops utilize the GI Bill and resettle into American life. My parents' heroes were Mahatma Gandhi and Martin Luther King, not John Wayne or the Green Berets. My father fulfilled his role and purpose as a man by turning away from violence and, alongside my mother, teaching the bravery of nonviolence.

Needless to say, I grew through boyhood and toward manhood with competing internal trajectories. I loved John Wayne movies, and with my brother, played GI Joe in the backyard when my parents weren't looking. When I came indoors or went on a peace march with my parents, however, I did so as a follower of Gandhi's philosophy.

One evening in 1968, I remember the two sides of my budding male self coming together. I was ten, standing with my family outside a jail entrance as my father and a number of other protestors against the war in Vietnam—mainly professors and students—were released following their arrest at a nonviolent peace march. Shouts of support rang out around us, but also, just a few feet away were shouts of opposition from protestors who supported the war—many of them dressed in camouflage uniforms. Some of them, Vietnam, Korean, and World War II vets, stood at attention, proud and ready for anything. I respected my father, my mother, and the other adults in our community for their brave purpose; I also envied the soldiers their uniforms and powerful role in beating away the forces of evil. I was a young adolescent boy who wondered which course would bring the most glory and respect, the most passion, the biggest thrill, and the most meaning and success.

I see myself now as somewhat emblematic of the confusion of the males of my generation. The traditional masculine role was being deconstructed, yet we boys yearned to hold on to its clarities of male purpose. A new role for boys and men was trying to germinate and grow, yet it was murky, and caught up in familial and social tensions not sufficiently resolved to help boys become men of clarity. So, for me, in 1968, and well into the seventies and eighties, my clear purpose in life didn't emerge as early as that of Dean, Margaret, Jack, or Julia. My situation back then, common to many men of my generation, is becoming even more confusing and potentially dangerous today for the boys, women, and culture of the X, Y, and Millennial generations.

What Is the Purpose of Boys?

As an advocate for children, I see a world in which boys are asking us every day, and mainly through their actions, "What is the purpose of boys?" And for the most part, our culture is answering, "We don't know." This is not an ideal situation, neither for male development nor human development, and so this book is about finding a better answer.

How This Book Proposes to Answer the Question

Those of you who care about boys today are poised to answer the question, "What is the purpose of boys?" in all that you do every day. This book is an eight-chapter tool kit for helping you. It is a map you can use to help your son wrestle with everyday life events and growth. It is a way to help your son seek a successful future, while still a boy, adolescent, and young man.

In Chapter One, "The Loss of Purpose in American Boyhood," I'll present research regarding what can happen to boys who are not helped toward a rigorous and joyful purpose during the first two decades of their development. I will show that if boys are not directed toward joyful roles and positive purpose, they can be manipulated toward a socially isolating or dangerous purpose later on—they may remain aimless and unmotivated, even lost, as adult males who grow male bodies but do not become fully loving, wise, and successful men.

In Chapters Two through Four, we'll look carefully at fascinating science-based information about what is happening inside your sons as they grow up, from birth through early adulthood, seeking motivation, self-confidence, purpose, and meaning, in both their biology and culture. I'll present new models for understanding boys' development and each chapter will include tips and tools for communicating with your son as he grows. These will help you develop, in concert with him, a deep and fruitful answer to the question of purpose in his life.

Part Two of the book includes four chapters of insight, practical strategies, and social and emotional tools with which you can develop and lead a team of family members to care for your son. We'll specifically explore the roles of:

- The nuclear and extended family
- Communities and neighborhoods
- The best schools for boys
- Specific rite-of-passage experiences

We'll look at tools that you and everyone around you can use as an organized "team" to ensure boys' success and happiness. In all these chapters, I'll feature practical strategies that have been proven—not just in the United States but around the world—to help mold successful sons.

Tools We Need to Develop Purpose in Boys

The models and insights in *The Purpose of Boys* are presented in such a way that you can apply them immediately. Their usefulness and wisdom grows from:

1. Research in new biological sciences, which are teaching us amazing things about boy biology and its "hardwiring" toward the development of purpose. As a researcher in brain biology since 1983, and a therapist who specializes in how males and females develop differently, also as author of *The Wonder of Boys* and *The Minds of Boys,* I have been studying the biology of boyhood for a quarter century. The models and insights in this book are based on human biology seen through a nonstereotyping, science-based lens.

2. Insights from social anthropology, which can help us understand the importance of building purpose into boys' lives from a historical and cultural perspective. Positive attention is being paid in our culture recently to the issue of purpose. *The Purpose Driven Life,* by Rick Warren, has focused readers on life purpose from a Christian perspective. Eckhart Tolle's *A New Earth: Awakening to Your Life's Purpose* has approached the topic in a more new age way. *To Kindle a Soul,* by Lawrence Kelemen, has explored a child's development of purpose from a Jewish perspective. Stanford University's William Damon has looked at youth and purpose development in more secular terms in his recent *The Path to Purpose.* *The Purpose of Boys* takes the growing social dialogue into a practical parenting vision specifically for *boys'* development.

3. Crucial sociological research regarding how many of our sons are receiving too little help from social institutions in developing a sense of purpose—purpose is too little understood in the male context—and therefore failing to thrive, whether in school, work, or marriage and parenting.

4.   Anecdotes from parents, teachers, and mentors like you, who have shared their success stories about raising sons with our Gurian Institute team, providing tried-and-true practical advice. Throughout this book, you'll find stories, anecdotes, and insights from parents and caregivers who have been guiding the male development of purpose with success and a beautiful, joyful sense of mission. You'll visit schools that have improved boys' lives by making curricula relevant and purposeful in male development. You will meet whole communities of people whose lives have been changed by their understanding of the development of a boy toward purpose.

5.   Words of wisdom from ancient and modern sources regarding purpose development in boys, such as Theodore Roosevelt, Mark Twain, Eleanor Roosevelt, Thomas Hughes, William Blake, and many others, whose teachings appear throughout the book.

6.   Insight about how to activate "a developmental journey to meaning" in both boys and men, including models gained from my own family therapy practice, and from other professionals who focus on the development of purpose and well-being in boys and men. Over the last twenty years, I have developed the CORE model (Compassion, Honor, Responsibility, Enterprise), the Ten Integrities Teaching Tool, the Three Families Paradigm, and, with my training partner Kathy Stevens, the Boys and Girls Learn Differently! curriculum. These tools have been utilized and tested by tens of thousands of parents and teachers in more than two thousand schools and communities.

Specific Questions to Be Answered

Our children's grandparents and great-grandparents answered the question, "What is the purpose of boys?" in ways dictated by necessity. Our generation and the generations to come are not as limited by that necessity, but without such compelling necessity, we've come to a time in history when parents and children aren't sure what the purpose of our sons should be. We often do not answer the questions our sons are tacitly, and in their inner worlds, asking us.

When we were in our mid-twenties, Gail and I taught in Ankara, Turkey, and completed research in male and female development in village and city culture. In Ankara we met a lawyer who had been raised in a village near Diyarbakir, in southern Turkey. "In our villages," he said, "everyone works very hard together to craft our boys into men. We become afraid of them, if we don't. The last thing we want is for men to carry empty souls in their big bodies."

As we spoke, I understood what he meant by "craft our boys into men." He meant, first, helping them discover their own natural gifts, and second, helping them bring those gifts to a state of worthiness in the community. "Purpose," we agreed, meant "reason for being here," and "purpose of boys" meant "reason for being here as a man, at this time, on this earth."

As this lawyer knew, boys are asking questions about who they are every day. Parents and other caregivers are asking questions which, though they might not realize it, provide their sons with wonderful answers. *The Purpose of Boys* is written to help you answer hidden questions. Here are some that will be answered specifically in this book:

- How can I help my late-maturing son?
- How do I raise an emotionally intelligent son?
- What does it mean to raise "a man of character"?
- What discussion starters can I use to reach my son, especially when he seems to be putting up walls against me?
- What does a purposeful family and community look like?
- How do I teach boys as much empathy as I do toughness?
- What kind of discipline destroys a boy's spirit, and what kind enlivens his inner drive to succeed?
- What practical things can schools do to make the classroom more helpful for boys?
- What specific rites of passage can we develop so every son can have a safe and powerful journey throughout adolescence to manhood?
- What is the role of video games, the Internet, and other technologies in a modern boy's search for meaning and purpose—and what limits are crucial for sons of different ages?

- What are the distinct gifts of mothers, fathers, and others in providing boys a path to purpose and meaning?
- How can we help boys integrate their sexual urges into a sense of purpose in love and intimacy?
- How can we raise sons to be good husbands and fathers?

We Who Care for Boys and Men

We who care today about the lives of boys and men have an immediate and profound mission, inherent in our position as mothers and fathers, teachers, mentors, citizens, and friends. That mission is nothing less than to help each boy develop into a creative spirit, trustworthy friend, moral leader, and meaningful man. Our mission is nothing less than to protect and nurture the future of humanity.

I believe every boy wants to find his purpose in life. Every boy is trying to overcome bumps on the road while he is a boy. We cannot walk the road for him every step of the way, but we must at least bring him to it and help point him in the right direction. This book is devoted to that adventure—for ultimately, I believe, we are each called to the practical task of helping one boy at a time awaken, direct, and animate his inborn and natural call to be fully human.

As you read this book, I hope that your sons, like your daughters, will make you most proud when they surpass you. I hope they will awaken one day during adulthood and realize, "I am on a path of service to my family, friends, and community, I am doing what I was born to do, and I could not have gotten here without the help I got along the way."

PART

Understanding the
Purpose of Boys

Boys are so filled with yearning and adventure, I don't want to lose a single one. I want to help all of them channel their energy creatively and wisely, like the heroes they read about in books.

—ALISON HARBAUGH, LIBRARIAN AND
GRANDMOTHER OF SIX GRANDSONS

The Loss of Purpose in American Boyhood

> How are our boys needed in the world? They need to be needed, but these days they aren't sure how to be needed. That's not only sad—it's potentially dangerous.
>
> —JUDITH KLEINFELD, PROFESSOR OF PSYCHOLOGY AND
> DIRECTOR OF THE BOYS PROJECT

AS YOU READ THIS BOOK, I hope you'll find it joyful and filled with hope about the future. Yet it can't be an honest book—nor can we be fully honest parents and caregivers of our sons—if we don't take a moment to look at what is happening to boys, men, and male development in our culture.

A mother of three children recently put it this way:

I have a son, fifteen, and two daughters, thirteen and nineteen. All of us try to help my son focus, but he just doesn't seem to care about anything. He's a great kid, there's nothing wrong with him morally or personally, but he just doesn't seem to go anywhere. He's getting Cs and Ds in school (his sisters do much better), and he skips a lot of classes. He does like Lacrosse, but mainly because he's good at it, and he likes his friends. Other than that, he plays video games, chats online, and listens to his iPod. He isn't disrespectful to me or any of us in his family, except when we try to prod him to go out and DO something. That just makes him mad.

After a talk I gave recently, a father told me,

> I think boys and girls are very different. My daughter will do what-
> ever is right in front of her, and try to do it well. A birth defect
> keeps her from being athletic, but that doesn't stop her—she works
> hard in school, and she started working in a Baskin-Robbins when
> she was sixteen. So it's not like life is easy for my daughter, but for
> my son, it's like he thinks life should be easy. He thinks stuff should
> come to him, and if it doesn't come easy, to heck with it. And he's
> really pie-in-the-sky. He thinks way ahead—I'm gonna be Bill Gates,
> he says—but he can't see right now. I think maybe I was like that
> too, at his age, but my work ethic was stronger.

Both of these parents are sensing a similar undercurrent in boys'
cultural lives today by observing their own sons.

Another parent's email began,

> I am the mother of three sons. They are twenty-one, nineteen, and
> seventeen. My youngest has struggled with school since the sixth
> grade. He went into the special education process in seventh grade.
> He gave up on school in his junior year of high school, and we
> got him in the alternative school. He dropped out of that and left
> home and now works at the beach. He has no plans to come
> back home or go back to school. Our whole family has been in and
> out of counseling with him for years, but still we can't figure out
> what to do. He just doesn't seem to find himself.

I have received thousands of messages like this over the last decade,
and I have talked with thousands of parents of boys and girls. In 2005,
after publishing an article in the *Washington Post* called "Disappearing
Act" (which asked the public to wonder why so many boys in culture-
rich America were "disappearing" from positive, motivated, and directed
life paths), I received more than a thousand emails in one week. Parents,
teachers, and policymakers wrote to express their love of boys and young
men, as well as their fear of losing them; their desire to help them, as well
as their lack of clarity on how to do so; and their sense that school and
life were feeling irrelevant and purposeless to many of their own sons.
The writers all expressed their feeling that easy fixes are not available.

Why Parents Want to Provide Purpose for Boys

In nearly every email of this kind that I've received, I hear a hidden song, one of great hunger that I've been listening to for decades, and one that I believe a whole culture is beginning to sing loudly: Parents realize that boys and young men need a purpose in life, and that far too many don't have one. Parents sense that a boy's lack of purpose—his lack of a drive toward a reason for being, important role, and sense of being needed—and society's gradual diminishing of its focus on providing what males need are the foundation of so many other issues that we face with boys and young men.

The following are some of the core issues of male purposelessness as noted by parents:

- Schools filled with caring teachers and staff, but schools *not* set up to care for and motivate boys in the ways many of them need
- Media imagery and social dialogues that attack males as defective and dangerous (and, quite often, just plain stupid) without also providing a variety of strong role models
- Single moms hungry to raise adolescent sons, but lacking a full range of resources to help them, especially when the boys are going through puberty
- Families in which men may be available, but where the men don't fully understand their crucial and specific role in bringing purpose to their sons' lives
- Grandparents and other mentors who care deeply, but are not fully embraced in their role as carriers of purpose, lineage, and high expectations for boys
- A culture that does not understand what an important role the whole community and neighborhood play in caring for a son
- Workplaces helping young women secure employment, but assuming young men will do just fine at landing a job, even though millions are not finding useful work
- The society as a whole pursuing child development issues without understanding how important are the naturally different issues that boys and girls face

The Impact That a Lack of Purpose Can Have on Boys

Ultimately, the parental message and voices I've encountered over the past ten years reveal an awakening across the country to the fact that boys are indeed struggling. Dr. Tom Mortenson of the Pell Institute, a founding member of the Boys Project and an expert in the changing state of males, has collected findings regarding boys' mental, emotional, physical, and economic health in a number of reports, including *The State of American Manhood*. (References for the Project and this very important report are provided for you in the Notes and References to this book.) Following are some of Dr. Mortenson's stunning statistics:

- For every 100 girls suspended from public elementary and secondary schools, 250 boys are suspended. For every 100 girls expelled, 335 boys are expelled.
- For every 100 girls diagnosed with a learning disability, 276 boys are so diagnosed.
- For every 100 girls diagnosed with emotional disturbance, 324 boys are so diagnosed.
- For every 100 girls ages 15–19 who commit suicide, 549 boys in the same range kill themselves.
- For every 100 women ages 20–24 who commit suicide, 624 men of the same age kill themselves.
- For every 100 girls ages 15–17 in correctional facilities, there are 837 boys behind bars.
- For every 100 women ages 18–21 in correctional facilities, there are 1,430 men behind bars.
- For every 100 women enrolled in college, there are 77 men enrolled.
- For every 100 American women who earn an associate's degree, 67 American men earn the same degree.
- For every 100 American women who earn a bachelor's degree, 73 American men earn the same degree.

- For every 100 American women who earn a master's degree, 62 American men earn the same degree.

The Dark Side of Males Without Purpose

It is crucial to remember that the statistics don't just grow from issues in one socioeconomic group. As Judith Kleinfeld, director of the Boys Project, has pointed out, "Even white males of high earning college educated parents are increasingly falling behind equivalent females." She is joined by Jacqueline King of the American Council on Education, whose research showed that just in the last ten years, even this group of privileged boys and young men are "checking out" of school—either not going or not finishing—at rates much higher than girls. And Boys Project researcher Melana Zyla Vickers points out, "White boys are the only demographic group whose high school drop-out rate has risen since 2000." Literacy researcher Richard Whitmire has collected findings on boys and education in his work at *USA Today*. He points out, "There are ten million women in college this year versus 7.4 million men."

Our sons are not only losing a sense of educational purpose in school and college. They are also losing a sense of social purpose in their behavior—filling our juvenile justice system and prisons. They are losing a sense of purpose in their hearts and souls—committing suicide and harming others at alarming rates. In each of these areas, they are increasingly falling behind or failing at life.

According to a new Justice Department study, seven million Americans are now in the criminal justice system. This is a fivefold increase over the last two decades. Ninety-three percent of American inmates are males. Among African American males, the loss of purpose is stunning. Between 40 and 50 percent of African American boys and young men will enter the criminal justice system sometime in their lives. Violent crime and violent death rates for this population of young males is now epidemic.

THE JOY OF PURPOSE

It Is Not Far, It Is Within Reach

Dear son, not I, not anyone else can travel the road for you,
You must travel it for yourself,
But it is not far, it is within reach,
Perhaps you have been on it since you were born and did
   not know,
Perhaps it is everywhere on water and on land.
O sit a while dear son,
Here are biscuits to eat, here is milk to drink,
But as soon as you renew yourself in sweet clothes,
Wash the gum from your eyes,
Habit yourself to the dazzle of the light and every moment
   of your life.
Long have you timidly waded holding a plank by the shore,
Now I will you to be a bold swimmer,
To jump off in the midst of the sea, rise again, shout
   and laughingly dash with your hair!

—Walt Whitman, adapted from *Leaves of Grass, Song of Myself*

The Breakdown of Male Purpose Development

In the past, young men learned strategies for success through concentrated efforts of parents, grandparents and other extended family, schools, faith communities, and role development (by "role" I mean "a sense of being needed, a reason for being, a purpose in life") in their culture. All of these formerly positive influences are in flux or breaking down. And though it has been important to overcome the limiting and oppressive male and female roles of the past, it is also crucial to note that each role change has ramifications for men, women, children, and society. We have looked carefully at the female side of the role changes of the last forty years. The following are a few of the crucial male issues in the breakdown of roles:

- The relationship between boys and their fathers is deteriorating. According to the Center for Media and the Family in Minneapolis, boys now relate directly to their fathers, on average, one-half hour per week, but spend over forty hours a week in front of screens (video games, TV, movies, Internet). As families break down and boys spend less and less time with either or both parents, their development of conversations and a sense of role modeling and purpose can be profoundly affected.

  Decades and centuries ago, boys often had absent fathers—this is not a new phenomenon—but when the father was away in another city to work, or to fight a war, or was dead, boys had grandfathers and other men to teach them how to be men, including what ideals a man should sacrifice himself for, and how a man remains motivated to succeed and set goals.

- Schoolboys, mismatched in school systems that are not set up for male energy, are being medicated for behavioral issues at alarming rates. Eighty-five percent of the world's Ritalin is used on boys in the United States. The use of antipsychotic drugs on children in general, and boys in particular, has gone up 500 percent since 1993. For some boys, medication is crucial for well-balanced living. But for many, it's a device to stifle their natural behavior, smother and prevent them from fully comprehending and utilizing their own natural assets, many of which are simply no longer understood in our culture.

- A century ago, the schooling of boys would have involved more debates, more competition, more outdoor learning, more hands-on apprenticeship, more coaching in purpose and meaning. Now, many boys cannot find relevance or the male learning style in their schooling.

• Boys are increasingly unsure of their roles as men, to the extent that they mature into adulthood one to two decades later than they did just one hundred years ago. The number of young men in their twenties living at home and unemployed increases every year in Western cultures—not only in the United States, but throughout Europe, Australia, and the industrialized world. Even in countries where you wouldn't expect this to be an issue, it is. In Jordan, for instance, which is modernizing quickly, many boys are growing up lacking college or life skills and without clear social roles. A new study shows that Jordanian women are "marrying down," that is, having to become both the major money earner and child-care provider in the new marriages.

UNDERSTANDING PURPOSE

The Impact That Boys' Lack of Purpose Has on Women

On the surface, the fact that males mature late, go to college at lower rates than women, and don't develop a clear sense of an educational or social role would seem to be empowering to women. But the difficulty with this view becomes clear when a woman wants to marry and have a family (and most women do). Now the children's mother no longer has broad options for mothering her infants and toddlers. In our changing economy, her husband often cannot earn enough money to support the family (just a college education alone increases one's earning power by over one-third). The man is also a less mature prospect for long-term marriage. Because over 95 percent of early child care worldwide is provided by mothers and women, the lack of male maturity, sense of purpose, and earning power become significant issues for women.

• Boys are increasingly eating and drinking without purpose. According to the American Medical Association, 40 percent of boys are now overweight or obese. Their food intake, and their lack of exercise and time in nature show a disconnection in their growing minds between the reality of their body's needs and a natural sense of purpose for that body's development and action.

Simultaneously, boys are increasingly binge drinking. And though boys have, of course, always engaged in drinking and binge drinking, the rate at which they escape life through binge drinking continues to increase, despite educational and public service programs that aim to help boys stop this dangerous behavior. These boys are often lost, self-medicating through food and drink.

• Increasingly, boys are randomly raging against, beating, and killing people. Across the United States, teenagers are finding baseball bats, golf clubs, paintball guns, knives, bricks, and other weapons and trolling the streets for homeless individuals to beat up. In Ft. Lauderdale, Florida, three young males beat up a homeless man while he slept, murdering him.

• This kind of purposeless violence—different in character from the kind of violence that young men like Grandpa Dean were conscripted into or volunteered for during wartime—is just one example of the new lack of male role and social purpose in male violence. For the young male perpetrators of today, thrill-seeking, dominance behavior, and initiation into gangs are not occurring in search of a life purpose that cares for family and society's survival, but quite often, and quite simply, to destroy society while gaining a temporary group success for which there is a high mortality rate. Ultimately, the gang becomes the role modeling agency, creating its own special kind of defensive self-protective "family" for boys tossed out by the larger society and culture; it also becomes the place in which the boys will die young.

The Wisdom of Purpose
THE ULTIMATE SPLENDID TRIUMPH

I wish to preach, not the doctrine of ignoble ease, but the doctrine of the strenuous life, the life of toil and effort, of labor and strife; to preach that highest form of success which comes, not to the man who desires mere easy peace, but to the man who does not shrink from danger, from hardship, or from bitter toil, and who out of these wins the ultimate splendid triumph. . . . In the last analysis a healthy state can exist only when the men and women who make it up lead clean, vigorous, healthy lives; when the children are so trained that they shall endeavor, not to shirk difficulties, but to overcome them; not to seek ease, but to know how to wrest triumph from toil and task. The man must be glad to do a man's work, to dare, endure and labor; to keep himself, and to keep those dependent upon him.

—Theodore Roosevelt, *No Man Is Happy If He Does Not Work*

There is a perfect storm brewing in the culture of boyhood. It is really three storms in one:

1. Males not knowing what their social roles should be
2. Families deteriorating around boys
3. Communities and schools not understanding boys' natural needs

We'll keep exploring these things as this book continues, and in each discussion we'll move immediately toward practical questions, answers, issues, and solutions.

Moving Forward with New Vision

The rest of this book will show how to help your son develop purpose— the "how to" begins in understanding how boys develop purpose and roles differently from girls, the subject of Chapter Two. Boys share many

Questions of Purpose
Son, Do You Know That You Are Important?

I hope you'll consider asking your son the following questions not once, but over a period of weeks or months. Ask one or two at a time while you and your son are doing something together, such as a household chore or a trip to the store, or enjoying a family vacation. Some boys enjoy keeping a journal, even if on a computer or iPhone, in which to express themselves, and ponder these questions.

- What is the most important thing you did today?
- What will be the most important things you do when you are a man?
- What kind of work do you want to do when you grow up?
- What is the role of a man in today's world?
- When does a boy become a man?
- What are the ways a man loves his family?
- Who are your heroes? Why?
- Is your school a good place for you as a growing boy? In what ways? In what ways is it hard for you?
- What do TV shows tell you about what defines a good man?
- What do your friends say a good man is? Can you ask them?

Discuss one or more of these issues by engaging your son in dialogue about grandparents, uncles, and aunts. Ask your son what he knows about what the men did with their lives "back in the old country." In every family, there are male and female role models equivalent to Grandpa Dean and Margaret in my wife's family, or my own parents in mine.

qualities with girls, but they also need us to recognize their differences in a fresh and exciting way.

A mother who is also a social worker brought up a crucial point about this dialogue in a parent workshop: "I get how important it is to talk about role and role models when you talk about boys, but as a feminist, I want you to know I'm wary of the word 'role.' If you are saying something new about the purpose of boys, that's fine with me—but I'd hate to see us end up in a place where men get to have a role that depends on women being weak. That would be just more of the same stuff that has been killing boys and girls, and oppressing women, for thousands of years."

This is an important point of view. Indeed, you'll notice in this book and in my work I use the word "purpose" much more than role, because the word "role" is laden with the kind of negative connotation that this mother was pointing out.

The Purpose of Boys presents a synthesis of two previous views of boys and men in what I hope is an uplifting, progressive vision. The traditionalist religious and biblical approach was the cultural "thesis" for the lives of boys and men. The feminist movement provided the "antithesis." For the sake of boys, it is time to absorb the best of the past in a synthesis, a combination and compromise that takes the best from both of these points of view.

In presenting a science-based vision of boys and men, this book combines the wisdom of the past, including our religious and ancestral lore, and the feminist deconstruction of conventional stereotypes of male entitlements, into a new vision of boys and purpose through both a scientific and common-sense lens.

I hope that, wherever you fall on the political spectrum, you will find theory and practical insight in the next seven chapters that resonate with your own experience of the boys around you. The vision of this book is based on my desire to help everyone gain a common language and find universal tools for caring for boys by understanding who they are and who we need them to be: men who know how to love, men who know how to "earn it," men whose role it is to be motivated by a deep commitment to service, success, empathy, and the common good.

2

How Little Boys Develop Their Sense of Purpose

Sam Witwicky, you hold the key to earth's survival.

—SPOKEN BY OPTIMUS PRIME TO SAM IN THE FILM *TRANSFORMERS*

IN HER WONDERFUL LITTLE COLLECTION of vignettes called *Up to No Good: The Rascally Things Boys Do,* editor Kitty Harmon asked men she dubbed "perfectly decent grown men" to reminisce about the rascally things they did as boys. One of those men, Charlie, recalls this vignette:

> Every summer I got together with my cousins who lived on a big farm in Iowa. I spent most of my time with "the twins," who were about my age, and for two weeks we were inseparable—playing Tom Sawyer and Huck Finn on a small crick, rodeo men trying to ride the backs of pigs, and so on.
>
> A favorite pastime was to torment another cousin, Mick, who was two years younger and visiting from California. One trick was to go out into the middle of the cow pasture and then sprint back to the barn. Since we were older, we could always get about twenty or thirty yards ahead of Mick, at which point we'd yell back: "Hurry up, Mick, the bull is running after you! He's about to gore you!" Mick would be running and sobbing. Poor guy.

The Empathy of Boys

When I tell this story at conferences of parents and educators, there is a sigh of empathy in all of us as we picture Mick sobbing. Men in the audience who were like Mick—younger, sensitive, naive, unsure of themselves (I was also one of these)—feel a special sympathy for him, as do just about all mothers of any son. There are such comments as, "How can boys be so cruel?"

Then, as our discussion about the boys in the story goes on, something interesting happens. Most of the men who were once like Mick also remember that sometime later in life they became more like the older boys. Many of the mothers admit that their own sensitive sons often became quite insensitive to other boys as they grew older.

Once, during a discussion, a mother asked the men in the room: "What do you guys get out of stuff like this? What are you after?" A mother of sons five and seven years old, she had seen this kind of behavior in her family and community many times, and it troubled her. "My husband treats my little boys this way," she said. "He's got no empathy, he thinks the boys are made of stone and can take anything he dishes out."

At this point I asked the group to let me continue Mick's story before we gave our answers. Charlie recalls:

> Then there was the electric fence that kept the cows in the pasture. I had my first lesson in physics when I touched the fence and felt a strong thump in my arm from the electric shock. I had the bright idea to try and get Mick to pee on the fence. I told him that it felt really great to have the electricity run through the urine up into your penis. Mick really wanted to be part of our gang, so he went ahead and peed on the fence. He let out a big yell and ran away holding his "thumped" penis. These days I'm careful not to mention the words "cow" and "electricity" around Mick.

Aggression Nurturance

After she heard this part of the story, the mother of the five- and seven-year-old sons cried, "I rest my case. How cruel can these guys get! No wonder boys feel like they always have to do battle!" Simultaneously, nearly everyone was smiling, chuckling, or laughing out loud. Even this mother herself was surprised to hear herself chuckling.

What a strangely humorous, paradoxical moment this was! Everyone in the room, even if unconsciously, wondered: How can we be laughing at this kind of cruelty? How can even the mother herself be smiling at the fate of a boy, just like her son, who was sobbing, then humiliated (and physically in pain), the butt of everyone's jokes?

The answers to these questions lie, I believe, in understanding the biology of boyhood, which I'll explore with you in this chapter—especially the male need to find guidance for his own innate drives toward role and purpose. When we guide male biology toward purpose, we help boys develop empathy and healthy power.

A key element in the biology and empathy development of boyhood is "aggression nurturance," the development of a boy's maturity through a form of teasing and aggression that can be perceived as quite hostile and cruel. You have probably noticed this aggression nurturance (which is different from the direct empathic nurturance girls often utilize) when a boy gives up nearly everything, including, temporarily, his self-esteem, in order to follow guidance on development of identity and purpose that gains him respect and status, such as via his participation in an aggressive game like that which Mick and his older friends engaged in.

Mick was willing to pee on the electric fence because he is honored to be helped toward manhood by the "cruel boys." In Mick's mind, he feels the humiliation and its incumbent pain, but he also feels that the older boys are actually being "friendly." They are treating him with respect ("you can survive this"). They are challenging this younger, lower-on-the-totem-pole boy to push himself through weakness—physical, mental, and emotional—toward strength, which will be his foundation for future success, performance, purpose, and engagement in life.

Because the older boys are still boys themselves, they don't think much about the consequences of their humiliation of Mick (this is the dark side of their behavior, which we'll explore in the next chapter). At the same time, the pain they are inflicting on Mick is not arbitrary: it's a form of ritualized aggression nurturance—a kind of male nurturing that is central to human survival, a distinctly male way of nurturing others.

What Our Ancestors Knew About the Cruelty of Boys

Sometimes we don't realize that everything boys play with and about can be laden with meaning for them. Every game they make up can be an experiment in the development of male roles, male empathy, and male purpose. Even though our ancestral cultures did not have access to brain science, they seem to have understood biological differences between boys and girls, including how to help boys through "aggression nurturance" somewhat better than we do. They had the instinct to respond to boys' aggressiveness (and even their cruelty) by building purpose into boys' everyday lives. Not to do so, they felt, was to rob boys of an essential place in the world, thus robbing the society of male talents, and ultimately creating danger for the society.

Here are some examples of what other cultures do and have done to help boys start, from early in life, on an organized journey of turning male energy into social good. Note the young ages at which they started these rituals. In a moment, we'll look at the biological and neural backdrop for their decision to do so.

- The Shavante tribe in South America begins boys on their initiation into adulthood at four years old. The elders of the tribe stand the boys in a line and compel them to learn songs and gestures of purposeful living that will become like mantras for manhood. The boys know that for about ten years they will be led in initiation rituals, many of which are much more difficult than this initial foray into social development. This long-term initiation by the tribe is empowering, both physically and emotionally, leading to the development of compassionate and service-oriented men.
- In various parts of the Middle East, Muslim boys enter adulthood training (often via a circumcision ceremony) at four or seven years old. The boys begin learning the prayer cycle they will practice as men, and begin learning themes that will carry them to

manhood. The Muslim ceremonies provide a communal direction of the boys toward service to the group. This kind of initiation is of course even more known by Western society via Jewish initiation rituals in which the boy learns, as early as possible, the prayers and story of the Torah, then becomes a "Jewish adult," by leading services as a bar mitzvah.

• Among the Masai tribe in Africa, boys begin learning the role of the sacred hunt as early as each boy can, even before puberty and sometimes as early as seven years old. This education leads to a sense of sacred meaning for males as adult caregivers and protectors of the society.

• In the Catholic traditions of Europe (and still to this day), boys are asked to begin serving the church as acolytes (in other words, "to carry the church") from very young. This "burden" is a way of directing their impressive male energy (energy often haphazard and undirected) toward service of community, family, and God.

I believe our ancestors understood some profound male-female differences. They saw something in boys' eyes—and they knew that although boys and girls needed a lot of similar socialization, boys need some different socialization, too. They saw three psychosocial drivers, rooted in male biology, inside every boy. I'll explore these drivers with you, via science and story, in this and the next two chapters.

These psychosocial drivers, primary elements of boy psychology, are the "magical boy," the "adolescent seeker," and the "heroic adult."

1.   A little boy's inner drive to develop self-esteem by identifying himself biologically and socially as a *"magical boy"* (he need not feel superior to girls, but he will feel different already). Before ten years old, he tries to develop male self-esteem via personal relationships and activities that bring both increased emotional literacy and competitive skill. (This chapter will explore biological and social aspects of this magical boy.)

2.   A pubescent and adolescent boy's journey in which he learns to channel his restless, complex, self-transforming energy by *seeking and finding* his personal maps and "truth" within his civilization's

hierarchy. It is as a young *seeker* that he develops self-discipline and pathways to success. Chapter Three will explore how the young seeker establishes himself in the world, and is helped on his journey during adolescence.

3.   The drive of a boy, adolescent male, or adult man (in whatever culture we find him) to become *heroic* in a "male" way that fits his culture. He hopes to seek and find not just a human purpose but a "male" purpose, an authentic, adult male self that is both equal to, but different from, the female. The purpose development of this adult male self will be the subject of Chapter Four.

Brain Differences Between Boys and Girls

Throughout this book you'll learn about evidence that boy psychology is not just socialized but also hardwired into our sons. I will argue that every boy is driven from deep within to try to become (in our metaphorical language) a magical boy, an adolescent seeker, and an adult hero. I believe these drives (which we can under-nurture if we don't understand them) to be central to human development: basic drives toward purpose that have been building in male genetics and the male psyche for almost a million years.

Thankfully, recent evidence from neurobiology can now help us see the inner world of boys. Neurobiologists have been able to track over one hundred biological differences between the male and female brain. The following are just a few that we'll see apply beautifully to the male way of developing empathy, social maturity, and purpose, and most importantly, to his need for our help in nurturing, fully, his development of these assets.

- There is 15–20 percent more neural activity in a girl's brain than a boy's at a given time. Neither the boy's or girl's brain is superior or inferior, but differences in brain activity enable different parts of the female brain to work simultaneously in ways that the male brain does not. The male brain tends to compartmentalize its brain activity into fewer brain centers than the female brain does.

- Girls and women have a greater number of nerve fibers in their skin as boys and men. Thus, pressure receptors on the skin and pain receptors in the brain are less sensitive in the male brain than in the female. Males feel pain, of course, but their bodies and brains feel less pain and move less experience of felt pain through the brain at any given moment than does a girl's body and brain.

- Boys' brains have more gray matter, and girls' brains more white matter. Gray matter, a kind of neurotransmitter, localizes, compartmentalizes, and keeps brain activity in a single place in the brain—for instance, in an aggressive part of the brain—rather than spreading activity throughout other parts of the brain, such as in an area that reads emotions. White matter, however, constantly networks brain activity to different parts of the brain, including emotion and empathy centers.

- A boy's brain "shuts off" (enters a rest state) more times per day than a girl's brain tends to do—as a result, boys and girls generally have different approaches to paying attention, visioning their future, completing a task, de-stressing, feeling emotions, relating to others, becoming bored, and even having basic conversations.

- In the male brain, especially in the right hemisphere, there are more neural centers than in the female brain that focus on how objects move around in physical space. Boys spend more time than girls manipulating and testing cubes, footballs, other kinds of balls, rocks, and other physical objects, and also relate to other people more than girls do with balls, darts, sticks, paint guns, bulls, fences, and thousands of other objects as "relational intermediaries"—objects that make relationship comfortable for males.

- A girl's brain processes information and experience in different parts of the brain at different times than a boy's does, including the aggression-emotion center, the amygdala. Because of such structural differences in the brain we all tend to sense that "boy energy" and "girl energy" are different. Boy energy tends more than girl energy toward physical hitting of each other as a bonding mechanism, jabbing at one another, bantering, and other dominance and aggression activities through which to relate and show love.

- A boy's hippocampus (a major memory center in the brain) is generally less active than that of a girl, especially during most emotional and relational experiences. Living out his developmental journey, a boy may not recall portions of it that a girl will recall, and not be sure what to do next, but a girl can often more fluidly multitask in memory and in her daily life. More than girls, boys will often wish they received more external guidance for what memories are important to their inner motivation, their future success, and their personal power.
- A girl's occipital, parietal, temporal, and frontal lobes are all generally more active than those of a boy. One outcome of this is less linkage in a boy's brain between memory centers and other centers that pick up sensation (seeing, hearing, touching), and to the word-making centers of the brain. Therefore, girls will often have a greater sensorial experience of their surroundings at any given moment, store more of this in their memories, attach more of the experience to emotions, and finally connect more of those sensorial experiences, memories, and emotions to words.

UNDERSTANDING PURPOSE

Biochemical Differences Between Boys and Girls

The structural differences between boys' and girls' brains are augmented by chemical differences, as follows:

- Boys have between ten and twenty times more testosterone than girls do. Testosterone is a risk-taking and aggression chemical.
- Boys have less of the bonding chemical, oxytocin. Boys certainly bond, but they do not tend to reach out to and bond with as many people as girls do. They often need more help in finding

crucial bonding opportunities and "moments." They will often need us to structure for them team games and mentoring systems in which they can form "boy bonds," where talk and emotionality generally follows action and doing.

- Boys often have less serotonin, a chemical that calms us down, and they often have less serotonin moving through their frontal lobe (the decision-making part of the brain). With less serotonin, boys are generally more physically and socially impulsive, have more trouble controlling themselves than girls, and their decision making is often less "thought through" than that of girls, especially in adolescence.

How Boys and Girls Need Purpose Differently

Brain and biochemical differences don't create superiority or inferiority for either boys and girls. Nor do they create "opposites." Girls and boys share a lot of characteristics, and girls and boys can do equally well in school, the workplace, and the home. To point out difference is not to engage in limiting any person. But to avoid difference would be to miss out on seeing into the souls of boys, and noticing certain things that boys are crying out for.

A Boy's Need for Direction

Think about boys' brain and biological differences for a moment. Look at how they add up to a deep need for boys to be directed toward emotion-laden experiences before many of them can become emotionally empathic. Consider how boys need to be led to motivation by role models before they become motivated to carve out an identity for themselves. Have you noticed how they often need to be led to purpose before they can lead purposefully?

Unlike girls, boys don't experience a hormonal cycle every month by which their blood and body and even biochemistry shift internally toward cognizance of a possible child within them. An African saying is appropriate to this point: "A girl can know that life will grow right beneath her heart—a boy cannot. He knows he will have to grow life with his hands." Even when quite little, boys already know this. In studies of day-care centers, boys have been recorded putting pillows under their shirts to try to show they can be pregnant, then realizing they never can be pregnant. Already at three and four they know they are biochemically different from girls, though they cannot yet understand the biological mechanics involved.

And given the fewer verbal-emotive centers in male brains, we are probably not surprised to notice that even when little, boys will often try to *do* something rather than *talk* about it. They will be more physically active and less verbally adroit about feelings and emotions. The outcome can be less opportunity to learn verbally from other people's experience; consequently boyhood emotional experiences are based more on trial and error, which leads to higher risk and failure rates.

Because of brain-blood flow differences, boys are also more likely than girls to spend larger parts of their day "zoning out" (or, in the extreme, "unable to pay attention"). The brain activity differences between male and female brains means that a boy may need extra help from parents, caregivers, and mentors in finding the right projects to attend to—projects that won't bore him, projects and mentors that motivate him, projects that he is daydreaming about, perhaps, but can't quite bring down to earth. He needs to find projects that he will pay attention to and this will help create a sense of purpose that he did not have before.

How Boys Learn Purpose from Without

Girls, too, need projects, mentors, maps, and purpose—but girls don't spend as much time in internal states of boredom, in situations of long restlessness. Girls don't generally tend to "daydream away their day" as much as boys. Girls multitask mentally and emotionally, and much more constantly, than boys may do. They "keep busy" from

THE JOY OF PURPOSE

Tom Sawyer's Day Dreams

A log raft in the river invited him, and he seated himself on its outer edge and . . . Tom presently began to drift. . . . What if he went away—ever so far away, into the unknown countries beyond the seas . . . (or) he would be a soldier, and return after long years, all war-worn and illustrious. No—better still, he would join the Indians, and hunt buffaloes and . . . come back a great chief, bristling with feathers . . . no, he would be a pirate! That was it! NOW his future lay plain before him, and glowing with unimaginable splendor. How his name would fill the world! How gloriously he would go plowing the dancing seas, in his long, low, black hulled racer, the Spirit of the Storm, with his grisly flag flying at the fore . . . and hear with swelling ecstasy "It's Tom Sawyer the Pirate!"

—Mark Twain, *The Adventures of Tom Sawyer*

internal motivations that many boys may not develop unless they get appropriate attention and maturation from their families and culture.

Boys don't have as much inner access as girls do to sensorial information, memory, or feelings. In order to gain complete empathic development, boys will often need cultural and social maps and rigorous rituals to make connections between their senses, important memories, and important feelings. They will need, in other words, parents, mentors, and other people to help guide them toward a plan, an objective, or a sacred text in which they can feel their emotions are useful, purposeful, meaningful.

What they may lack in conversation, boys may need to find in outer relationships and groups and debates and role development.

When parents, mentors, schools, and communities direct them toward religious institutions, or sports and athletics, or schools, or rites of passage that teach "the good," "high character," and "virtues," each caregiver is instinctively trying to help boys find safe places for emotions, places of good memories, and places where they can use their senses purposefully.

Understanding these things is crucial for raising our sons. Overall, compared to a girl, a boy's brain and biochemistry are not set up as well to self-develop an empathic sense of important pathways and relationships in the world. When boys ask, "What is the purpose of boys?" they are ready to make a journey on which, for many years, they are led. So are girls, but much of the mirror for their female journey comes naturally from within their biology. For boys, much of that mirror must come from clear, direct, concerted efforts of home, school, society, and culture to connect male growth to "purpose growth."

Your Little Boy's Need to Save the World

A way to bring together these observations and insights reveals itself if you walk by a video game arcade or watch your sons and their friends play video games in the other room. You may notice that boys create a raucous environment of battle around them. They enjoy it to its limits! Whether they are playing *Resident Evil, Doom, Ninja Assassin, Halo* (and when older, *Grand Theft Auto*), or any number of other games, the boys are fighting enemies who threaten not only the boy, man, or warrior, but also the people this boy loves—his friends, his community, his nation, and ultimately, his "world." This boy and his group of other boys are trying to save the world from enemies.

The benevolent robot in *Transformers* tells young Sam Witwicky, "You hold the key to Earth's survival." This key, it turns out, is his grandfather's set of glass spectacles on which a code is written. When I went to this movie with my own children and my friends' six- and nine-year-old boys, it was beautiful to see their eyes light up as they identified with Sam. By the end of Sam's adventure, Sam learns that the real "key," of course, is hidden inside himself—and the boys watching the movie feel it too. Maturing into a man is something deeper, they can already sense, than just being interested in a slick car, or seeking to be independent of eccentric parents: it is about having an essential purpose in the world, which, for a young boy, translates into accessing some kind of magical power or treasure, and utilizing it to "save the world."

Preparing for Responsibility

What we are seeing in male stories, fantasies, games, and dreams is the extension of "purpose psychology" that begins in the little boy. Whatever he has gained from family and close caregivers about who he should be is immediately tested and added to through his stories, games, and dreams. In the boy's young, ever-growing psyche, a foundation for self-esteem and identity is becoming established, one that he will build from so that boyhood is not a mundane, "boring" encounter with air, people, buildings, or whatever is around him, but in fact becomes more: a place of personal transformation wherein young males can change, every day, into miraculous beings who can save the world, alter the course of planets, rescue and protect the vulnerable, and become admired for having been good, true, and purposeful throughout the journey.

Our sons, and we ourselves, may not realize that every video game maker is demonstrating a knowledge of the male psyche when they design the video games and tools and weapons our sons play with. They understand the spatiality of the male brain, its testosterone, its pull toward dominance systems and hierarchies. When I have provided consulting to film producers, and toy and game designers, I've been impressed by how fully these professionals want to know about male-female brain difference. They understand their audience.

So do many successful writers of comic books, books, and films written for young males. If your son doesn't play video games, he might be entranced by "saving the world" books like the *Harry Potter* series and action movies like the *Terminator* or *Transformers*. Even if he cares nothing for these, you may have noticed your son or the boys around you gazing into heroic comic books. Have you seen their interest in science fiction battles, and films about warriors and kings? Have you seen their eyes light up when they win at something? Have you seen even your gentlest little boy stare up at the stars dreaming about doing something important, something that will save the world?

If you have, you are seeing in your son a prepubescent confluence of his developing brain, his biochemistry, and his male socialization. Understanding this internal "fairy tale" or "fantasy world"—one can call it many things—is potentially as life-defining to him and useful to you as was the urge directed by Grandpa Dean to fight real evil.

To test this matter out, try sitting down with your young son and reading a heroic comic book with him. Try playing a video game (one you feel is the right fit for his age) with him, or read a book together. See if you notice a "saving the world" dream in your son's eyes as he experiences the imaginative world of the comic book, game, or book. Watch how he identifies with heroes. Watch how satisfied he seems to feel when there is a heroic victory, a competitive notch achieved, a demolition of bad guys. Whatever culture you are reading this in, on whatever continent, the identification with magical or powerful male heroes occurs in boys. For the most part, you do not see boys aligning themselves for prolonged periods with bad guys (though they can certainly enjoy those characters at various times temporarily); ultimately and generally, you see little boys ending up aligning with victorious and magical good guys.

This male identification, noticeable even among toddlers, is a psychobiological driver through which boys seek their purpose in life from quite young. This driver is part of why our ancestral cultures started boys out on their journeys of initiation and transformation between four and seven years old. Boys are searching for their own power to help others by identifying with those who help. They are searching for their own innate talents and abilities by projecting onto heroes who are or have developed their talents and abilities. They are gaining courage to become important young men by watching and enjoying heroes who are constantly tested and challenged.

For your son and the boys around you, boyhood and then manhood is not meant to be an empty map—it is meant to be a tumultuous adventure in which they learn to create a meaningful life from their family and world. Boyhood is meant to be clear preparation for a manhood that is empathic and purposeful to others, family, the self, and the world.

The Wisdom of Purpose

FIGHT FOR WHAT IS RIGHT

If you will not fight for the right when you can easily win without bloodshed; if you will not fight when your victory will be sure and not too costly; you may come to the moment when you will have to fight with all the odds against you and only a small chance of survival. There may even be a worse case: you may have to fight when there is no hope of victory, because it is better to perish than to live as slaves.

—Winston Churchill

In many ways, our ancestors on all continents, and the makers of our sons' heroic stories and games, understood the need to help young boys perhaps better than we do. The rituals and games show understanding of the inner struggles of boys. They show understanding of the fact that boyhood, even when the boy is a toddler, must prepare the male for the highest responsibilities he can imagine (in our metaphor, "saving the world"). These rituals, stories, and games understand the drive in boys to find "kings" to mentor their "knighthood," and then to try to become kings themselves; to find warriors to mentor them, and only then become true warriors; to find explorers to mentor them, and only then become true explorers themselves; to be loved by people who care about them, and then to develop empathy and love in the world; to find magical Merlins to care for them, and then to become themselves the skilled, talented, magical transformer of reality.

Helping Fulfill Your Son's Need to "Save the World"

You and everyone around you can revisit, revise, and then gain from this understanding. Right now, all around you, the media, the Internet, video and reality games can be mined by you so that you can guide yourself, other parents, extended family, and the larger community to help your boy seek and find these elements of "saving the world." You can help guide his brain development, his biology, and indeed his male soul toward:

- What natural talents he can develop as a young boy on which to hinge his accomplishments, his service, and the world's spoken or tacit approval of him. We shouldn't expect our boys to be good at everything. But by ten, your son will show certain skills and talents. Perhaps he is very physical or verbal, musical or mathematical, sensitive or empathic; perhaps he shows a proclivity for chemical experiments or drawing pictures. He might already show a talent for computers, or he might possess an independent spirit of inventiveness. He might be a diligent worker, or a good caregiver to his siblings.

    You can help him every day to develop these natural and clear proclivities by finding the "magicians or mentors" around him who can guide him in taking his skills further than they are now.

- His future place among milestones of male purpose, such as what service he can provide to peers, community, and society. Boys need to be directed to apply their one-upmanship and their aggressions toward others with greater empathy, and with social and spiritual goals. You can see how mad your son can get, how he can bully or be bullied, what kind of "mistakes" he makes in his interactions with others. Seeing these, you can help him develop strength and various skills for handling conflict in a way that doesn't hurt anyone else and brings himself new friends and alliances.

- What strengths he has in him, both by birth and by life experience, and what weaknesses he must push through and turn into strengths. We need to help our boys understand their deepest fears so that they can one day direct their whole selves toward goals larger than simply their own naturally confused feelings. By ten years old, your son is able to understand what his fears are. Maybe he is afraid of his teacher or gets nervous and embarrassed in class when singled out to read or answer questions. Maybe he fears big kids or girls or not being good at sports. Talking to trusted adults about these fears can be wonderful medicine. It is the conversation with purpose-givers who tell their own magical stories through which he can learn how weakness is turned into strength.

• The capacity for love and intimacy that is already in him, and must be developed further so that he can be compassionate, empathic, and generous to those who need him. To fully socialize a little boy toward the beautiful love and intimacy you want him to be capable of, you will truly need your team of "magical" caregivers—mother, father, uncles, aunts, day-care providers, teachers, and coaches. All of these individuals can offer your boy wisdom and modeling, conversation and challenge, thus helping to build up his capacity to love and be intimate, purposefully, as a small but heroic part of family and community.

Questions of Purpose

Son, What Do You Need?

- What are your favorite books, comic books, and games? Which characters do you like in them (It's OK, you can tell me you like the bad guys!)?
- What are your "magical powers," the things you think you are best at?
- Who are you having the most feelings toward today? Which feelings scare you?

- Which activities make you most happy?
- What do you need from me right now?
- How do you want to help people?
- Whom do you want to help this week?
- Is there a teacher you really want to spend more time with? Why?
- Whom do you like playing with the most these days? Why?
- What do you want to be when you grow up? You can have one answer or lots of answers. What interests you the most right now?
- What chores would you like added to your list right now—which ones do you think are really important?

Asking the Deep Questions of Boys

Sometimes people will say, "We can't ask questions like these to little boys. They won't understand them." Certainly you must alter each question to fit the developmental maturity of your son, but don't be surprised if five-year-olds like to be asked important questions. You may have to ask them over and over again in order to get useful answers—that is part of the joy of these questions of purpose. Boys' minds want the challenge of important things. A boy's answers will be different at six, seven, eight, and well into early adolescence, but he will always enjoy the respect you pay him by asking him to try to reflect on who he is, how he is in real life getting set up to try to "save the world," and what help he himself needs.

Any teaching, questioning, and helping that you can do in the first ten years of life get stored up by your son for the next phase of life, adolescence, when developing a sense of purpose may become more exhilarating and confusing, as boys start to develop healthy self-discipline and become seekers of their adult purpose.

3

How Adolescent Boys Seek Their Purpose in Life

If you want to help teach boys to succeed, make things difficult; teach them the details of leadership; require excellence. Teach them to be effective communicators. This is not kids' stuff.

—DEAN DENNISON, BUSINESSMAN AND SCOUT LEADER SINCE 1968

KELLEY KING IS A MOTHER OF A SON AND A DAUGHTER, a former school principal, and the coauthor of two workbooks on helping boys and girls succeed in school and life. She recently told me this wonderful story regarding her fourteen year-old son, Connor:

Connor is a wrestler on the high school's team. One day he came home with a bruise on his left eye and cheek. I asked him how it happened, and he relished telling me about a tough match he had won. Listening to him, I could tell he felt like a young knight going into battle. I hugged him and got some meat to put on his wound, which he allowed me to do for just a few minutes, then he gave the meat back to me, and he went to his room where I could hear him telling a friend on the phone about what happened.

About two or three days later, his big blue bruise started to turn yellow and go away. I watched him when he was looking in the mirror at it, prodding and poking it, wishing it back into existence. He was already grieving the loss of internal feelings the wound gave

him, and the attention and respect he had received through that
"shiner." Though I was glad he was healing, I also felt something
as his mother and a woman. It's hard to describe, but I could
understand a little more now the need that adolescent boys have
to compete, push, pull, fight, wrestle. There's something really
big going on, and incidents like Connor's shiner make me want to
understand it and direct it, because it obviously means the world
to these guys.

Have you been in a similar situation with a boy or young man?
Boys going through puberty still have some of the younger boy in
them, making anything into a weapon, brandishing their arms in the
air, creating battle plans with their friends, feeling the magic in and
around them. Yet now, too, they sense even more intensity in their
own lives, even more at stake. They see the world's dangers and opportunities with a somewhat more mature vision, and wonder what they
will have to do during their journey through the world in order to discover glory or truth, and what maps they will follow to their future
treasures.

In this chapter, we'll see how pubescent boys are trying to become
young *seekers,* looking for power, empathy, loving relationships and
intimacy, and life direction as they set out on their complex male journey. I was speaking to a parent group about male adolescence and a
mother of two boys, thirteen and fifteen, said, "I can tell you a story
that illustrates how rich are those hidden inner lives of early adolescent boys. I got some bad news one night and I was crying. My sons
were playing a video game I hate, *Grand Theft Auto,* in the other room.
One of them saw me crying. They dropped their sticks, came immediately, asked me what was wrong, and hugged me. My thirteen-year-
old started to tear up in sympathy. It was so touching, and the switch
between the aggression and the tenderness happened in seconds."

Connor with his love of his battle wound, these boys with their battling and empathy . . . these are illustrations, I believe, of the complex
and fascinating forces with which adolescent boys wrestle inside themselves, forces that hit them quite hard at puberty (we'll look at biological reasons for this in a moment), forces they want to integrate into

their lives via a journey of strength, vitality, empathy, and truth. These pubescent boys need help from us as they try to organize their life journey from within. They are fighting—through their games and their insights, their fantasies and confrontations—against their own fears; simultaneously, they know they have to build a self that will be compassionate to others' fears and weaknesses. They are "wrestling" not just with other boys or girls or parents or others, but with every one of their own potential energies, weaknesses, and strengths. Everything is in flux for them, and they are becoming conscious seekers after specific ways and tools of control and excitement and thriving.

Puberty is an internal learning experience that begins around nine or ten, then increases in intensity through hormonal and brain changes well into a young man's twenties. The changes are so extreme that adolescent boys often live life and try to determine their futures as men via extremes. They are introduced to their own developing brain and biological changes early, and notice in themselves the psychobiological energy sources and maps of adolescent purpose. As we now explore male development in this next phase of life, we'll need to be as brave in dealing with it as our boys are trying to be themselves as they face adolescence, for what they face is the battle between the primitive and the civilized, a battle that will inspire them (with our help) to move beyond "fighting" into "seeking."

The Young Seeker Among the Primitive and the Civilized

Romans 12:21 says, "Do not be overcome by evil; overcome evil with good." All the world's religions and thousands of male-oriented stories from every continent provide admonishments similar to this one. If you look at stories about pubertal boys with an eye for this, you'll notice that in the stories, inspirational aphorisms are integrated into a call for young men to put forth their best, most mature selves by setting out on a journey of maturation in which they will seek a path to truth, strength, and purpose. This is the case for Jesus, Moses, Arjuna

(Hinduism), Buddha, Batman, Superman, Spiderman—the list is long and we hope each boy has his own list.

You'll also notice that in these stories the evil that the adolescent (and the later man) "conquers" is not just an enemy army, but generally it is also his own urges, appetites, and issues—what his mentor tells him is the "raw" or "primitive" inside him. He must not "give into it," he must direct its energies, even transcend it. The wounding that the young man goes through, the struggle, the search for truth, the battle with dark forces, and the time in the wilderness are as much about discovering identity and purpose through and beyond the primitive forces in him, as coming in contact with the divine.

The Buddhist Lotus Sutra gives a perfect example of this: "It is not enough to conquer in battle a thousand men if you have not first conquered yourself." Even to the Buddhists, for whom there is no sin, just suffering, the end of suffering does not necessarily come when we defeat finite enemies, but when we remove from our thoughts and actions our self-debilitating practices such as angers and primitive urges—and discover maps and a path on which we can seek to become fully civilized.

Becoming the Seeker

If you watch any martial arts film, whether made in the United States or abroad, you can see all this clearly. The adolescent boy can only win his battle against villains by seeking a path on which to gain self-discipline. This self-discipline can only be achieved with a kind of spiritual practice and training that helps him lay a foundation for his life purpose by conquering the demons of fear, evil, aimlessness, and restlessness in himself. The young warrior is not considered ready for battle against evil until he has become fully empathic for himself and the others he serves, comprehending a map of his purpose—so that his battle (at the climax of the story, that is, the end of boyhood and beginning of manhood) is not an individual's effort of arrogant prowess, but a seeker's purposeful and powerful service of family, friends, and community.

THE JOY OF PURPOSE

Bring What Obstacles You May!

Difficult? No matter! "Let the heart fly into pieces," he roared, "let the shoulders come unhinged, let heaven and earth collapse, but a man must not stray from his path!" Obstacles are unimportant. On the contrary, the more of them, the greater the merits of trying. Little does it matter if, going from discovery to discovery, one comes up against even an unknown God who does not compromise, still one must continue one's quest, nothing else counts. What is important is to accept the challenge, to fight the battle! What is important is to choose an opponent more powerful than oneself.

—Elie Wiesel, *Souls on Fire*

As a student of adolescent male psychology, I believe the adolescent male seeker-warrior stories reflect an evolutionary mechanism of the journey that the human brain has been making for a million years. Our brains were first only a brain stem, filled just with survival and fight-or-flight instincts. A limbic system developed to wrap around that brain stem with more emotionality and sensuality than the brain stem possessed, and our ambitions and drives became more complex. We were, however, easily absorbed in raw emotion. In the last few hundred thousand years, a cerebral cortex—the four lobes at the top of our brains—are developing rapidly. We now try to think and manage our emotions and instincts toward the greater good via this newest part of the brain, which wraps around the limbic system and the brain stem, battling with and utilizing instincts and emotions to assert power that will help humanity and civilization.

In adolescence, our brains expand their capacity for brain stem power, limbic system emotionality, and cerebral ability. Of course, both girls and boys go through adolescence, experiencing leaps in brain development. Both boys and girls increase their power during adolescence, and both care about being good and seeking truth. Much of what we say about adolescent boys in this chapter can certainly be said about girls too.

At the same time, boys make the neural, evolutionary journey between the primitive and the civilized in their own way—they gain self-discipline, personal power, and a sense of purpose somewhat differently than adolescent girls do, especially in early adolescence, when their brains mature more slowly than girls. Let's explore this further, for we too are seekers hoping to understand what is happening inside our adolescent males.

How Adolescent Boys and Girls Seek and Develop Purpose Differently

Research from a number of scientific fields can help us develop an understanding of the "male" way of seeking purpose during adolescence.

Seeking the Self Inside His DNA

Zoological and genetics sciences are now providing insight into male adolescence by studying male biochemistry in not just humans, but other species as well. Researchers such as University of Toronto zoologist Susannah Varmuza have compared DNA evidence from humans and other primates and discovered that, as Dr. Varmuza put it, "At the level of DNA, a male human is more similar to the male chimpanzee than he is to a female human, because of the Y chromosome."

This kind of research is controversial because of its stark comparisons with other animals, which can seem to make males look unsophisticated, inferior, or defective. Researchers like Dr. Varmuza, however, are studying DNA patterns on the Y chromosome in order to help us understand the needs of both boys and girls, and the patterns of nurturing that are required for males and females to be successful. The Y chromosome sets males up for surges and spikes of testosterone during adolescence that need a certain kind of care and supervision.

Among chimpanzees, for instance, the social process of acquiring power, then acting in socially helpful ways, is taught differently to young males than it is to young females. All young chimps commonly learn about power and service via experimental behavior, and then communal response. Civilized behavior is modeled from older chimps, and punishments by senior males and females are meted out for wrong behavior, as are rewards for right behavior.

For males in particular, however, when their testosterone begins to flow at puberty, there is special attention to discipline and self-discipline via role development. Males challenge other males hierarchically to figure out where they are in the pecking order and what role they should play for the survival of the group. These males receive "wounding" (rebuffs) like Kelley's son Connor received. This kind of wounding and aggression-nurturance is a part of the development of males' sense of empathy and boundaries against too-extreme risk-taking. The community wants male energy directed rather than haphazard, seeking after healthy roles and goals, rather than constantly warring against other groups or within the group.

This kind of research is useful to us in helping our boys. It need not limit our sons, and certainly our sons are not chimps! But they are being hit—via five to seven spikes of testosterone per day—with high levels of a chemical that stimulates aggression and risk-taking behavior. Their need for hierarchical supervision (especially if they are more aggressive than other boys) is absolute: without it, they may well not be able to channel and discipline their energy—the very energy that can, if supervised, help them achieve a valuable life purpose and seek and find a path of worth. Helping pubertal boys manage their aggression (helping them "battle the primitive" with the "expectations of civilization") is a very human duty, and one that takes courage and a lot of people who are ready for the challenge.

Differences in Stress Response

Adolescent boys and girls handle stress differently. This difference, too, should raise our antennae as we think about how to help pubertal boys become conscious seekers after a healthy male self.

Research at UCLA, Rutgers, and Macalester College has discovered different biochemical arrays in boys and girls when they feel threatened. Both boys' and girls' levels of cortisol, the stress hormone that regulates crucial body chemistry, fluctuate depending on their level of stress. But for boys the fluctuation is directly tied to their adrenaline levels. Thus, more of their brain's stress response focuses on the dangerous fight-or-flight mechanisms in the body and brain stem, in order to help them impulsively and instinctively regain physical and social stability of power.

Girls' brains secrete more oxytocin, a hormone that also acts as a neurotransmitter released during hugging, touching, orgasm (for both sexes), and bonding, trust, and generosity. Higher oxytocin tends to help girls focus more of their chemical response to stress on the socially safer reacquisition of power and equilibrium through verbal connections with others. This is not a fight-or-flight mechanism, but a tend-and-befriend strategy. Unlike boys, girls generally do not need as much direction toward a potential "path of seeking," or specific "map of goals," because they are more constantly directed by a bonding chemical to gather and build selves through their ever-expanding verbal and social relationships.

The 2007 Nobel Prize winner for Medicine, Mario Capecchi, recently provided a personal corroboration of the male-female stress-response difference. Brought up in hard conditions in Italy—starving and homeless—Dr. Capecchi recalls himself as a feral boy who beat up other kids in order to make friends among the other boys and gain food, shelter, and gang-like survival bonds. When he felt the stress of his physical and social conditions, he handled it by aggression techniques and even violence, ruled not by tend-and-befriend instincts but by fight-or-flight mechanisms.

Now, of course, he is an established and renowned scientist who received much-needed adult mentoring and education through and beyond his lonely adolescence. But his telling of his story is courageous and inspiring for those of us who look at stressed-out adolescent boys and girls and wonder, "Why do stressed-out girls tend to cut themselves, whereas stressed-out boys tend to try to hurt others?" Or: "Why do boys shoot up their schools, whereas girls tend to get on the Internet and try to destroy one another's relationships?"

Some (not all) of the answer lies in the fact that boys are driven by an adolescent biology underlaid with aggression and adrenalin. Students of gang behavior have corroborated this idea, noting how many gang members today do not get the mentoring and assistance they need to seek and find a socially adaptive path of worth. Lacking this path and training, they nonetheless seek direction and support toward something like it, and form violent, high-risk, highly adrenalized groupings in order to at least approximate what they need.

In neural terms, gang members do not respond to the stress and trauma of their life experience by bringing the civilized to the primitive. In biologically stark terms, they become unable or unwilling to discover socially acceptable pathways to purpose for their adrenalin and testosterone such as those ultimately found by Dr. Capecchi. Yet still they seek out male groupings in which to process and "civilize" their energy toward a common goal—survival of the gang and its territory. They create their own high-risk, highly aggressive structures, and encounter early death. The average life span of a gang member is twenty-five to thirty years old.

UNDERSTANDING PURPOSE

Adolescent Boys and Girls Respond to Social Rejection Differently

One significant stressor on our early adolescent boys (and indeed any child) can be social rejection—feeling isolated from, bullied, or constantly ridiculed by a dominant social group. Studies at Stanford University and U.C. Berkeley have shown that adolescent males and females respond differently to this threat. Specifically, when he feels that his social identity is threatened, less of the adolescent boy's brain activity involves frontal lobe activity—which includes making "good decisions," thinking out a response, talking out a response with a friend, parent, or mentor—and more of it involves brain stem and lower limbic activity, which links directly to uncontrolled impulse and violence. Girls' brains often react to the same threat with increased frontal lobe activity, leading to more tend-and-befriend efforts.

One contributor to this neural process is a little almond-shaped part of the brain called the amygdala. It is in the middle of the brain and swells up with fear during social rejection. More signaling from this amygdala passes downward to the brain stem in adolescent boys; more goes upward to the talking and thinking centers of the brain in adolescent girls (frontal and temporal lobes in the cerebral cortex).

A recent case in New York provided insight into the male-female difference in stress and social rejection response. At fifteen, an outcast boy planned an attack on his high school (and got another rejected boy to help him). Thankfully, the two boys were caught before they could murder their schoolmates, but the fifteen-year-old's journal (confiscated later by police) read: "I will start a chain of terrorism in the world. This will go down in history. Take out everyone there. Perfecto." The violent plans were precipitated, investigators found, by the adolescent boy's feeling that "everyone was against him. The world was against him. He was upset at life in general and the world in general."

We're all painfully familiar with cases like this, from Columbine to Virginia Tech—adolescent boys, especially unloved and lonely ones, who are on no path of seeking, and have no map of purpose except the highly aggressive, highly adrenalized, and destructive stress response. These adolescent males are more likely to make fewer social connections on their own than girls, and thus can feel their whole identity destroyed when they are rejected by a friend or social group. These boys may also seek more physically violent "solutions" to their loss of status than girls. Girls suffer immensely from rejection, but often have more access to nonviolent responses, both in the brain and in the world.

This area of social rejection of adolescent males is being studied carefully around the world today. New research continues to find that one-on-one mentoring and crisis intervention with these males is crucial. One or more powerful, instructive, understanding people can help set a young male on a healthy path of seeking. These young males are lonely for contact of this kind, contact that shows them maps for developing respect, increasing status, and developing authentic selves. They are hungry for others, including older peer boys and adult men, who can bring them into a relationship in a workplace, family, or social group, where they can feel themselves to be a purposeful part of society and civilization, the family and community, and not just left alone to battle their own primitive responses to the pain of rejection.

The Issue of Status and Respect in Adolescent Male Development

The brain and biological differences we have just looked at help us understand adolescent boys from the inside out. I hope as you've read them, you've felt a pull toward your son, a sense of wanting to know how he is doing as a "seeker" after relationships and maps that will guide him through his own choices between the primitive and the civilized. I hope you sense his inner hunger to be led to possible paths that can lead him to become a man of purpose. Adding to all this is the fact that adolescent boys develop a sense of self-motivation somewhat differently than girls. We are learning this from studies of male and female social groupings during puberty and into adulthood. Research at the University of Missouri has found that the male brain and biochemical base creates a greater need in boys than in girls for developing, in the words of researcher Dr. David Geary, "motivational and behavioral dispositions that facilitate the development and maintenance of large, competitive coalitions, and result in the formation of within-coalition dominance hierarchies."

Dr. Geary's research has found that whereas all humans, male or female, can seek dominance and status in large groups, males tend to pursue not only close one-on-one relationships, but also large, project-driven groups (such as Boy Scouts or gangs) that potentially hone their skills and teach them right and wrong via maps of purpose and paths of seeking truth, justice, and self-worth. Geary and others surmise that the male's need at a certain point during adolescence to become a seeker after status within a large group may derive from the male brain's evolution along a hunting trajectory, with males working, for hundreds of thousands of years of our history, in large hunting groups. In these groups, males became more civilized, directed, motivated, and purposeful by cooperating and competing in hierarchical structures where status, respect, and authentic power could be earned and utilized.

The importance of status in large groupings among adolescent boys cannot be underestimated. Recently, I was working at Morehouse College on educational issues facing black youth and asked the educators what was the single most important thing sought by the adolescent boys they worked with. Nearly every teacher and administrator agreed: a path by which to gain *respect*. Adolescent boys come to school, athletics, neighborhoods, extended families, sports arenas, streets, or parties at a friend's house looking for ways to gain respect. They will do high-risk things in search of that respect, and they will turn away from structures such as schools when they feel disrespected in that school—that is, when they feel that the school or other institution is not set up for them to be able to seek and gain respect there. They will say, "School sucks, it's for girls, it's not for me." They are ultimately saying, "I am compelled from within to find maps, people, and structures through which I can gain status and respect—if this school (or home) isn't the place, I'll find another. I will push and push against every limit of every place until I find paths and places that will help me gain status and respect."

Seeking Respect Through Authority

In all the areas we've looked at so far in this chapter—aggressiveness, stress response, social rejection, status-seeking and respect-building, let's make sure not to group all "adolescent boys" as if each individual fits a stereotype. Hormonally speaking, some adolescent boys at any given moment are higher or lower in testosterone. This can matter. For low-testosterone boys, adolescence might be difficult because of challenges these boys might face in climbing high-testosterone male hierarchies. These particular adolescent boys are not as driven to try to gain status and respect in large groupings—they may get deeply involved in a single solitary activity (a lot of the obsessive video gaming of shy adolescent boys fits in this category). These boys may not be as adrenalized and aggressive as the more high-testosterone boys.

At the same time, adolescent male development, whether at its lowest testosterone levels or its highest, and whether the boy is shy or quite extroverted, can benefit from authoritative leadership from strong male influences. This piece of "hardwiring" seems to transcend all variety, and speak to all adolescent boys at some time in their development. Each will tend to need some kind of authoritative instruction in how to find paths of worth that are purposeful and gain the boy respect. Even the solitary boy obsessed with video games is seeking in the virtual world his own way of "winning" and raising status.

Studies in South Africa and Zimbabwe have noted that, similar to male humans, male testosterone expression among elephants, whether high or low, becomes socially disruptive if unchecked by alpha authority during adolescence—much more so than female elephant adolescent development that is unchecked by alpha authority. When young males have been either withdrawing socially or attempting to acquire power through socially violent behavior, putting them in the presence of a strong male authority can affect them profoundly. The authority "puts them in their place" via instruction, encouragement, and anger management techniques which establish pecking orders and vehicles for appropriate respect and status acquisition. The withdrawn young males tend to come forward more, and the overly aggressive young males tend to desist from their disruptive and violent behavior.

And quite interestingly, for adolescent females, empathy and power development often follow their understanding of the pain they are causing others—but this is not as often the case with males, especially high-testosterone males. Often, these particular males need intense authoritative structure, supervision, and discipline in order to change their behavior from primitive to civilized. They need authoritative males who have clearly gained respect and status already to "take them under their wing" and show the young male how to seek real status, real power, real purpose, and real worth.

Seeking Respect Through Sex and Intimacy

In few areas of male development do ALL adolescent boys need more help in developing their purpose than in the area of sexual intimacy. Much of a man's future sense of success and earned respect will be tied to his sexual ability, sexual success, and intimate alliances. Sexuality begins in boys far younger than puberty, with first erections happening even in the womb! Boys have sexual fantasies when they're still quite young, feeling confused and excited by them. Then, at puberty, as surges of testosterone rush through the male brain and body at a greater frequency, sexual fantasies, desires, curiosities, preoccupations, and infatuations become an almost everyday happening for boys.

Sometimes, feeling that we are ill-equipped to get involved in our sons' internal lives or that it is not our place, we forget that our sons are becoming sexual seekers, and wrestling with the primitive and the civilized in the arena of sex. But we really need to be aware that these young boys are already trying to work through primitive drives and feelings and find appropriate and civilized outlets for sexual energy and desire. Simultaneously, they are setting goals for sexuality and intimacy that will bring them respect—trying to have sex, and later, an intimate partner (or more than one), and a spouse and children.

We'll deal in more detail with practical strategies for helping boys develop sexual values and purpose in Chapters Four and Five. In this chapter on the young seeker, I mention sexuality in order to ask you as a parent to rethink male sexuality as a normal part of his search for purpose, respect, and meaning.

As you raise your son through adolescence, you are raising a young man for whom sex is a mysterious vehicle for respect and purpose in direct proportion to how "shameful," "confusing," and "thrilling" it seems to him. As your son discovers the irresistible allure of another person's body, masturbation, pornography, sexual storytelling, fantasies, projections, puppy love, and love, each becomes a big part of his seeking and finding himself. Even though some of his urges can frighten us to the point where we forbid them, each is also a challenge toward bonding: the more we talk to our son, ask him questions (a list of questions is provided in Chapter Five), and join with him in exploring sexual boundaries and respect for other people's bodies, the more we help him seek and find civilized values for sex. In doing this, we show our son that we respect him as a young sexual seeker.

Many of our ancestral cultures spent much more time than we do teaching young men about their own bodies and helping them understand "rules" for relating to women sexually and intimately. As our society reinvigorates a sense of the purpose of boys, we will keep increasing our dialogue with boys, over the ten years or so of adolescence, about what is good and joyous in their developing sexuality.

What Motivates Different Boys

A mother and teacher, Trudy Shmeller, wrote about changing churches to help follow her instincts about what both her high- and low-testosterone boys needed. She exemplifies quite beautifully the need for seeking and the helpfulness of authoritative structure for all kinds of sons. She recalls wanting to make sure the diversity of her sons was nurtured appropriately during the difficult years of adolescence, noting that one of her sons was shy and withdrawn, did not like team sports (was, in our language, probably a low-testosterone male in this developmental period of his life), while her other son was very athletic and pretty aggressive. She writes:

> To protect and help both our sons, we left a large church they were becoming bored in and searched for a smaller congregation where mission work was an integral part of the church. We were led to St. Matthews, where all children have opportunities to be involved with projects both in our community and in Mexico. Our sons love the pastor and the staff, and really look up to the committed men on missions.
>
> This work helped us keep our sons focused on their purpose— to always give back, now and in the future. The closeness they got with these men who were already on a mission to help others gave our sons a greater sense of mission themselves.

The Path to Self-Civilization

Trudy and her husband understood something about male motivational psychology for which there is now new and interesting scientific corroboration. It may partially explain why adolescent boys seem to respond so well to strong, respectful, and caring authority systems and individuals.

Peter Erikkson, of Sweden's Sahlgrenska University Hospital, is a specialist in "neurogenesis" in the human brain's neurons. He has discovered that although many parts of the brain are set and patterned before a child is even born, including large parts of our personality and the gender of our brains, there is one particular area of the human brain that is constantly creating new neurons, especially during adolescence—the hippocampus, or memory center, of the brain—and not surprisingly, in adolescent boys and girls, there are differences in the development of these neurons.

All young people, boys and girls, develop their ability to mature in direct proportion to what goes into their memory banks. A child's mother, father, caregivers, mentors, teachers, peers, games, play, activities— all of these influences produce experiences within children that they use to self-civilize. If a child lacks crucial people and activities needed for character, moral, and empathic development, that child will tend not to have filled his or her memory banks with "good, virtuous actions," or with "lessons from good people," and thus will not have as much access, especially during tumultuous early adolescence, to internal frameworks for elevating the self toward values, goodness, and purpose.

For girls, however, there are three developmental advantages in the area of hippocampal development. First, when girls are little and have sensorial, emotional, and relational experiences with parents, caregivers, teachers, and the world around them, their brains develop and retain more neural connections for those experiences than boys' brains do. Second, their brains develop more "memory neurons" for the multitude of these emotional, sensorial, and relational experiences. Third, their brains develop more "verbal neurons" for the sensory, emotional, and relational experiences they had.

The female brain in general is more active than the male brain (with fifteen to twenty percent more neural activity in the brain at any given moment), and the adolescent female brain develops and matures its empathic memory centers more quickly than the adolescent male brain. The adolescent female hippocampus, for instance, with its wealth of stored emotional and relational memories of good behavior and empathic choices, becomes connected to the female frontal lobe (the part of the brain that controls impulses, guides good judgment, and helps people make good decisions) more quickly than do her male counterparts.

When Trudy and her husband made sure to find appropriate adolescent environments—a small church and mission projects—to help motivate their sons toward becoming seekers after purpose, they were literally helping them seek and find a path by which to civilize themselves, a path on which they could fill their minds and their memories with activities that taught purpose. These parents sensed that although girls certainly need similar activities and projects, this need may be more urgent for many boys because adolescent males are not doing as much of this maturing from within as quickly as adolescent girls are. They need more structures, maps, and authoritative systems "from without."

Helping Our Sons Seek Respect in Adolescence

I hope that in taking this somewhat "scientific journey" you have seen enough to agree that if the family and community around the adolescent male are not helping him seek and find a journey between the primitive and the civilized, the "unrespected" and the "respected," the "aimless" and the "purposeful," the young male may be profoundly underserved. He may become so desperate by fifteen or sixteen to figure out how to be good and true and strong in the face of his internal confusions that he may not attend to the busywork of school or other areas of value. Because he is, by nature, fighting a deep battle for relevance and purpose during confusing biological development, and because the world around him may be providing him with only cosmetic solutions to cosmetic problems, he may not be getting the deep help he needs.

Listen for a moment to Ruth Price, a pediatrician and mother, who spoke at a parent workshop with and for her deaf husband, Carl Price, a cardiologist. Together, they provided the group with both grassroots and science-based insight into their two sons and two daughters. Ruth said:

> These issues about adolescent boys and respect are absolutely science-based to us. Menstruation and ovulation are intrinsically self-civilizing for our daughters—they were for me also. Estrogenic hormones, including oxytocin, self-civilize girls. But boys in puberty don't have this internal advantage. Their brains, their hormones, their sex drive, their aggression, their fear of aggression, these things are not as internally self-civilizing. They are more like internal cries for help. People tend to think adolescent boys don't cry—well they don't cry tears as much as girls, it's true, but we see them crying for us in lots of other ways.

The Wisdom of Purpose

THE COURAGE OF A MAN

If you can keep your head when all about you
Are losing theirs and blaming it on you;
If you can trust yourself when all men doubt you,
But make allowance for their doubting too;
If you can wait and not be tired by waiting,
Or, being lied about, don't deal in lies,
Or, being hated, don't give way to hating . . .
Yours is the Earth and . . . you'll be a man, my son.

—Adapted from *If* by Rudyard Kipling

Robert Kodama, a teacher and administrator at Crespi Carmelite High School in Encino, California, echoes the Prices' wisdom, and illustrates beautifully how much our adolescent boys hunger for appropriate care. He told me:

> I have been coaching soccer for the past nineteen years. I've found that all boys, even the most sensitive ones, are looking for a sense of discipline, and have been for years. There are forces inside them they need help with. Over the years, I've had to go toe-to-toe with

a number of the guys, over team issues, attitude issues, and moral issues. It is these guys in particular who come back to me today for advice. They are the ones who visit me and the school most often as men.

Robert looked into the eyes of these adolescent boys and rose to the occasion by helping them seek and gain respect in moral and disciplined ways. These boys, now men, may not even realize why they liked Robert so much as a coach—they may just think, "He was cool." In fact, Robert's "coolness" came from his courage to help boys seek and find discipline, motivation, morality, and service. Adolescent boys are so hungry for paths toward these aspects of maturation: they will allow themselves to be put in their place by a coach, as long as the coach helps them become real and good men.

Questions of Purpose

Son, Are You Living the Adventure of Purpose?

You will know when each of these questions is right for your adolescent son. Timing and trust matter greatly. Get help in asking these, as you need it—help from friends, family members, counselors.

- Do you have someone in your life you trust enough to talk with about anything bothering you? Would you come to me for help?
- Do you have someone to talk to you about sexual stuff, even the confusing stuff?
- Who is relying on you right now for help? Are you helping them? How? How could you help them better?
- Do you have activities in your life that show you're becoming a good and important man?
- When have you seen a man cry? What do you think about that?
- What parts of yourself must you manage better so that you can succeed? Who can help you learn to manage these parts of yourself?

Moving Forward with a Map in Hand

In this chapter, we've looked at the young seeker living in your home. In the next chapter, we'll notice how this seeker evolves even a step further, into a "hero." In every culture, adolescent boys must become HEROIC in order to fully mature. What do we mean by "heroic"? Perhaps not what you think! The "heroic" model in the next chapter is a developmental tool for guiding a son to seek and find the treasures of Honor, Enterprise, Responsibility, Originality, Intimacy, and Creativity in his own unique, beautiful, and wonderfully male way.

You are an integral part of the HEROIC journey. Therefore, together with your son or student, you yourself are the "co-subject" of our next chapter.

4

Son, You Are My Hero

Every man is an original mind . . . there is some peculiar merit which
it is his to seek and find.

—Ralph Waldo Emerson

"SON, YOU ARE MY HERO." I have heard these words spoken by both a
mother and a father to their respective sons. Few words have seemed
to touch the heart of each boy more.

I was judging a high school debate tournament recently and,
after a varsity round, heard a group of parents talking to their young
sters. The winners (and losers) of the last round were announced.
A particular middle adolescent boy, fifteen, tall, gangly, covered with
acne, discovered that he had gotten second place. He looked despond-
ent, but his mother gave him a hug and said, "Son, you are my hero."
Embarrassed by her attention in public, his face reddening, he moved
away from her embrace, but not too quickly. He heard her words, and
he clearly savored them.

The second time I heard "Son, you are my hero" was at a bar mitzvah. The time in the ceremony of the parent speeches had come, the thirteen-year-old boy having completed his reading of the Torah (the Old
Testament in Hebrew) and his other adult duties. His father, voice shak-
ing with the emotion of the moment, said, "Son, you are my hero."

From these opening words came a speech to his son about this
young man's accomplishments of both work and heart—how the boy

cared for his grandmother, fulfilled his responsibilities at home (even if imperfectly!), went out of his way to learn his Hebrew lessons, and when rebellious, often seemed to have a good reason for rebelling. The father then directed the son to how he hoped he would grow in adolescence and adulthood. When the father finished his speech, the whole congregation understood what this man meant by *hero*. There were tears in many people's eyes, for everyone who had a son or a daughter felt comforted and moved, at that moment, by the endless possibilities of youth.

I've heard a boy called a hero and worked with many young men and women to help them develop a sense of the heroic. Each family, each mother and father, each grandparent, each teacher, will mean something different by the words hero, heroic, or heroism. In this chapter, we won't erase any of the different meanings that are possible for the words, but we will find a model of the HEROIC in the everyday development of your son's mind, heart, and purpose in life that fits well with the challenges of manhood in the new millennium. This model reflects, enhances, and provides a seven-stage developmental map to the science-based material of our first chapters, and then moves from adolescence into male adulthood.

The Heroic Son

I was once introducing this heroic model at a workshop and a woman said, "You know, I don't like the word 'hero' very much. I don't want to raise the kind of son who wants to be an action figure or a soldier. The word 'hero' feels weird to me." Her comment led to a powerful discussion, one in which we all came to understand how crucial it is to transcend stereotypes immediately when we decide to use the word "hero" in the new millennium.

In this chapter, I'll use it in the way a person might use the word "purposeful, respectful, seeking self." I hope you'll let "hero" help you understand your son's natural drive to be purposeful. I hope, too, that you will feel the power of the word in your own development as a woman or man. It is an "old" word but it is also a crucial word that we can make new and helpful for our world. Our sons are hungry to become heroes in our eyes and the eyes of the world.

UNDERSTANDING PURPOSE

The Hero Can Be Defined

When I use "Heroic" with boys and families, I am looking for boys of all ages to be and become:

Honorable
Enterprising
Responsible
Original
Intimate
Creative

Each of these terms can be nascent potentialities in young boys, each ideally becoming more powerful for pubertal boys who are led successfully toward path-seeking, and all should be well established in youth who discover purpose in life.

By honorable, I mean a moral boy who becomes a man of conscience and duty.

By enterprising, I mean a busy, industrious boy who becomes a man who gets things done.

By responsible, I mean a boy who cares about others' needs, and becomes a man of service.

By original, I mean a boy who is moral, busy, and caring, but in being these things, does not lose himself or enslave himself when he becomes a man—but instead expresses his own unique gifts throughout his life.

By intimate, I mean a boy who learns how to love, then becomes a man who can love another as an equal partner.

By creative, I mean a boy who dreams, and pursues his dreams—even one day, as a man, all the way to creating and loving the next generation.

The mom at the debate tournament and the dad at the bar mitzvah were trying to provide these two boys with the blessing of the essential goal of purposeful living in boys—to become a hero, to become heroic, to seek heroism. They and their sons were on, I believe, a seven-stage journey toward heroism. They may not have been looking at science, but still they sensed their sons' internal need to be heroic. They may not have had sociological evidence of disrupted boyhood at their fingertips, but still they wanted their sons to develop in sync with their highest expectations and the boys' highest potential.

We are all like these two parents. We want our sons to be heroes. Let's explore a HEROIC model and celebrate where we already are in this journey with our sons, and take whatever new steps we need to take to alter what we do with boys. To help us explore this heroic model, let's use the story of Joseph from the Old Testament. Through this story, we'll trace how boys all over the world are seeking the same sort of positively defined, yet struggle-filled map to "earning it," and "being a good man"—beginning when they were born.

The Story of Joseph

Joseph's life is typical in its story of the development of male heroic purpose, and occurs similarly in Christian images of Jesus; Hindu tales, such as Arjuna's journey in the Bhagavad Gita; fairy tales such as those of the Brothers Grimm and Hans Christian Andersen; ancient Asian tales of the Buddha's boyhood and youth; and African and Native American tales of young hunters initiated into manhood.

Indeed, Joseph's story of heroism includes elements so universal to male development that there is not a culture that has not told its own version: the boy who is loved but then must seek, wander, and struggle, even experience a loss of freedom, then discover his natural and somewhat "magical" powers, then seek and find his originality, his path to intimacy, his creativity, his honor, his responsibility, his enterprise, and his purpose in life.

Students of mythology, including Carl Jung and Joseph Campbell, believe that archetypal tales like Joseph's appear all over the world because patterns of heroic development are biologically universal to human brain development. My work with boys and their families confirms that this belief regarding our sons is accurate.

Stage One: The Wanted Boy and His Birthright

To follow the story of Joseph in its original version, you can go to Genesis 37 and then read all the way through to the end of this first book of Moses.

In Genesis 37, Joseph is born the youngest son of Jacob who loves him as the "child of my old age." Like every hero, Joseph is born to parents who love him, a boy who is important to the world around him. By "important," we mean he has a *lineage*, a family or tribal past, a birthright, and a legacy to pass on. In this early detail of Joseph's life, he is like nearly every other prophet. Jesus, for instance, was born to an ordinary carpenter but also a woman who, in some Christian traditions, was inseminated by God. Buddha was born to the palace of the highest lineage, where his father led his people. A Native American warrior in a native story is often born to the chieftain. The hero of a European fairy tale is born to a princess or a queen. Joseph is born to Jacob and Rachel, the patriarch and matriarch of the Hebrews.

Even the first words of the Joseph story in Genesis show the importance of his birth, and how much he was wanted by these important people of purpose. "And God remembered Rachel, and God hearkened to her, and opened her womb; and she conceived, and bore a son, and she said, 'God hath taken away my reproach'; and she called the son Joseph." The purpose of boys starts here—in being wanted, and the early love given by parents who want and love their child. From this stage, he will later say (even if unconsciously, and without spoken words), "I came here wanted by people who themselves had a purpose in life to pass on to me." Every son's development of purpose needs and demands to begin with this inner motivation, so that as he grows from infancy into early boyhood he is aware of being adored and already important. His sense of purpose begins in being the object of his parents' and community's purpose, as well as the vessel of purpose carrying messages of importance from the past.

When an infant boy does not experience this first stage of birthright, his whole journey can be derailed. I worked with a family of a boy who was adopted in Hungary. The boy had been abandoned at birth, raised in an orphanage until seven, then adopted by the American family. This boy couldn't find his way—and now in his twenties, he's in prison. He was not the wanted boy and thus could not become the hero of his adoptive parents, even though they were filled with love and ready to provide him anything he needed. He could never learn about who his parents were, what his birthright and legacy were, what treasures of the past he needed to carry along with him as he developed his own independent self.

Most adoptions, of course, do not turn out this way, but many adoptees do show signs and effects of Post-Traumatic Stress and Attachment disorders. Two pieces of the puzzle we are calling "purpose" can be missing in these adoptee cases: (1) healthy, loving attachment to caregivers early in life, which is the foundation of good mental health; and (2) loss of lineage—a loss of the sense, from deep in our cells, that we know we have come from a bloodline that struggled, survived, and has a deep story to tell.

Carey Johnston, a psychologist who works with babies adopted from Africa, told me, "We try very hard to make sure the children learn everything they can about Africa, especially the country and the village from which they originally came. It's not only important to help the growing child gain a black identity in our white American culture, but it's important for the child to be connected to his roots. His roots can be a big part of what he will hang onto and refer back to when he's unsure and insecure later in life."

If you think of your son as a "Joseph," does he know enough about his ancestors, his origins—the foundation of his originality on this earth? Does he also know well enough, and deep in his heart, that you who created him want and love him? His ability to be intimate with a mate later on may depend on how well he knows he is loved now. His ability to find his originality in the world may be more difficult if he doesn't know from whence he has come.

Stage Two: The Rise and Fall of a Boy's Self-Esteem

In the next major incident in Joseph's story, the hero is now the loved boy whose father, Jacob, gives him a coat more beautiful than the garments worn by his many brothers. This young hero experiences the egotistical pride of his own "importance," "adoration," and "birthright." He goes to an extreme of birthright, we might say. The Bible storytellers made sure we saw that Joseph's purpose must come from feeling adored and important, but now they warn us that when a heroic boy feels too important (too entitled) there are severe consequences.

Look for a moment at the effects of the multicolored coat on Joseph's life. Through the coat and the attention it receives, Joseph feels "I'm cool, I'm the greatest"—he gains what we call today "high self-esteem." This is a crucial step for a boy; he feels his own "magical powers," his "magical boyhood." As a toddler, a preschooler, and a school-age boy, he needs to feel that he is important. We all know this as parents, because we try to guide our son to a school that will protect his self-esteem, and activities that will fit his nature, and help him dream big, and feel magical. Through our many efforts, we hope our young Joseph will see a future in which he is written well—one in which he can save his own people, or even, in the language of Chapter Two, "save the world."

And Joseph feels his self-esteem so strongly that he does indeed dream about his coolness, his importance to the world, his heroic possibilities, his future purpose in life. In one particular dream, a sheaf of corn that he plants rises up above the sheaves of his brothers. He interprets this as showing how he, Joseph, will one day have to be obeyed by others. Joseph gets the dream we all wish for our young boys—the dream in which he will lead others purposefully.

At some time, like Jacob, your son is (or has been or will be, depending on his age), a Stage Two heroic dreamer. He may feel the bursts of self-esteem felt by young boys who are focused, by parents and others, on their potential importance. Boys grow, compete, learn, seek their own assets, and compare their assets with their brothers and sisters. These boys are ready not only to be a loved boy with a birthright and ancestry, but also to envision themselves as heroes who will set out on a journey. They're too young to actually leave home at this age, nor would most of them say they want to leave home, but their maleness, their growing brains—their emotions, their heart, their soul—are expanding.

For Joseph, the struggle of the boy-hero comes as his many competitive half brothers turn on him in jealousy. They plot against him, challenging him to grow up and see that he's no big deal—just one of them; they become cruel to him, disrespecting him in mean, provocative ways, throwing him in a pit, then selling him into slavery in Egypt. Joseph's brothers, boys and men themselves, are so mean to him, so bent on wounding him that they even put blood on his beautiful coat, and tear it up as if an animal has eaten him. They return to their father, Jacob, and say, "Your blessed son is dead." Jacob is destitute with grief, and now Joseph is living as a slave, utterly humbled in his struggle to grow up.

As parents we might realize that our son can become the prideful, hated, envied boy, the boy who is enslaved by what we have given him—his beautiful things can actually kill off his identity, just as Joseph is "dead" because his coat is torn apart and destroyed—and his youthful dreams can be imprisoned because he doesn't understand how to be disciplined, responsible, honorable, and loving.

We gain wisdom from the Joseph story by watching for opportunities not only to adore and praise and give things, but also to provide responsibility, chores, and incentives by directing boys to hobbies, schoolwork, athletics—projects they can do in tandem with others as equal partners who both lead and follow. It is important to hold our sons close, but not so close that they don't understand the signals of struggle coming at them from the world. To build a boy's self-esteem without also giving him the tools to survive and thrive in the struggle between the primitive and the civilized is to create only half a man, a prince who will never become a king.

Stage Three: The Struggle for Freedom and the Love of Mentors

In the story of Joseph, the heroic journey toward maturity continues as the Jewish slave child is sold to the Egyptian captain of the guard, Potiphar, a prosperous man who sees something in Joseph's eyes. Genesis 39 says, "Potiphar saw that the Lord was with Joseph." This is a biblical euphemism for "this boy has many gifts and an important purpose." Seeing this in the young Joseph, Potiphar does not immediately set this new asset free to lead the world—instead, he teaches Joseph how to be a good *servant.* Joseph, who is depressed from being thrown into a pit without water by his own brothers, grief-stricken at not seeing his family again, in deep pain at now being a servant of a foreign empire, also begins to adapt, to bond with the man whom he is now serving, and starts to mature from this struggle.

Your son, as he moves toward or into puberty, feels like Joseph: at times he feels saddened by how difficult he can now see the world to be. Perhaps by now he has been betrayed by one or more friends he thought would be his "brothers" forever. Perhaps he's beginning to pull away from the adoration (and the discipline) of mom and dad. He may give up an athletic program or sport he once cared obsessively about—losing this avenue for building self-esteem.

The third stage of your son's development toward his ultimate heroism is fraught with potential anxieties, feelings of being scorned and trapped, yearnings to be free. Although these will only get stronger as family, friends, school, and society require severe adjustments from him, these feelings become internally palpable to your son during Stage Three.

The Wisdom of Purpose

SERVITUDE IS CRUCIAL TO MALE DEVELOPMENT

Jesus said, "And they shall be my disciples." One crucial thing we often don't realize as we see Stage Three feelings take hold is that a hero—thus, every boy—must go through a time of servitude. It is not by trying to free our sons from the complexities of growth that we build a hero—it is by making sure our sons become servants, apprentices, interns, and students—to ourselves and others who will guide the boys through these feelings, and this time of growth.

Every culture has a mythic story that involves a pubescent boy's servitude to one or more masters—or mentors. These mentors can be grandfathers and grandmothers (kings and queens of our family). They can be the "other parent," for instance, when a boy has not had much contact with a divorced father and has begun acting out against the mother; the father may now become the king or mentor of the young, ebullient, but undisciplined son, who goes to live with the father. The mentors can be coaches, teachers, counselors, or older boys.

The mentors are like John the Baptist for Jesus, or Merlin for young Arthur. The mentors can be like the many teachers of Harry Potter in that classic tale of male development. The mentor can be a computer geek who teaches your son about computers—and while gaming with him, working with him, coaching him technologically, also teaches him about the ways of life.

In all cases, we will know our son is on track with his journey to heroism if he is "serving" the mentors. Boys in Stage Three know, deep within them, that though they posture, they are not yet ready to lead; though they may be immensely shy, coming out of themselves will require them to be "servants" of others who have both led and set themselves free.

Stage Three is also the time when, if we say to our son at a perfect moment of accomplishment or love, "Son, you are my hero," he can feel the intense vibration of truth in that comment, and be prepared to spend a number of years (a decade or more) of trying to live up to the sound of those holy words.

Potiphar, the Pharaoh's captain, makes Joseph feel "heroic" in his servitude, which matures the young Joseph. Potiphar's healthy care of Joseph helps the boy gain purpose by seeing beyond his suffering toward a future, possible mastery. Inside the boy is the sense, "I am the servant now so that I can be a master later." Similarly, your son has perhaps been hurt by you in your parenting, or by other children, or by a series of his own failures—but his servitude to a hero (or heroes like yourself) can become his way of making sense of his struggle. Much of his making sense of it will take place with you as his parents, but much will also rely on mentors—coaches, teachers, or caregivers. Some of it will take place in his being alone, in solitude, to reflect on his own being. This aloneness is a final "takeaway" we can all gain from this point in Joseph's story. Joseph, even mentored, feels alone as a servant.

This aloneness will actually set him up for Stage Four of his heroic journey. He does not know that now, however; he just feels the moments of what we might call, regarding our sons, "going into his room, immersing himself in music, or in a book, or in nature, and not caring about anything else." Pubescent boys want and need to feel alone. Our culture, one that fills boys' lives with constant stimulation, often forgets how important it is for young heroes to experience loneliness during their development of purpose. It is a developmental gift in their journey. Even boredom, which is a form of loneliness, is important for them. If boys are well parented and mentored—if they are required to be both praised young men and servants of others who have already been down the road of heroism—their solitude, boredom, and loneliness will not be dangerous to their self-development, but will provide a time of self-knowing that will in fact nurture them.

Stage Four: The Progress of Intimacy

Have you noticed that just as your son is pulling away from you—going within, finding mentors, shifting his allegiances, and trying to find his particular gifts and talents—he is also nervous around girls (I will assume here that your son is heterosexual), who can, almost in an instant, completely throw your heroic son off balance?

Do you remember how this happened for you during the first glimmerings of your own sexual curiosity, whether you are a woman or a man? This is what happened, quite literally, to Joseph. In his case, it is the wife of his master, Potiphar, to whom he is emotionally and physically attracted. Your son will probably not have his first attraction to the wife of a coach or mentor—we need not take on this literal piece of the Joseph story—but your adolescent son will feel immense inner feelings now toward one or more girls and older women—the neighbor, the young teacher in middle school, a celebrity film star or pop singer—regarding love and intimacy.

He must go through these feelings for a number of years in order to become heroic and purposeful. This struggle will feel to him like a prison at times—just as Joseph is imprisoned by Potiphar when Potiphar finds out about the feelings between his wife and his young servant.

Joseph's words to the woman who desires him reveal, quite cogently, a hidden piece of what is going on inside your son during his struggle with intimacy in adolescence (and well into adulthood). In telling Potiphar's wife why he cannot be with her, he says, "Behold, my master hath committed all that he hath to me—how can I betray him by wickedly loving you?" Young Joseph is developing a sense of honor in intimacy, an ability to make the right choices at the right time—choices that (1) ensure integrity for himself, (2) show compassion for others, (3) provide a healthy and purposeful stake in his community, and (4) seek the most free and powerful outcome possible for the world as a whole.

Honor is the way a hero survives every suffering—he can say, "Though I suffer, I acted honorably." Honor is a pact the hero makes, saying, "I will carry in myself throughout my life an invisible covenant with justice and purpose, and thus will know I have always done good, even when I'm passing through attractions of love and sex."

A sense of honor is a crucial mark of maturation and civilization in young men. During adolescence, boys are enormously stimulated but also confused by many things, from what happens in themselves when they are attracted to lovers, to the process of reproduction and sexual pleasure. Through their families, many boys belong to religious organizations that increase the boy's confusion by overreacting to things like masturbation. It is possible that even these religions are responding to the confusion the male priests and others felt as boys themselves.

The adolescent boy who struggles through his confusions about sexual desire has to learn both how to restrain himself and, gradually, how to have an honorable and respectful relationship with the individual of his curiosity and desire. He learns that it is honorable to sacrifice himself for his lover and new best friend (and, later, the woman who may become the mother of his children); and he learns that it is honorable to hold on to a strong, independent self so that he can constantly remain of service to his lover, his children, and his community. He learns these heroic lessons through three bases of adolescent experience with intimacy:

1.   Teachings about love, both from teachers and books, and from people of his own lineage—stories of how love has always been and used to be for men like him
2.   Examples and models he sees around him, most intimately among his own parents, close family, and mentors
3.   Experiences with peers, in the banter, talk, and goal-setting intimacy of other boys, and then with girls and women in romantic experiences that affect him deeply

Meister Eckhart, a theologian of the Renaissance, wrote, "It can often seem that he who suffers for love does not suffer at all—suffering, in fact, is forgotten when we are in love." For the adolescent boy and the young man learning about what a crucial, life-defining role intimacy will play in his heroic journey, a joy seemingly like no other fills him up completely, for he discovers a way, if even only temporarily, to see beyond every struggle of adolescent boyhood and feel only immense love.

But also, as he grows through adolescence and learns how to relate, how to be close, how to let go of someone with whom he is not in love, or even someone whom he adores but does not adore him— these experiences all include times of embarrassment, rejection, a feeling of inadequacy, and humiliation. He may, in the end, have only his honor to hold on to.

As our sons enter and explore Stage Four of the heroic journey of purpose, we can be available to them as good listeners and tellers of our own stories of intimacy. We help our sons by setting good boundaries and expectations regarding their relationships and romances— setting limits for cell phone use, looking at their MySpace account if we think they are behaving inappropriately or someone is being inappropriate with them. Although you must be the one to choose the right dating age for your son, a good rule of thumb is to not let a boy date alone with a girl until he is around sixteen years old. Your values are your honor, and you pass them on to your son as guidelines during his times of experimenting with intimate joy, painful frustration, and dreams of future marriage and bliss.

If your son is going down a path with a girl that appears to lead him totally away from his heroic journey and instead into an obsessive feeling that he can't be happy without this girl, you might have to get help from counselors or other mentors. If your adolescent son is so wild with enthusiasm and desire that he wants to elope or "get married" to the first girl who responds to his efforts with tolerance or affection, you will be called on to restrain and contain his enthusiasm, with clear parental boundaries. By acting in these ways with your boy, you are not only helping him through his own confusing feelings, but also helping him see that the fourth stage in the heroic journey of purpose development is not meant to last forever. At some point, it will be time for a "next step," a new stage of wonderful struggle for your young hero.

Stage Five: The Discovery of a Boy's Inner Power

Joseph learns a lot during his stay in the Egyptian prison. Though he suffers and struggles, he is a young man whom "the Lord was with," and for whom the Lord so cared that Joseph was able to still be purposeful and of use, even while imprisoned. This happens through a relationship with a new mentor, the prison keeper. This mentor sees (as had Joseph's own parents, then Potiphar, then Potiphar's wife) something divine, an inherent birthright, some essentially good and important qualities in this young man.

Then, through an opportunity presented by a baker and butler who are thrown in prison with Joseph by the Pharaoh, Joseph discovers or, in truth, rediscovers his ability to interpret dreams. This rediscovery and its reflection of Joseph's personal development of original power, is the fifth stage of a son's journey of heroism and purpose.

THE JOY OF PURPOSE

Feeling the Truth of Who He Is

A boy lives through things in order to feel the truth of them.

—Indian poet, Kabir

No bird soars too high, if he soars with his own wings.

—William Blake

The power which resides in a man is new in nature, and none but he knows what that is which he can do, nor does he know until he has tried.

—Ralph Waldo Emerson

Have you noticed that your adolescent son can become almost obsessively focused on one or more particular expressions of himself—intimate relationships, academics, athletics, music, inventions, or computers—as a way of "building his own wings" even as he feels the ups and downs of adolescent social relationships and experimentations? As you notice your son's focus, you are seeing or hoping to see his sense of real power—his maturation from boyhood fantasies to actual talents, skills, and powers that will, in part, ground him and also free him in his adult life.

In Joseph's case, you may recall that when he was just a boy, the ability to interpret dreams—his original power—actually led him into difficulty. His family over-adored him and did not provide enough discipline, thus he became arrogant, interpreting his dreams in ways that alienated him from those he loved. At the same time, the misinterpretation (or egotistical interpretation) of his own dreams propelled him forward on his heroic journey. His original gift and the essential creative power that grounded him in his particular and future purpose in life (which, we will soon learn, is to save Egypt from drought), actually showed up early in his life. Now in the story, as it shows up again in Stage Five, the power he may have misused in immature boyhood is better used as an adolescent.

So it may be quite clearly with your own son on his heroic journey. He is now fourteen, fifteen, sixteen, or older, and moving into a deeper sense of purpose for his life. You can sense him entering this fifth stage when you see him discovering his inner powers, and focusing on paths of self-esteem and achievement that are real for him.

In today's world, many of our sons don't enter this stage fully until their twenties. They are late maturers for many reasons, including not having been servants earlier in life, or not having had sufficient responsibility and discipline earlier in life. But still, they try to mature, and we try to help them mature, by helping them find realistic "powers." And so often we notice these sources of power and achievement not only when the young man pursues girls, not only when he finds one or more new mentors for his emerging individuality, maturity, and creativity, but also when we hear an echo, as in Joseph's story, of a "voice" speaking from the boy's past (or even from our family's lineage) that says, "I have powers that others have had, and powers I have had myself, when I was younger, but now I need to understand them and use them in my own original way."

Some boys don't break through at all—they aren't motivated to seek and find their power or to do anything of much worth. They remain obsessed with a girl and have no other self. They get immersed in technological entertainments that lead them nowhere. They do very little schoolwork and rebel against you and society with no seeming purpose or heroic power. They may even get into trouble with the law. Later in this book, we will look more closely at how to help these boys, providing practical ways to get them back on the path to heroism and purpose.

At this point in his story, however, Joseph is not one of those boys—he interprets the dreams of his fellow prisoners, and thus gains (and regains) his "magical powers," the power that will be a useful foundation of his achievement of life purpose. In the butler's dream, he predicts a long life. From the baker's dream, he sees death coming in three days. The Biblical story shows how right Joseph's powers are. In the story, the butler is set free by the jailer and returned to his post by the Pharaoh. The baker, however, is hanged exactly as Joseph predicted.

Of all the many powers an adolescent boy can gain in his boyhood, adolescence, and young adulthood—good looks, athletic ability, and intelligence that attract girls to him and provide him with achievement and opportunities; an ability to be socially adept; a specific talent and skill set for computers, or filmmaking, business, music, art, or writing—those that will guide him into the next step of his journey of purpose will feel like a special kind of "magic" for him.

A mom talked to me about her son who had seemed somewhat lost in middle school. He spent all his spare time gaming online, but not doing much else. Then, in high school, he took up chess. In fact, he became obsessed enough with chess that it worried her. As I worked with this family, the mother began to see the part that chess might be playing in her son's journey.

During a session, she said, "Yes, it is becoming almost magical for him." She was surprised that he liked it even more than video games. He began to hang out with friends who played chess; he met a boy who wanted to be a filmmaker, a girl who was a math whiz, and an older teenager who could do anything at all with a computer. He learned from each of these young people, and his horizons expanded.

Boys are immensely project-driven: they don't tend to multitask among as many ways of becoming adult as girls do. As we noted in Chapters Two and Three, there are a number of neurological and biological reasons for this. If you have this kind of son, you may notice that it is through a project of deep interest that the boy walks through a doorway into adulthood. He can develop other talents than chess, of course, or than dream interpretation, but later on in his life we will notice that this almost magical power he gained through his concentrated project is intertwined with his adult purpose.

For the boy who loved chess, it became technology—this mother's son is now working as a computer support "techie" at a major university. For Joseph, it was interpreting dreams. In the next stage of his journey toward purpose, he will meet the mentor who will transition him into adulthood, the mentor who clearly needs his youthful magic.

Stage Six: The Mentoring of Adult Purpose

Think back for a moment to your ancestral cultures. Make a list of all the ancestral places you and your boy's other parent are from. The following is a list that was provided by a mother of three sons during a workshop on mentoring in Washington, D.C.:

ME:
> On my father's side: Ukraine, Romania, Poland
> On my mother's side: Spain, Portugal

MY HUSBAND:
> On his father's side: Kenya, Zimbabwe
> On his mother's side: India (South Central)

I've purposely picked a multiracial example in order to show how universal to all cultures is this sixth stage. When you make your list, and even if you just use the list this mother provided, think back to the original cultures in each of these places. Go back all the way to villages and small towns. Think about what fifteen- to eighteen-year-old boys were doing then. They weren't playing video games, or podcasting, or going to YouTube and Facebook. They were apprentices to masters of trade, craft, or work. In Eastern Europe, the adolescent boy was apprenticed to a tailor or a shoemaker. In Spain or Portugal, the adolescent boy was apprenticed to a fisherman or a carpenter. In central Africa, the adolescent boy was apprenticed to a hunter or a planter; in India, to a metal worker, dam builder, or monk. No matter where we trace back our ancestry, our great-great-grandfathers, during their "adolescence" (which was really young adulthood for them, as most were married by fifteen), focused their raw and powerful energy through the guidance of parents, extended family, and "masters" or "mentors."

No matter where your people are from, it was assumed that young men needed masters and mentors to complete their psychosocial development, and to make sure they were trained for a form of work that would sustain their families. When these boys were lucky, they would become apprentices and be given over to the care of masters whose guidance fit their inner drives and yearnings of individual purpose.

Michelangelo and Leonardo da Vinci became apprenticed to artisans and artists. A boy good with horses was, ideally, apprenticed to a man good with horses. The "magical power" inside the boy was an inner guide for the boy and his family to find the best master to whom to apprentice him, and help his original energy find its fuller purpose in the world. The boy's apprenticeship to the master of the craft or trade is somewhat like the "servitude" we discussed earlier in Joseph's journey, but also different. This apprenticeship happens later in a boy's development, during his young adulthood.

Of course, in many cases our ancestors did not get to pick and choose to whom their young "Joseph" would be apprenticed. The families had to just assign sons to work and workplaces from a very young age, and the sons, in the interests of sheer survival, had to become apprentices to any man who would teach them how to make any kind of living. Fortunately, today, most of your sons in adolescence and early adulthood will be able to pick and choose their masters and their mentors, with your help and guidance.

Questions of Purpose

Are You a Hero, Son?

If your son would write down answers to the following questions over a month or so, and then share parts of those journal entries with you (or another trusted mentor), his own inner dialogue and struggle with issues of heroism and purpose could be engaged in powerful ways.

- What are your strengths as a young adult?
- When you think about the future, what excites you the most?
- When you think about the future, what scares you the most?
- What are the gifts you have inherited from your father? Your grandfathers?
- What are the gifts you have inherited from your mother? Your grandmothers?
- What are your core values? What beliefs are you most devoted to right now? Why?
- Who is helping you to master each talent you have? Who is helping you to move beyond each negative part of yourself?
- Do you need more help? What particular people do you wish you spent more time with?
- How are things going with girls (or with_____; fill in the name of a friend here)? Do you need help from me or anyone else in understanding love? Do you have sexual questions to which you need answers?

Because of his "magical" ability to interpret dreams, Joseph is brought as a young man before the Pharaoh, the representative of the magical god of the Egyptian world, to interpret dreams that had been confusing the ruler.

Pharaoh dreamed that he stood at a river, and seven famished animals rose out of the river, and they ate the grass in the nearby meadow, and became fat; then, seven other animals came up out of the river and ate the fat animals, but they were still not satisfied, they were still famished, and the Pharaoh woke up frightened.

Joseph "saw" for the Pharaoh from these dreams that there would be seven years of plenty, in which the Pharaoh would need to store up grain and other food, for after that, there would be seven years of drought and famine. Egypt would not survive unless it stored up its food.

Upon hearing Joseph predict this from the interpreted dreams, Pharaoh paid close attention to this young Hebrew, took him under his wing, saved his country by heeding the young man's advice, and ended up giving the former Hebrew slave great political and social power.

Stage Six of your son's journey to purpose will often require and be best expressed through a new apprenticeship toward a mission or purpose. Perhaps it is a new teacher who becomes a mentor to your son—or perhaps a coach. A mother and a father at a workshop told me about their adolescent son who had been having anger management issues. He had already been kicked out of one school. Among the other techniques this family used in order to help the boy was to get him into karate. This helped, but he couldn't get along with the sensei (teacher) The sensei himself suggested that the boy play football, given his size and personality. The boy, now sixteen, took to football immediately. The physicality, the rigor, the discipline, the camaraderie—it was a perfect fit for him. He excelled under the care of coaches and older players. This boy later joined the military and then, upon returning to the states, decided to get a degree in education, which he is now pursuing—he wants to coach football and tennis at the high school level.

Our sons cannot fully develop their own sense of purpose if we don't help them find the masters and mentors of late adolescence who will encourage their newfound and honed power and guide their "magic," their "gifts," their "temperaments" toward service and work in society. Parents provide love, support, and discipline; earlier mentors focus on helping the boy experience servitude to greater ideals; and experiences with intimacy build character through joy and struggle; in contrast, the mentor of the late adolescent generally apprentices the young man to a specific work.

Stage Seven: Devotion to Family and Community

The section of the Joseph story that involves boyhood, adolescence, and early male adulthood ends in a seventh stage of development. Pharaoh decides that "God is with Joseph," seeing in this young man the gifts that others have also seen, and deciding that Joseph would become the leader of the hard and important work faced by Egypt. Joseph accepts the honor of office, and begins a long path of fully adult purpose. He saves Egypt from destruction, marries, has a family, and becomes a devotee of family, community, and the nation. He will also later save another nation—his original bloodline, the Hebrews—by bringing them into Egypt, where they can survive the drought.

By the time your young hero reaches Stage Seven, he has gained

- A sense of honor, having overcome his weaknesses (for Joseph, as for many boys, these were arrogance and a sense of entitlement)
- A sense of enterprise, having seen what he is good at, and found the opportunity and help to bring his inner assets to bear where they are needed
- A sense of responsibility, having struggled without power until he realizes that true power comes as much from taking personal responsibility as it does from the desire to succeed and gain status
- A sense of his originality, having seen what his "special pow- ers" are, and bringing them into his manhood consciously, and through his work
- A sense of how to be intimate with and respectful to a mate, having experimented, learned, and grown a life of the heart
- A sense of creativity, having understood that he has gifts, and that he is now living in a situation where he can creatively expand, organize, and devote these gifts toward the good of the world around him

In short, your young hero has become a good man.

If we can ensure these developmental stages for our sons, we can be very proud. We will have launched our sons on their way to successful lives as young men who are good at certain things that are worthwhile to them, their family, and the world. They will be poised for success, in whatever their interest area—whether in college or not, whether working at an art or a craft, whether working with their hands or their intellect or both. Our boys will be successful Josephs now, succeeding not just at "anything," but specifically at what they believe are their individual paths of purpose.

Things may change for each young man in the future. He may have many different careers by the time he ends his work life. But when he looks back on his life, ideally he will see that he advanced through the seven stages of healthy boyhood, and, through the power and grace he gained in them, devoted himself to living well in a complex world. Among his many careers, he has been heroic: honorable, enterprising, responsible, original, intimate, and creative.

Even the young man who has no other assets or opportunities except to work to feed his family—at seventeen, in a coal mine or on an assembly line—that young man is still Joseph or your son in the seventh stage. Although what he does for work is more physically, mentally, and emotionally grueling than dressing in robes and being the king's advisor, it is still heroic, for he is sacrificing some of his own dreams in service of those people and the ideal for which he believes he was born: to be devoted to the opportunities of the next generation. And within the structure of coal mining or working on an assembly line he can achieve a level of responsibility, leadership, and selflessness that will help him rise within those ranks to higher positions. There have been many cases of such workers eventually running the company or a good part of it.

No matter what your son's seventh stage of heroic development looks like, you will know he has arrived at that place of maturity when he becomes devoted to helping his family and community thrive. You will see that you have raised a young man who has arrived at the threshold of full adulthood, and sees that he must do what is necessary to help the world. You will sense he has learned a lesson—one that he may rebel against for a time, or may need time off from for a while—that nonetheless enters his heart and soul to stay.

The lesson is: "When you live your adult life purposefully, in service of the world, you will not need me to say, 'Son, you are my hero.' You will understand all on your own how important and heroic you are."

The Story Ends, for Now

As we end our study of heroic development in Genesis, the mission of Joseph's life is not over. A reading of later chapters of Genesis shows that he must not only care for Egypt through tough times, but also work on his own inner life: in his case, he must make peace, emotionally and spiritually, with his own family and people.

There is a saying from the Talmud: "When you conquer your own heart, then you become somebody." Joseph is carrying around a great deal of pain from what happened in his childhood. Much of his adult journey involves conquering this pain, making peace with his half brothers, and being reunited with his father.

THE JOY OF PURPOSE

From Success to Significance

You fully discover the joy of life not from success, but from success that you have made into significance.

—Ambassador Andrew Young

Joseph's story continues through seven more stages of male adulthood. Throughout these stages Joseph discovers and explores new kinds of inner and outer freedom. His adult life of purpose ends up bringing the Israelites to Egypt where, almost parallel with Joseph, they too will be imprisoned and enslaved for a time. His life ultimately becomes central to the Jewish journey toward freedom, the enslavement of the people in Egypt and later, in Exodus, their liberation from slavery and foundation of the Jewish people, who eventually settle in Israel. As we move to Part Two now, let's carry forward the map of heroism, the seven stages, the understanding of magical boyhood and adolescent seekers. Let's bring them with us as we look at how to take the science and the story of your sons' lives even deeper into everyday adjustments and practices, so that you can fully feed the boys' need for purpose, and guide them as they make their heroic journey through each stage of life.

PART

Helping Our Sons Find Their Purpose in Life

A child is a person who is going to carry on what you have started. He is going to sit where you are sitting, and when you are gone, attend to those things which you think are most important. He will assume control of your cities, states, and nations. He is going to move in and take over your churches, universities, and corporations . . . the fate of humanity is in his hands.

—ABRAHAM LINCOLN

5

Creating Families of Purpose for Boys

What cannot be achieved in one lifetime will happen when one lifetime is joined to others.

—HAROLD KUSHNER

KAREN ALBRIGHT, A GRANDMOTHER FROM GEORGIA, wrote regarding her two sons, born two years apart:

> Jeff and Alan are in their thirties now, with kids of their own (they have given us five grandchildren), but I still remember how busy they were as young boys. My husband and I both worked, and for a number of years, we had to juggle seeing one another in order to see the boys, but we both tried to instill a sense of purpose in them. We made sure they knew why we worked so hard, and we expected them to work hard, and become somebody.
>
> We didn't live near any relatives, but we both remembered a grandmother and grandfather who had influenced us as kids, so we tried to make an extended family out of our friends. Our boys had so much energy, we needed help! And both of them were quite sensitive, especially my youngest. I think I was harder on him than my husband (which surprises people), but I wanted him to be his best, and I pushed him even harder than my husband did when he was young.

Now that we have grandkids, I'm glad we can live near them and help with the kids. We have created the "parent-led team" we heard you talk about, the "three-family system." My husband is retired and I work part time, so we can be around, and we try not to be bossy. We work very hard to love and cherish our daughters-in-law. They and our sons are the leaders of the team. Jeff's wife is a doctor and works long hours. I baby-sit for her as much as possible.

Raising boys today is complicated. I can see how easily they can get lost. They seem completely self-sufficient, but they aren't. They need a team around them. Now that I have grandsons running around, I am so glad they have lots of people who care about them, and guide them. They love to be loved, and I see a successful future for them.

Karen's email continued, and the love she had for boys and men was clear. Also clear was her reflection back on her family life when she was young. She remembered it as so busy that she couldn't really catch up to what it all meant and what worked well until now, in her early seventies.

In Part One of this book, we explored boys' developmental journey, focusing on the deep and crucial need they have to be seekers and finders of an important purpose in life. In Part Two, let's focus on new tools and insights for the family toolbox—practical ideas and strategies for parents, extended family members, community members, teachers, friends, and social systems. These tools will help you manage, guide, and fulfill all the promise of the purposeful boy we explored in Part One, thus helping ensure a heroic journey for your son.

Creating a Three-Family System: The Parent-Led Team

At the top of the list of innovations that help boys grow up well is this one: repositioning the word "family" away from a pure nuclear family model (mom and dad and kids) to a larger concept of family. The logic behind this can be introduced this way: Boys are such explorers and so filled with the energy and imagination we discussed in Part One that they need *both* close-up contact with their nuclear family parents *and* wide-lens intimacy and experiences guided by a set of other "family members" who provide significant help. One vision of family without the other is generally not enough to ensure we are raising purposeful and successful sons.

In Karen's email, you may have noted the terms "three-family system" and "parent-led team." This team and multifamily approach to parenting can be one of your greatest allies in making sure you raise a boy of purpose. I introduced this concept twelve years ago in *The Wonder of Boys* and refined it in *A Fine Young Man* and *The Minds of Boys*. When it first came out, it was a concept without a great deal of success under its belt yet. Now, over a decade later, I can say that emails like Karen's come in weekly, sometimes daily. Parents and other caregivers of both boys and girls are putting it into effect and refining it as they do, and, thankfully, sharing their successes, insights, and innovations with me and my professional team. You'll meet many of them in the next four chapters.

A New Kind of "Family"

Kathy Stevens, mother of two sons and grandmother of three, has utilized and taught the three-family system. She shares her insight: "If my decades of work with boys have taught me anything, it is that they are hungry not just for mom (though some days it's only mom they want) nor just for dad (though quite often they need their fathers desperately) nor just a teacher, or mentor, or group of peer friends, or community, or school, or church. Boys want and need all of these."

She's right. Boys are struggling so powerfully (and often so nonverbally and unconsciously) with emotional intelligence and cognitive development, the shames and joys of the growing body, the burdens and joys of education, and the vagaries of romance and love, that their human journey needs the care of many parents, many "leaders," many "elders" who will value, admire, and guide them.

In this model, boys need their parents to be leaders of a family system that is composed of:

- The First Family (the nuclear family)
- The Second Family (three or more other leaders who are or become extended family)
- Social institutions, such as schools or churches, men's clubs, athletic programs, that are so well matched to boys' needs that they feel like a "tribe" attached to the family

If you think about everything we learned in Part One, you might see immediately how difficult it is for one parent or even two to help fulfill all of a boy's primary needs. You might also see that even when one or two parents can fulfill primary needs of food, shelter, clothing, love, and attention, the whole expression and discovery of purpose that a boy strives for would still be limited if only one or two people tried to help him refine it.

Finding Emotional Support

Sara, a mother in Austin, Texas, wrote regarding her success in branching out for emotional and other sources of guidance for her two sons. "One of the most important things I did when I became a single mom was to reconnect my sons to their grandparents and uncles and aunts. From that time on, my sons always had an adult to go to, no matter what they were feeling or experiencing. I understood that my ex-husband and I loved them, but we weren't enough for them. Admitting this was one of the most important things I've ever done."

Sara's family came to a point where they were compelled to reach out to others. Because these families utilized some of my work and language for their process, I was able to meet the families and talk to them. These parents all said variations of something I've heard for decades. "Boys need so much more than we realize—and one person's way of getting at their feelings and emotions just isn't enough." To reach out, these families needed to become brave and open, to allow themselves to be honest and vulnerable about their most personal feelings and problems.

What I mean can be illustrated by a story. After a parent workshop I led, a group of mothers came up to me, and each said similar things, which I have melded together in these words: "I as a mother have felt terrible every time my son does something wrong, isn't empathic, or can't express his emotions, or can't find his way. I feel like it's my fault for not teaching him what he should know. What I've learned today is that it is not my job alone to help him be 'the seeker'—I need to find lots of good people to help me. This is a different way of thinking. It's going to take me some time to figure out how to be as much a team leader as a mom."

It takes a first step of bravery to admit "I am not enough," and indeed, it takes time. It means a reorientation of the nuclear family, the other extended family and community resources available, including schools and faith communities, toward the son's energy of seeking and heroism. It is initially difficult to break away from individualized parenting in our culture especially, where boyhood (and girlhood) have been placed on the shoulders of one or two parents exclusively. The moms in the story came to see that no other culture in the world has bought so completely into the illusion of the nuclear family. In every culture, one parent is only one part of the template that raises the good son, an emotional and purposeful man, and two parents are only two parts—they are not the only major source of purpose and success for the boy (or girl). It is mainly in our culture—for social, economic, historical, and other reasons, such as fear of predators—that we have highly "individualized" the human family into a nuclear unit. In so doing, we tend to think we should "do it all" as parents.

As you go through this chapter and the subsequent ones, I hope you will feel a new freedom and a new effectiveness in building success and purpose into your son's everyday existence, and I hope you will experience some deepening and enlightening new ways to look— through a three-family lens—at such issues of purpose-building as "values," "morality," and even "destiny."

The Development of a Boy's Sense of Destiny in the Family System

Malidoma Some is a Dagara teacher from Burkina Faso, Africa, who came to America with a purpose. He begins his autobiography, *Of Water and the Spirit: Ritual, Magic and Initiation in the Life of an African Shaman*, with this explanation: "My name is Malidoma. It means roughly 'Be friends with the stranger/enemy.' Because the Dagara believe that every individual comes into this life with a special destiny, some names are programmatic. They describe the task of their bearers and constitute a continual reminder to the child of the responsibilities that are waiting up ahead. A person's life project is therefore inscribed in the name she/he carries."

Dr. Some holds three master's degrees and two doctorates from the Sorbonne and Brandeis University. I met him in the mid-1990s. He was and is a learned African teacher who has lived in Africa, Europe, and America, a man who has definitely seen the world, a free spirit, a generous person, a role model for many young men and women around him. As he notes, he came into this world with "a destiny" defined by his tribe and people—that is, he was given a purpose in life from early boyhood. You might think this was a burden to him, but if you meet Dr. Some, you do not meet a man who feels oppressed by his destiny. For him, this destiny grounds the values he knows and teaches, and it is a way toward emotional and social freedom. He was born with a "group destiny" which he has molded and shaped to fit who he is as an individual.

Spending time with Dr. Some was, for me, akin to spending time with many of the people I met as boy when my family lived in Hyderabad, India. Many of my parents' adult friends were men and women who seemed to have a sense, from earliest childhood, that they came into this world with a tribal, historical, and personal reason for being. They used the word "karma" for destiny. Like Dr. Some, they were inspired by their karma to develop values that freed them to become fully human and whole as individuals, within a defined social and religious context.

Our American attitude toward our children is often different from this, isn't it? We worry, for both boys and girls, that talking about destiny will hurt them, oppress them, enslave them to their ancestor's or parents' destiny (and therefore, to old tribal errors and mistakes). We are a highly individualistic culture at the family level, even trying to make sure that no one else tries to teach our children "values"— because we feel that only mom or dad should have that ultimate responsibility.

Although African and Asian views of family, destiny, and values have their own flaws, they offer a depth of understanding of extended family life—and of the purpose of that family life—from which we can learn. Plumbing its depths can feel risky to us, for it requires us to say, "Maybe my son needs a destiny," and if we say that, we will have to say, "Well, I sure need help teaching him that!" Indeed, "destiny" is a huge concept, a huge feeling, and some of it comes from far beyond one or two parents.

Your son's destiny is not something you need to know at his birth— but what might it feel like to raise him, every day, with openness to the idea that he is destined for greatness, some of which is tribal, comes from "a people," and grows from "the past"? And if we are open to the feeling of a destiny, the sense of a boy's value growing from networks of people who came before him and are now all around him, wouldn't we perhaps alter our thinking about what we teach our son, even how we raise him? We would see his greatness as part and parcel of something much greater than our singular efforts as an individual parent.

This is a very empowering way to see a son, and leads to a tool for raising boys that teaches "values" in both a three-family context, and as part of the purpose of boys.

The Ten Values Tool

When we expand our minds as parents to think about such things as destiny and tribe and three families, we expand our role as parents to include being leaders of a parent-led team of people who will explore our son's destiny with him. We look to set up structures for his development that will guard his greatness, protect his journey toward it, help him along the way, be there for him when he needs help, and provide him with values, emotional intelligence, character development, and social success. We even begin to wonder if a son may fall short of his destiny if he only has one or two approaches to life stored in his psyche. We expand to wanting the help of uncles, aunts, cousins, grandparents, family friends, schools, teachers, coaches, trainers, peers—all of whom are needed if a son is to "gain his name," "find his destiny," "develop his purpose," and "find himself."

To help make this expansion of parenting practical, I have developed and used a "Ten Values" model, or tool, which you can use to help define "destiny" in the context of the ethics and values of *your* family. As you make sure to help your son gain these ten basic values of purpose development—what he needs to fulfill his destiny—you will be able to gauge how you do or do not have enough of an extended family system in place. Where you need help in teaching a particular value, you will generally be able, quite quickly, to see what other person you need to bring into the three-family system to help your son.

The Ten Values

Here are ten values with discussion starter questions and statements. After listing these, we'll go further into each one. Be creative when you think about three families teaching these crucial developmental values. Even if grandpa and grandma live far away, think about how the Internet and email can be used to create more contact between them and your son. Think about schools, neighborhood groups, clubs, athletics, and individuals all around you whom you can enlist for help.

1. *The Value of Legacy.* What's in my name? What important legacy do I carry from my family's past into my own destiny?
2. *The Value of Give and Take.* Will my family teach me how to value giving as much as taking, so that I can always feel I am fairly earning my destiny in this world?

3. *The Value of Failure.* Will my family overprotect me, or will those who love me help me learn that failure is a crucial part of my destiny, for it is through challenge that I learn how to change and grow?

4. *The Value of Independence.* If I can do it myself, I hope people will let me—if I can't, I hope they'll teach me how to do so; my destiny will not fully grow in me unless I find my own power.

5. *The Value of Identity.* I was born with a certain core personality and set of assets, which I must "meet" and value in constantly new ways as I seek and grow—will my family and caregivers each help me understand who I am?

6. *The Value of Self-Reflection.* There are some crucial insights no one can give me, but I cannot gather them to myself either, if I have not been taught by those who love me how to be silently engaged in thoughtful self-reflection.

7. *The Value of Ethical Action.* Everything that I do occurs within an ethical society; will my family help me learn how to advance my destiny through ethical actions that both fit and mold that society?

8. *The Value of Self-Discipline.* My anger, grief, sadness, and joy are all part and parcel of who I am, but I need help managing and expressing them to the good, for my destiny can become stifled or even imprisoned if I cannot express and discipline my emotions.

9. *The Value of Self-Doubt.* I am human and imperfect—my destiny is not to be perfect; I need those who love me to love me unconditionally for who I am, but also teach me how to judge myself conditionally when I deserve critique.

10. *The Value of Faith.* Whatever higher power I have faith in, I must remember always that I cannot go it alone in this world—that to push myself toward freedom, goodness, and love, I need help learning trust, the humility of faith, and the importance of service in my destiny.

Using the Ten Values to Expand Your Family

Let's explore the ten values more deeply now, one by one, and as we do so, let's look at how each one cries out not only for your own parental innovations, but also for help from a three-family system. In each case, we'll consider practical ideas for teaching these values not only to your son, but to a whole team that comes together to lead, coach, and admire him in his discovery of each value.

The Value of Legacy is a hidden starting place of destiny in your son. Boys love feeling like they came from a bloodline, a past, a previous world of meaning. They like dreaming about "the old worlds." They like knowing about lineage, ancestors, and magic that might still exist in their blood as a hidden seat of power. Our culture has somewhat turned away from the value of legacy because we turned away from the gender unfairness of "passing on the farm to the oldest son." And because many of us live in a "new world," away from "the old country," we may unconsciously see "legacy" as a burden rather than an innovation.

Legacy can be a burden, but rarely do the bad memories of life in older places outweigh the good of making sure a boy knows where he came from, and thus, who are the heroes in his own lineage. His family heritage is in some ways the foundation of his present adventure. He yearns, even if unconsciously, for people to transmit and inculcate the passions and purpose of the family's past into him. This kind of family history can be taught by mom and dad, but other relatives can add depth, flavor, and inspiration. Grandparents are a source of such information and often enjoy the role of showing old photographs or telling stories of "the old country" or the old farm or that apartment in the ghetto or life in the Depression. Quite often, to teach the value of legacy, a family needs to create rituals—family reunions, weekly visits to grandpa and grandma, watching old home movies that you've compiled and converted to DVD.

If a son carries the first name of someone in your family who is still alive, that person can write a letter or email to your son (or many over the years) regarding how he or she understands a person's journey through this world. If the namesake is not alive or able to help, you as parents can still help your son understand the value of a *name*, why you gave him that first name and what it means to you and your family.

per... ...ly connected to a
...why you chose it,
so ...I was carrying you
in r... to be very musical
bec... ...usic you stopped
kick... ...Frederick after
Cho... ...g *Oliver Twist* just
befo..., ...we named you Charles, after Dickens . . . What
a gr... ...ars from you and others the family history ... ...eded him, he not
onl... ...but he also gains a
dee...

...boys in our society.
We ... ...rial possessions to
ou... ...ease of life we have
wo... ...we might give too
m ... ...ng the more gener-
o... ...n more at home and
re... ...a great deal in three-
family systems is a literal give-and-take ritual.

THE JOY OF PURPOSE

What You Give

We make a living by what we get, but we make a life by what we give.

—Winston Churchill

Your son can quite literally expand his sense of family by giving one object to a charity organization that supports impoverished families for every gift or toy he receives from you or others. The value of equitable exchange that surrounds this innovation can be taught in part by one or two parents, but it also helps to have a number of "parents" echoing its necessity. When a boy is old enough to work outside the home (as we'll explore later in this chapter), extended family and community can become like "parents," helping him by hiring him to rake lawns, cut grass, do anything that teaches give-and-take, and thus help him learn more about his own real power, destiny, and purpose through work.

The Value of Failure is often forgotten in our families because so many of us have been convinced somehow that sadness or guilt or shame will automatically bring adult failure to our children. Most of us want our sons' self-esteem to be as high as possible at all times, and we worry when he seems unhappy.

Clinical depression is certainly a reason to worry, but it is also generally true that failure is *not* a reason to worry, especially when there is a strong safety net of parents and caregivers to help a boy navigate through his failures. Failure is a unique kind of sadness for someone who is seeking his destiny, a sadness that ideally inspires deep, helpful changes in the self.

Acknowledging the value of failure without jumping in to rescue our son may be more difficult for us as mom or dad than for another extended family or community member. Because it's pretty instinctive for a parent to want to keep a son's success ratio very high, we parents may need help from extended family members in making sure we don't overprotect.

And although no one can tell you how much to let your boy play "dangerously" in this world, the book *Dangerous Book for Boys* is a great help in creating your measuring stick. It is filled with relatively safe "dangerous" old-fashioned activities for boys that include helpful possibilities for failure, and that bring in other people, beyond one parent, who can help a boy recover and succeed.

The Value of Independence is directly linked to the value of failure. As we don't want our sons to fail (or not be chosen first for a team or be good at everything they try), we will drive them anywhere, give them anything, feed them anything they want, let them do anything they seem to need, even if it's a whim. We love our children and will bend down for them at every moment, whether they can help themselves up or not.

Yet doesn't a boy want to feel his own independence and strength? Doesn't he want to lift himself up? Isn't there a seat of passion and destiny that he cannot recognize or muster unless he feels helpless sometimes, and must raise himself up without help?

If your son can do something himself, it is often good to let him, even if he does it less well than an adult might, the first fifty times. In those situations where you feel that your son's failures are crushing him, it is of course crucial to step in, and even at these times, you may find you need three families, including mentors who can do the teaching you may be unable to do.

The Value of Identity is gained to a great extent by boys themselves as they make their journey through life—living at home, playing outside, going to school, bonding with others. Especially in adolescence, boys themselves take some control over their own identity by trying on new clothes and fads, trying out new kinds of relationships, and separating from their parents to "become adults."

Throughout this process, each boy (and each girl) has inborn assets, talents, personality, strengths, and weaknesses. The outside world exists to test these—to test and challenge the inborn identity of a human being—and the family exists to protect and help the child through the challenges (as well as provide tests and challenges of its own).

The process of identity development is a difficult one, and one parent generally can't fulfill it as well as many parents can. One or even two parents may not have the time, especially if both are working to support the family, they might miss an inborn asset or undervalue it, whereas another parent or family team member might say, "Let me help Brandon with math, I know he can do it," or "Let me take Bobby on a road trip, he'll love the maps and landmarks," or "I'll take Tim to the library every Friday and we'll read books together." Any small or large piece of the self can develop through three-family care that might one day become a touchstone of identity development for a boy.

The Value of Self-Reflection becomes even clearer as a boy grows up toward an identity, a sense of who he is. Boys who are gaining a sense of identity seek to reflect on that identity, shape it, and mold it themselves as much as it is being molded by family and society. Boys are, thus, very spiritual people, even though they may, at a certain point, come to resist what they see as the boredom of religion.

In your own life there are self-reflective moments, which you can model for your son. You also know other people who spend time thinking about themselves and their own development. These are often people who can show your son how to become thoughtful and contemplative. These might be religious people who can teach a sacred language of self-reflection, or even a teacher who loves books that are spiritual in nature.

Teaching the value of self-reflection builds a boy's strength in his world, for it provides him with the internal ability to mature and become a man. Every seeker must at times be thoughtful. Every hero, even as he tries to save the world, must stop to understand himself and the powers he serves.

If a boy can't sit silently in nature (or another quiet place) and look carefully at who he is and who he will become, he will not be fully capable of finding his destiny and purpose. He will be easily swayed by anyone whose mask of purpose he wants for himself.

Because self-reflection is a value that needs to be constantly taught and retaught to boys in various settings by various people, it can be crucial for you to lead a family team meeting to decide who is best at teaching it and in what ways. As you do this, you might keep in mind something parents have probably always suspected, something that brain scans are just now confirming: many of the parts of the brain that are involved with self-reflection also control ethical and moral decision making.

The Value of Ethical Action is taught by teaching good character, morality, and ethical debate. Boys need a great deal of help, as we saw in Part One, linking their future visions of their own power with the basic moral structure of their society. They need a lot of help in developing a moral code that will not only keep them safe during their decades of risk taking and achievement, but also serve humanity. Boys cry out for a variety of assistance in learning (often through trial and error) what is moral and ethical. One person generally cannot teach these things to a son. Quite often a mother can teach morality, but especially as adolescence comes, her son wants to rebel against her vision. Or perhaps the father is teaching morality, but the boy needs to argue constantly with the father. Or possibly the boy is developing in a vacuum of moral development, wherein mainly his peers are his morality teachers. In all these cases, ethical action cannot be fully taught by one person to energetic boys—a number of people need to teach it. Like the teaching of emotional literacy, the teaching of ethics and morality is most successful when it is a team effort.

And therein lies a potential issue. You may say, "But if I open up moral and ethical teaching to a team effort, I don't know what I'll get. My morals and family values may be so different from those of the church, the school, the community, or even my relatives that I'll confuse my son's development. I need to just teach him family values and morals myself."

It is indeed very possible that others will teach different and distinct morals from what you teach. You must be the final judge of what three-family assets you expose your son to. At the same time, we are sometimes overprotective of our sons' moral training today. We fear that a boy taught by a homosexual will become homosexual, or a boy taught by a person with different social values will corrupt our son. Actually, if our moral training of our boy was sound and serious in the first five years of life, his development of ethical action will rarely be derailed by the opinions of a person whose specific religion or values are somewhat different from ours. Especially if our son is ten or older, access to people who are different from him can actually help him develop a sense of what he believes and does not believe, and how he will become an ethical man.

As you work in your family team to teach ethics and morality to your son, I hope you will always be protective, but also look for a few people with whom you do not necessarily agree, and let these people become teachers to your son. You can then carry on your own discussions with your son about these individuals' values and ways of doing things.

A son begins to learn the *Value of Self-Discipline* from parents who impose discipline on him, but soon he will seek out others who will also impose and inspire discipline. A mom wrote me about her son who "was a hellion growing up. I was a single mom, and he was my biggest challenge. He fought all the time, wouldn't do what I asked. He got in trouble with the law, and that's when I switched schools—I sent him to a boys' school, where he got a lot of healthy discipline." She concluded, "My son is now a cop. I never wanted that, and I worry about him all the time, but at least he has a purpose. He turned all his anger at his father and me into something useful in the world."

This is a stark statement that speaks volumes. This son found a destiny that did not go in the direction the mother may have hoped, but he found it—he developed self-discipline and purpose. This parent couldn't help this boy alone; she needed a community to help change her son's path toward health and happiness. She expanded her vision of family as she tried to teach the value of self-discipline, and the larger "family" came through.

As you look at your son's life in your family system, ask these two questions:

1. Is my discipline of him just punishment (or just rewards), or is it also helping him learn self-discipline?
2. Do I have three or more other trusted elders helping me help him develop self-discipline?

Punishment is useful and important, but it must also lead to changed behavior, which shows that the boy is learning self-discipline. Punishment that leads to deep fear and rage in the boy is not developing self-discipline. If such punishment only leads to escalated acting out, it is not useful.

Rewards are also good tools, but they must lead to changed behavior. If rewards and incentives keep getting showered on the misbehaving boy, and he does not alter his course, they are leading to more trouble in the end, rather than less.

And so, any repeated discipline technique—using time outs, taking away privileges, spanking, giving incentives, paying cash for good behavior—all must lead to better behavior. Although one parent may be able to provide the whole path of self-discipline development for a boy, usually one parent cannot, especially from puberty onward. Boys desperately need three or more people to take charge of them and show them how to build enough self-discipline to fully achieve their destiny.

The Value of Self-Doubt. We parents love our children unconditionally, but should we respect them unconditionally? Talking about this can be very important as you look toward a vision of multifamily influences. One parent may give love and respect equally, no matter what a child does, always saying "good job" from the soccer sidelines, even when the boy fails. Both parents together may not be able or willing to help their son criticize himself and experience healthy self-doubt—protecting him from the pain of the very self-criticism that is crucial for healthy identity development, ethical development, and for self-discipline and purpose.

These parents especially need a host of other "parents" who will withhold respect for their son until he earns it—these others will give love and care, but show love in different ways than a parent might. These others will be tacitly saying: to become a man, you have to earn respect—respect won't be given to you just because you exist.

It is important to find these people for your son (and encourage him in bonding with them when he finds them himself). A coach, a karate instructor, a clergy member, an employer, a counselor, a grandparent, a parent of his best friend, a teacher . . . any and all might fit this profile. And this person (or these people) might seem a little "harsh" with the boy at times—but so long as the boy's development is safe (that is, his self and will are not being crushed), these other people can be crucial to developing his strength to find his destiny despite and even through his own flaws.

The Value of Faith is often thought of as a religious value, and thus "faith" is generally used in the sense of "faith community" or "faith in God." As such, faith is seen as a part of spiritual development. It indeed can be, and much of the value of faith is taught through religion and spiritual search.

At the same time, we can't assume that faith is always connected to some kind of formal religious observance or belief in God. This value is also about a boy's faith in the concept of his own destiny, and thus, a boy's faith in himself. Faith in oneself, the sense that one's individuality is a crucial and necessary part of the whole universe's progress, is the deepest level of self-confidence—it is a sense that "I am here on this earth, at this time, for a reason." This kind of self-confidence lasts even when the deepest pains are experienced. It lasts in a ghetto, through slavery, in a concentration camp, through the traumas of others' deaths, divorces, and losses.

This kind of faith cannot be taught by one person alone, or even by two busy people who love a son. This kind of faith needs many influences, each of whom is teaching a boy in his or her own way that this kind of faith is possible, in a variety of difficult circumstances. Boys seek and find this kind of faith in apprenticeship to not only parents but others who model faith in themselves. Thus, parents, grandparents, coaches, teachers, mentors, religious leaders, ministers, rabbis, and family friends . . . any and all of these individuals can help teach your son to believe that "I will survive and thrive because I am linked to a purpose in life that is beyond 'me,' and about something greater."

As you look at yourself and at those around you who are helping your son develop this kind of faith in his destiny, you may be asking and answering these two questions:

- When have I felt the most self-doubt, the greatest sense of being an imposter, with no real reason for being?
- What has helped me turn that self-doubt into fearlessness and faith in myself, the world, and higher power?

If your son is old enough to talk with you about these questions, do so. Bring in other people's stories, too. Let your son hear keys to faith in the voices of those who love him. Ask people to tell him stories of how they became seekers and what they found, how they tried to be heroic, and what heroism really is. Your son will gain keys to faith in himself—keys that will open doors to destiny and purpose in life-giving ways.

Three Challenges to Finding a Boy's Destiny

There is so much a boy will never understand about this life, and that's okay—he needs help being satisfied with his own destiny. If he can find a destiny and be satisfied that he is walking and even running in its pursuit, he will be a free spirit, and he will succeed in his own unique way.

As he makes this journey, he will meet and need to manage three major boyhood and adolescent challenges. You as a parent are being met by these very contemporary challenges, too, as you raise boys. There can be many challenges, of course, and though we've looked at many so far, I've found it crucial in working with parents right now, in the new millennium, to look carefully at these three issues:

1. How to deal with boyhood sexual issues
2. Whether and when an adolescent boy should go to work
3. What limits to set in our homes regarding the ever-increasing use of electronic media by our sons

These three challenge areas can help set aspects of a boy's destiny and each connects with family values and the three-family system. Simultaneously, each challenge, if not met by a strong family team, can seriously affect a boy's development. Let's explore these challenges, and integrate answers to questions about each one into our greater sense of wanting to help our son find a destiny and purpose in this world.

The Value of Teaching Sexual Purpose

Because sexuality is a large part of every boy's life, and because it is certainly a family issue, let's look carefully at sexuality now from a values perspective. Your son, even as a toddler, gets his first erection (and it can happen, as we said before, even in the womb); later, before he is ten, when he discovers his first moment of arousal from a picture (or internal fantasy image) of a naked potential sexual partner, he finds himself in a lifelong journey of joy, fear, power, morality, amorality, seriousness, and humor that will drive everything in his life from masturbation to economic decision making, love and marriage and life purpose.

Pubescent and adult males daily have up to ten times the number of sexual fantasies that females have. The primary science-based reason for this is probably the ten to twenty times higher amounts of testosterone in the male body and brain than the female. Another reason for adolescent male sexuality lies in lower amounts of oxytocin.

UNDERSTANDING PURPOSE

Oxytocin Rises but Falls Quickly in Males

A fascinating biological fact regarding the bonding chemical oxytocin can come in handy when you and your family team are helping boys deal with their own urges. Oxytocin is a female dominant chemical in the way that testosterone is male dominant, but certain moments in a male's life wash the male body and brain with oxytocin. Biochemical tests have shown that when a man gets married or has a child, his oxytocin increases—human bonding requires it biologically—and also during the sex act male oxytocin hits a peak. The jolt of pleasure that both males and females feel during sex and upon orgasm is in large part an "oxytocin jolt."

But a difference in the post-orgasm experience between males and females is very important. After sex, the male, even if he is a guy of few words, may whisper, "I love you," and he might hug the woman to him, or try to caress her softly as he drifts in his bliss into sleep. But then, minutes or hours after that, his testosterone rises again and his oxytocin diminishes considerably.

For his female partner, a different experience can occur: oxytocin levels generally stay up and high, and can do so even a few days later. Thus, the adolescent boy and girl can start out feeling, right after sex, as if they are "one" with each other, but the girl may carry the feeling forward and the boy may not only let the feeling go, but in fact begin to fantasize about other girls, becoming callow to or ignoring the girl the next day.

When I've discussed biological differences, such as the impact of oxytocin on adolescents, I often find grown men and women having "aha" moments regarding their teen years and early twenties. Men remember bonding though sex, and feeling intense moments of intimacy—but often, only briefly. Women recollect that quite often their young partner quickly abandoned them. Both genders often look back with a sense that they were out of sync with the opposite sex during that youthful period.

When working with young men in particular, an explanation and discussion of this oxytocin difference can be an effective way to say to a young man, "The sexual desire and passion that gives you such a rush and makes you feel powerful can become sad and degrading for your partner, if you just have sex and run off and are not in love with her. Thinking about sex purposefully is necessary for true intimacy and love. It's why every ancient social system, like our religions, wants kids not to have sex until they're married, or at least until the couple is devoted and committed to a relationship they hope will last."

This kind of teaching does not suddenly make every boy want to be abstinent, but it helps young men understand better what is going on in themselves and their sexual partner, and how to think with sexual purpose rather than just impulse. It helps them understand why their minds so crave sexual fantasy, and their bodies, sexual release. Testosterone and oxytocin are doing battle in the boy, one trying to get him to ejaculate as much as possible to keep the human species alive, the other trying to get him to bond as much as possible to keep the human species alive. And surrounding all this are media messages and competitive peers who tease, goad, and brag about their own alleged exploits.

Abstinence or Contraception

Some abstinence programs have had success in increasing dialogue with young people today. At the same time, contraception programs are working to keep sex among young people safe. Ultimately, both messages are needed by adolescents, and sexual training of young men is a clear case of three-family systems desperately needing to be a parent-led team. There are so many sexual messages coming at boys, from within themselves and around them, that they need more than one person to help them develop their own compromise messages.

Think right now, as you read this, about how you can enlist three families in training your boys for sexuality that is values oriented and purposeful. If mom teaches respect for girls and women, dad needs to teach comfort with the male body as well as respect for girls and women. Schools, faith communities, and other mentors can answer boys' questions about sexuality honestly, frankly, and without shame or fear. And it is crucial that all the members of a teaching team be comfortable with their own bodies, sexuality, and relationships. Boys are already nervous enough about their own urges—they don't need everyone else around them to be nervous to the point of silence or shame.

Questions of Purpose

How Can We Support You, Son?

Here is a tool that can help you create a team approach to the value of sexual purpose.

Call together a "family team meeting" that involves significant players: mom, dad, a trusted uncle, grandfather, or other mentor, a trusted teacher or counselor from the school, a spiritual mentor of some kind, perhaps a progressive minister or rabbi, and maybe another trusted adult, male or female. If your son has an older brother who has matured or is maturing sexually, he could be this other adult.

Here are some questions to ask one another in your family team. These questions require brave answers, and this bravery is good practice for the questions that each or some of you will later ask of your son:

1. What were our first sexual experiences? Masturbation? Petting?

2. Were we involved in or did we see locker room teasing, bragging, competition for who had the most experience among our peers?

3. When did we start looking at pornographic magazines or movies?

4. Did we have an obsession with a teacher or classmate?

5. When did our first fumbling toward intercourse occur?

6. What were we most nervous about?

7. What did we wish our parents and friends had told us that they didn't talk about?

Once your team has shared and discussed these questions, you can strategize how you want to teach the values of sexual purpose to your son, deciding who will speak to your son about which parts of sexuality. The following are discussion starters for your team members to use with your son:

1. Whom are you most comfortable with right now in discussing sexuality?

2. What have you been thinking lately about masturbation? Is it OK with you?

3. When have you been thinking it will be OK to have intercourse?

4. Have you been making any decisions about oral sex?

5. What is safe sex? What is the most important contraceptive for you as a male?

6. What is abstinence?

7. What are your friends saying about sex? Are some of them bragging?

8. Can I tell you what I've learned about respecting girls and women?

9. Can I tell you what I've learned about what girls need from boys?

If you meet as a team to discuss these questions and agree on a plan for helping your son, you'll help him begin to integrate sexuality into his life in a healthy and purposeful way. It is crucial not to rush: go a little bit at a time, as much or little as your son asks for. Over a course of years, your attention will make sure it happens—not in some single moment of magical integration, but as an ongoing process within a friendly and familiar support system. You will help the shy boy and the aggressive boy, the high-testosterone boy and the low-testosterone boy. The parent-team approach creates a safety net for any boy dealing with sexuality. It provides so many voices of support that it can include the issues of seeking and finding, destiny, values, and purpose—and not just teach basic mechanics.

It is important to set this team approach in place before your son is ten. Although you can do it anytime, if you do it before he enters puberty you will have a structure in place that is ready for his changes when they begin. You will be more effective inculcating him with such ideas as:

- Pay attention to everything that is happening to your partner— what she's saying, how she looks, any other clues to what she's feeling.
- Remember to be kind to girls, don't exploit them, be very personal and sensitive—they aren't just sex objects or a collection of anatomical candy.
- Don't do anything with anyone until you are ready—follow your own lead.
- Sex is meant to be beautiful, so don't spend a lot of time being ashamed of your body or your urges. Like any aggressive part of you, they exist to become a matter of self-discipline, self-control, and joyful, purposeful self-expression.

Sexually Aggressive Girls

By using the team approach—with parents always leading the way—you can face whatever challenge comes, including a new one in our age: sexually aggressive girls.

A father wrote this email: "My fifteen-year-old son is smart and good-looking and he is being called and texted by girls! This is different than when I was young. And it's not just him, but other parents in the school talk about this. A lot of girls have gotten very aggressive, sending him little pornographic notes, telling them what they'll do for him. It makes him uncomfortable."

This father's story illustrates the importance of a team approach to sexuality. Every year, a new way of sexualizing our youth is emerging—using the Internet, MySpace, Facebook, iPods, cell phones, uploading erotic and pornographic pictures, sometimes of the aggressive girls themselves, through schools and social networks. Whether we like it or not, sexualization is increasing rather than decreasing among kids, and sometimes the sexual aggression comes from girls. A parent-led team that helps a boy through the years of ten to twenty is the best safety net possible for helping a son become a man of sexual and romantic purpose.

Helping Our Sons Find Purposeful Work

If sexual teaching is one key area of boys' development that needs a three-family system, helping boys find honorable work is another. In cultures that came before us, it was assumed that a boy would learn about sexuality relatively young (he would be marrying around thirteen); it was also assumed that he would go to work as soon as possible, and thus gain much of his values, destiny, and purpose through the strength of his working hands, body, and mind. Just as kids are marrying later today than they were centuries ago, our economic system has changed for many families. It is not absolutely necessary today for most American families to put sons to work at puberty or just beyond. Thus, our sons go to school, do athletics, relate to peers, involve themselves in electronics, and generally explore life today without having to involve themselves, as soon as they are able, in the rigors and joys of work.

Is this a good thing? You must decide what's right for your son. In making your decision, I hope you'll consider how much more of a sense of motivation, destiny, purpose, and self-confidence a boy can develop if we all came together as parents and family teams to change the "no work" trend. I hope you'll feel, after reading this section, that one of the benefits of a three-family system should be the development of a boy's purpose through healthy, developmentally appropriate work.

As I have discussed the purpose of boys with many parents, social policy makers, and corporate leaders, I've felt a quiet but growing social movement toward revitalizing boys' access to honorable work, and I hope you'll join this movement. I can think of no son who cannot gain from going to work.

The Importance of Work in Building Destiny

Dan Labell, forty-one, president of the Westfalia Corporation, a successful dairy equipment business in York, Pennsylvania, told me this story of his teenage years:

> My parents always had a strong work ethic, so I started working pretty young. I was good with my hands, so I got a job with a carpenter. He taught me how to sand, and so that's what I did. I was going to high school, of course, so I could only work in the afternoons and on weekends. I'd go to work about three in the afternoon to see where my employer had set out for me the wood he needed sanded. I would get going sanding each piece of wood by hand or with the sander whenever I could.
>
> There I was, sixteen, covered in pieces of sawdust, my arms aching, my back aching, my nose plugged, my eyes itching. For hours at a time I did this, and I did it well, gaining a good skill, a good work ethic, enough money to help pay for a car. I remember something else, too, though: I gained a vision of what I didn't want to do in the future. I knew within a month of doing this work that this was not my purpose in life. I have great respect for the carpentry and woodworking profession, and I still love working with wood, but that job helped set a course toward college and business success. I learned by trial and error what I needed to do in the future to reach my highest dreams—I didn't want to sand wood all my life.

As Dan and I discussed our boyhoods, he also shared his desire that his boys (nine and eleven) get jobs when they are old enough. We agreed that sixteen would be the latest—but that his sons could help him around the office well before that. By sixteen, Dan said, he wanted his boys getting the same experiences he got, not only to build skills, but also to start understanding what they did and did not want to do with their lives.

I shared Dan's wisdom with a parent group, and a mother of three grown sons recalled this story:

> My boys went with me to work cleaning houses as soon as they were able to control themselves and be useful. My middle son saw a weight lifting room at one house we cleaned and was intrigued. I think this was because he was twelve, and had always felt weak because he was small for his age. Anyway, he would rub the dust cloth on every dumbbell and every piece of equipment in that weight room. One day he told me he wanted to lift weights. So my husband and I met with his phys ed teacher at school and got help teaching him the right way to do it.
>
> Now he's nineteen, he lifts free weight, and does all sorts of body building with his friends—there is a whole community of these kids, who take care of each other and do things together. Two of them and my son work at TJ Maxx lifting the large cartons. My son pays for his car insurance, his gas, and all his expenses. He's taking this year off from school, then next year he wants to go to college and get a degree in occupational therapy. If I hadn't taken him to help me work at that house, I wonder if he would have gone down this path.

Financial Priorities

Perhaps you remember your own first job. In my home, chores were my first job. Then, when I was able, I got a job in a Continental Trailways bus station, cleaning toilets as a janitor's assistant. From there, I became a busboy in restaurants, then moved up to waiter. The experiences I had at work were so many, both good and bad, that I learned pieces of what I wanted to do with my life, and what I didn't.

Over the last decades, there has been confusion in our culture about whether boys should work, when they should work, why they should work. For some boys, like me, whose families didn't have resources, work was a must—I paid twenty dollars rent into the family money pool during the years that my family fell into hard times. But for some boys today, not only is work not a financial necessity, there is a sense that if he is engaged in after-school athletics—or debate team, science club, church groups—it's OK to substitute these other activities for working as a teenager.

Every family has different needs and values. Some of us really need the money a teenager can contribute to the family survival; some don't. But in addition to your financial situation, I hope you will look closely at the issue of boys and work from the perspective of purpose development. As you decide what is right in your family for your son, I hope you'll consider two very important things:

1. Throughout human history, boys have worked as soon as they were physically able, thus there is a long, wise tradition in our ancestry for putting boys to work as soon as possible.
2. The global marketplace is constantly changing, and the situation in that marketplace, as we noticed in Chapter One, can be dangerous for young men who don't grow up learning how to compete in the workplace as soon as possible.

My children have each begun working outside the home as soon as possible—baby-sitting and later teaching younger children at our synagogue. This early work has matured them greatly. At sixteen, they each began working twenty hours a week as servers at a nursing home, earning minimum wage. They have curtailed media time and some athletic and social activities in order to work. However, they've found serving food in a huge cafeteria to be very good exercise indeed, and their sense of social activities has been increased rather than decreased by their exposure to another generation. My eldest daughter, Gabrielle, has shown interest in gerontology or a similar profession.

In the same way that CEO Dan Labell gained exposure to an elder carpenter and a vision for the future through working, and the boy who lifted weights was exposed, through work, to an outlet for his energy and passion, your son too could enter real life—the life of earning a wage and valuing money as a direct component of thriving and surviving every day. Dan got the name of the carpenter through his extended family; the housecleaner ran a family business and brought in her son. My own first job was set up through friends of my parents. In the same way, your family team can help your son find honorable work.

What Your Son Might Lose by Not Working

As you ponder how to do this and whom to ask for help, it is useful to look at the issue of entertainment—especially electronics—and how entertainment has taken over the "work time" of our ancestors. For some families, there is the sense that if a boy involves himself in electronics, this in itself is good training for the future world, which will be increasingly technological. There is also a tacit approval of "letting boys relax while they're young, the world will be hard enough later."

Though only you can decide what is right for your son, consider this: Boys who spend their time entertaining themselves via media or peer society instead of working may in fact end up many steps behind others in the future workplace.

They have not gained daily access to

- Learning how to meet requirements of a job in terms of being on time, doing a prescribed and often measurable task, taking responsibility, learning cooperation and collaboration in teamwork on which their future and that of their own children will depend
- Being mentored and learning new skills, whether physical, mental, emotional, or social
- Being exposed to people of purpose and wisdom who can share stories of purpose development
- Discovering markers for building self-esteem that are directly linked to performance, such as praise for a job well done, not for just being around

- Experience getting critiqued, judged, failing, and succeeding beyond the criticism
- Visions of the future, both what purpose might be appropriate and what might not be

When I bring up the issue of boys and work while consulting to corporations, CEOs are often the first to remark, "I am amazed at how unprepared boys are to enter our workforce today. You just can't count on a lot of them." Some CEOs have said, sadly and wishing to remain anonymous, "Truthfully, girls these days seem more mature and better prepared than boys."

Here is perhaps one of the most important reasons you might consider reaching out to your extended family, your own workplace, or your community to help your son go to work: girls do, on average, mature more quickly than boys. Human history has insisted on boys working from as early as possible because it helps them mature—without it, many boys are not challenged enough to mature at a rate similar to that of girls. Although it is wonderful for our daughters that so many are finding their place in the workforce, it should worry us that their brothers are not gaining the skills and self-respect needed to do the work they will need to do. These boys are one day going to become husbands and fathers.

Try to start your son thinking at around twelve or thirteen about what kind of work he could do. If he is an athlete, he can work coaching his sport to younger kids. If he is busy with academics, he can work as a tutor. Being accomplished in one area is not necessarily a substitute for but an opportunity to do honorable work. And if your son is having trouble in high school, work is again an option to look at carefully—it might be just the right time to help focus his energies toward seeking and heroic effort, and provide him purpose in his life.

And even if he is having no trouble at all, but may not want to go to college, you can look to your own state government for programs that direct high school students toward trade apprenticeships. The state of Washington, for instance, has just allocated one hundred million dollars to expand regional community college and technical college campuses to make possible alternative tracks for young students, with specialized trade-based courses in aerospace manufacturing, computer networking, and health care. There is a social movement developing toward providing young people with a variety of alternatives so that they can start apprenticing and working as early as it would be good for them.

The Wisdom of Purpose

DO A MAN'S WORK, EVEN IF YOU FAIL

Each man must choose so far as the conditions allow him the path to which he is bidden by his own peculiar powers and inclinations. But if he is a man he must in some way or shape do a man's work. If, after making all the effort that his strength of body and of mind permits, he yet honorably fails, he is still entitled to a certain share of respect because he has made the effort.

—Theodore Roosevelt, *Men Who Greatly Dared*

Helping Boys Find Purpose in Their Media Use

Life coach David Bartholomew, now in his fifties, recently wrote, "Many of the activities boys engage in today don't contribute to social skills, personal interaction, work ethic, motivation, or future success. For hours and hours a day, boys are well entertained, but they are not well trained for life." Bartholomew mentors families on how to succeed, and has found a boy's use of the media (and his family's awareness of media effects) to be one of the primary determinants of a boy's future success. He has also noticed that a lot of the time boys used to spend doing the things we've just discussed—values development, work, and moral learning (for instance, about sexuality) from extended families and institutions—is now spent in "media time."

In my own work with families, male media use comes up as a primary area of interest. After issues regarding possible trauma and family dynamics, it is the most raised by moms especially.

Overuse of Electronic Media Is Potentially Dangerous

According to the Kaiser Family Foundation, in the United States today, adolescent boys (7–12 grade) are using electronic media the same amount as they would be working a full time job (44.5 hours a week, 6.5 hours every day). These boys are using electronic media 300 percent more than they see parents, 600 percent more than they spend in physical activity, 1,200 percent more than they do chores or other work.

- 68 percent of these young men have a TV in their bedroom
- 54 percent have a VCR or DVD player
- 49 percent have a video game player
- 31 percent have a computer

All young people, male or female, may enjoy electronic media, but boys are more likely than girls to have in their bedroom: a TV (72 percent versus 64 percent); a VCR or DVD player (59 percent versus 49 percent); a video game console (63 percent versus 33 percent); a computer (35 percent versus 26 percent).

Should we worry about media use? Yes, we should. As David Bartholomew is hinting: it is beginning to affect boys' abilities to become fully functional men. When boys grow up spending most of their time in front of a screen, their brain development is being affected. They lose out on the development of purpose in favor of mainly purposeless entertainment.

Screen Time for Infants and Toddlers

As brain-based research is now showing us, when little boys stare into a TV, computer, or other screen, they are not actively playing and building with their hands, and thus their organic brain growth is negatively affected. Circuits in the memory centers and thinking parts of the brain that would normally develop do not develop as fully. In part, this is because playing and building are purposeful activities; staring into a screen is passive. The areas of life in which our boys need help developing, the areas of active interaction that build their frontal and temporal lobe functioning, are diminished by most screen time. Organic brain growth defects affect later educational success, as well as social and emotional literacy.

Because 40 percent of our three-month-olds and 90 percent of two-year-olds regularly watch TV, you and your family team need to make decisions early regarding a boy's lifelong use of the screen. You can set the stage for the rest of the boy's screen life in his infancy. The American Academy of Pediatrics, and all other similar medical associations, suggest that no child under two years old watch TV or spend time in front of screens. Any screen time for infants and toddlers can have lasting effects—it's that simple. Although some boys will not have noticeable effects—and a tiny bit of TV here and there is probably OK for most kids—do we want to take substantial chances with the growing brains of our children? If your son goes to a day-care center that uses screen time as a way of pacifying children, that center may not be a good three-family member.

As Boys Grow

As boys grow, they will generally tend to engage in more screen time, and it would be an overreaction in most families to forbid all screen time—especially when there are educational options in TV, DVD, and computer use. However, it's also important to remember that two-thirds of preschoolers and kindergarteners sit in front of screens two or more hours a day. If this is your son, he is probably spending triple the time in front of screens as he is looking at books or being read to.

Play time, outdoor time, family time, and reading time are far more crucial for successful brain development than screen time. Even teaching a boy in this age group how to use a computer is unnecessary. Recent studies show that boys who learn computers at twelve years old perform just as well at computer tasks within two months of learning the computer technology as boys who learned how to use computers at three.

The less time a kindergartener spends in front of the screen the better. When thinking about "how much time is OK," think in minutes, not hours, and think only about educational programming, not violent or sexualized programming. It can be crucial to discuss this in your family team, so that grandparents, day-care providers, and all other members are in sync with your values.

Boys in Elementary School

Over half of children eight years and older have a TV in their bedroom, and eighty-one percent watch it alone and unsupervised. These children are not only entranced by the screen time, but they are taking in thirty-three thousand acts of murder by the time they are teenagers. Boys of this age who spend three or more hours in front of any kind of electronic screen are more likely to have attention and learning problems, as well as behavioral issues.

Simultaneously, boys in elementary school begin to sleep less than they should because of time spent online and onscreen. As they get TVs and computers in their rooms, and as they now start to get cell phones and iPods, they spend more and more time electronically wired. Brain development is affected not only because boys lack organic outlets for their development, but because they sleep less. Lack of sleep leads to cognitive delays and behavioral problems.

The fear we need to have for these young boys is ultimately that they will move further into trouble and further away from success, destiny, and lifelong purpose. Uncontrolled use of the screen in elementary school can lead to boys who don't read or do homework, don't interact with a variety of people, don't work around the house, don't help mom or dad cook dinner, don't visit grandparents, don't sleep enough, don't play outside, don't get enough physical exercise, don't help dad or mom fix the lawnmower . . . the list is endless.

Some screen time is fun and fuels the mind; too much retards a boy's time spent in activities of purpose. Families that protect the development of purpose in boys may be families that curtail screen time during the crucial elementary school years to around an hour a day.

As a Boy Goes Through Adolescence

As your son becomes pubertal and his hormones—especially his testosterone—begin to kick in (around ten), he may spend less time reading and doing homework or other activities that are purposeful and more time playing video games that are violent and competitive. It seems amazingly normal and natural to us that adolescent boys (and grown men) are attracted to these entertainments—which are so spatial and competitive. Indeed, any kind of competitive, hunting, or spatial activity like this is natural for many boys (as are competitive athletics, gaming, and, later in adolescence, driving fast and other high-risk behavior).

Worth noting, however, is that overuse of screen time can bring a false sense of purpose to an adolescent boy, and this can actually derail his long-term development of purpose. Here's what happens in the brain: when a boy "wins" (moves up to a new level in a video game), his brain's reward center (in the caudate, in the middle of the brain) registers a flash—like a hit of cocaine to the brain—of SUCCESS. The boy feels like he has accomplished something. He will want this brain-flash over and over again and will play the game over and over to get it. His brain will keep saying, "I'm accomplishing something today!" because its innate reward center, a seat of his lifelong sense of motivation and purpose, feels filled up with success.

Simultaneously, in the real world, he has accomplished very little. He is not building motivational strengths in the worlds of family, school, neighborhood, work, and life. He is not doing homework or chores, not exercising, not learning how to ask life's deepest questions. He is having fun and getting a brain-flash of reward sensation, but from activities that lead to no purpose except the possible honing of eye-hand coordination and enjoyment of virtual competition.

Our job as a family team is to ask constantly, "What world am I presenting to this boy?" If the world presented to a boy is limited in its challenges, the boy may adapt down to those limits. We may end up with a twenty-five-year-old who lacks the social, emotional, cognitive, and physical skills to become a successful man.

What You Do Matters!

A father wrote:

> I have two boys, thirteen and fifteen. The screen time became an issue for us because both boys started having "learning problems." I put it in quotes because both boys are smart and what the teachers said about them didn't make sense to my wife and me. We had the boys tested, we met with the teachers, we saw doctors. We tried all sorts of interventions.
>
> Finally, we decided to do the one thing that would most change their lives around. We unhooked the TV and the video games. They were spending hours every day playing SOCOM III (an online Internet-video game), they weren't doing much else, and they were losing sleep, too. We just got rid of it. They were mad as hell, but we stuck to our guns. It took two months to reprogram them both. The whole thing was like a bitter and sad and angry drug intervention.
>
> It worked. Our lives are different now. These guys are succeeding again. I feel like I was stupid before. I was the one telling my wife the video games and TV didn't hurt the guys. I was their defender. Now I'm the one sitting with them until they get all their homework done. I told them, "No car and no driving privileges till you do well in school." This really scares my older boy. He wants a car. He's working hard to succeed. We've turned a corner.

This family's experience shows what we all know instinctively: What we do matters, and sometimes we must be brave in our leadership! About half of all eight- to eighteen-year-olds say their families have no rules for screen time. Studies also show that parents who impose rules and stick to them get results. Boys in homes with TV rules report two hours less daily media exposure than boys from homes without rules. (Read a full Kaiser Family Foundation report at www.kff.org/entmedia/.) These boys increase their social, emotional, cognitive, and internal development in the active world—and these boys are more likely to develop a deep sense of purpose and mission in the real world.

Figuring Out the Right Amount of Screen Time

No one can tell you how to run your family system, and you may have a son who spends hours in front of the screen and yet has turned out to be a very directed, motivated, and purpose-filled young man. If you have any questions at all, however, about how to integrate screen time into a boy's life of purpose, this ten-point checklist might help.

If screen time is more important to your boy than these activities, then perhaps you should make some house rules and extended family rules about what should come first.

1. Mom time. Meaningful time spent with mom, learning her skills and wisdom.
2. Dad time. Meaningful time spent with dad, learning his skills and wisdom.
3. Elder, extended family, adult friend time. Meaningful time spent with elders, extended family, care providers, others who teach skills and wisdom.
4. Spiritual development time, in religious community, or even just in nature. Time spent in environments of quiet and community that build internal questioning of faith and self-reflection.
5. Chores and work time. For younger boys, work will be chores around the house and helping parents at tasks. For adolescent boys, work can be actual money-earning labor.
6. School time, including homework. This work comes before screen time because even when it is boring, it builds a sense of purpose. If your son has trouble with it, make sure he does it in your presence until he completes it.
7. Reading time. Reading is better for the brain, the heart, and the soul than most screen activities. If our sons don't read, they

have not earned the privilege of video games, TVs, iPods . . . This is a tough rule of thumb, but very useful. And remember, reading time can be a form of "down time." Boys get wound up and need down time.

8. Play time, exercise, athletics. Even if your son is not athletic, he needs to value exercise above sitting in front of a screen. The purpose of the human body is to move, not just to sit.

9. Care time. Siblings, elders, neighbors, friends, pets . . . all need the care of a boy, and your son needs to develop his own loving self by providing that care. If screen time cuts away care time, this time needs to be reestablished, even if it means something like the menial task of changing the kitty litter.

10. Sleep time. Many of the behavioral issues that boys face today are related to lack of sleep. If your son isn't sleeping enough, one of the best ways to cure him of this dangerous bad habit is to take away screen time.

If you are helping a boy position these ten elements of daily life above media use, the length of time he spends with media will generally take care of itself. He will not have time to spend three hours in front of screens. He will have time to be a young son in search of his own heroism, with the media a helpful but moderated part of his search.

A Boy's Search for Freedom

The families of today are often places where boys experience a great deal of personal liberty. Giving this gift to our children is something many generations have worked hard to accomplish, sacrificing everything so that the next generation would be free to become men and women of ever greater purpose.

As you raise your sons in your family team, I hope you'll take measurement of the liberties your son enjoys, and I hope you'll reflect on the possible differences between liberty and freedom.

At a parent workshop, an elderly man came up to me and said, "You know, I think too much freedom is killing our boys." We talked for a moment, and he left me with a distinction to ponder.

Now, years later, I believe I understand what he meant. I am rewording his sentence to say: too much "liberty" is killing our boys.

If boys are able to do whatever they want when they're young, many of them will simply not be prepared for life. These boys will be anxious and unsure of what it means to be a truly "free" man. In other words, they will not have learned that having the liberty to do anything is not the same as gaining the freedom to serve humanity.

Freedom, in this distinction, is the empowerment of a human being to give and take resources in service not only for his own good but also for the common good. Freedom is the ability of a person to achieve his or her purpose in life. When our sons have too much liberty, they often do not gain direction toward destiny, guidance toward seeking and finding their heroism, and the freedom to fulfill their purpose in life. They often feel spoiled or withdrawn, rather than free. They enter into relationships and workplaces without a deep sense of maturity, and at some point they may withdraw from those relationships or workplaces, seeking more liberty somewhere else, perhaps abandoning the people who thought they could rely on them, or leaving behind people they deeply love.

In the next chapter, we will look carefully at the role of the community and neighborhood in raising boys of purpose and character. I hope that as you leave this chapter, you feel inspired to hold your sons and your family to the highest standards of purpose development, with the intention of molding truly free men. Freedom is a call from deep within to keep growing. Our sons need to seek and find their heroism in ways that unite them with this powerful call.

6

Creating Communities of
Purpose for Boys

Merely being equipped with moral programming does not mean
we practice moral behavior. Something still has to boot up that
software and configure it properly, and that something is the
community.

—JEFFREY KLUGER, *WHAT MAKES US MORAL*

"WE ARE TALKING NOW OF SUMMER EVENINGS in Knoxville, Tennessee,"
begins the lyrical short story *Knoxville: Summer of 1915* by the American
writer James Agee. "On the rough wet grass of the back yard my
father and mother have spread quilts. We all lie there, my mother, my
father, my uncle, my aunt, and I too am lying there. By some chance, here
they are, all on this earth; and who shall ever tell the sorrow of being on
this earth, lying, on quilts, on the grass, in the summer evening, among
the sounds of the night?"

This evocative passage comes near the end of the story and provides a preface to Agee's novel *A Death in the Family*. The "sorrow" to
which Agee refers here is not only the beautiful, confusing feeling of
having a family and yet knowing one must one day leave it, but also
a foreshadowing of the father's death and mother's grief. At the end
of this short story, just before the action of the novel begins, Agee
writes, "After a little I am taken in and put to bed. Sleep, soft smiling,
draws me unto her: and those receive me, who quietly treat me, as one

familiar and well-beloved in that home: but will not, oh, will not, not now, not ever; but will not ever tell me who I am."

Already, though not yet an adolescent, this little boy knows he cannot fully become himself, cannot seek and gain his purpose, mission, meaning, and identity in his first or even second family alone—he will need help from the expanding circles of people he will meet and places he will go in his boyhood, adolescence, and adult journey.

A Death in the Family is an especially poignant book to read now, in the new millennium, even though it was written so many decades ago. It is poignant not only as a good story and record of America in an older time, but also on the two levels of the boy's foreshadowing, taken forward into our era:

1. Every one of our boys today searches, like this boy, to define himself in his larger community. Every boy knows that his mother and father and even aunts and uncles are not enough to fully build purpose into his life.
2. Millions of our millennial boys live like the boy in Agee's novel after his father dies—they do not grow up with their fathers actively in their lives. They are starved for community in ways they can only articulate through withdrawal from life purpose, or dangerous risks without purposeful goal setting, or late maturity, lasting even into their thirties, or early death from self-destructive behavior.

Every boy needs ever-expanding circles of care, and some boys may need them with even more urgency than we may realize.

The Loss of Communities of Purpose for Boys

Almost twenty years ago, when I was beginning my counseling career, I worked on a part-time basis as a consultant in various prisons, and as a group counselor at a federal prison. Prison work was eye opening for me, not only because the clanging doors, the cells, and the feeling of being trapped are a shock to the uninitiated, but also because both the depths of darkness and the most intense human light shared space in the minds of the men I worked with.

Some of the men I met had done terrible things; most of the men regretted what they had done, and nearly all grieved every day the loss of their families, especially their children. One prisoner, incarcerated on drug charges, told me, "I feel like I've killed not just my life but my family's life. My wife and kids are ashamed of me and sad all the time—it's hard for them to move on. I'm not sure I want them to, but sometimes I do. I will never be happy again, and I don't know if they will." His raw pain was palpable and shared by many men in the group.

The Loss of Purpose in Our Communities

I have not worked in a prison for fifteen years, but I have worked with families who have lost boys and men, whether to prison or to lifestyles that kill men at a young age, or to divorces that remove men and families from love, bonding, child care, and happiness. When men are lost to families, the children, women, and men involved generally experience anger, sadness, and grief. The situation of these families is often made worse rather than better by the community's and society's lack of clarity about who boys are, how to help them develop purpose, and how to help them succeed in marriages and in parenting.

I believe one reason we are still so "stuck" regarding boys—and why we are incarcerating increasing numbers of boys and men—is that we've handled boys' issues too much as "nuclear family" concerns, and too little as community concerns. With one in ninety-nine males now incarcerated, we are clearly not meeting boys' needs as communities. When we do decide to fully develop our three-family system for boys, we will help not only more males but also more females.

A single mother wrote, "I don't hate men, I miss them. I grieve that my husband wasn't better for me. I grieve that I am raising my kids alone. I worry about what they're doing when I'm working. I worry all the time. I really want my girls to find good men, men who will take care of them. I don't want my girls to fight unhappiness all the time the way I do."

Although many single mothers are happy, many share some level of this woman's grief and regret, and yearn to care for men and be cared for by men who have themselves been cared for fully. A powerful article by Paula Becker in Seattle's *ParentMap* magazine recently looked at some of the reasons for the issues that single mothers experience. Interviewing single moms, Becker found that it is common for single mothers to experience significant stress regarding the loss of support from the husband and significant anxiety about their sons. Sons feel a special (and often unexpressed) grief at the loss of their father in their lives, and mothers know it.

In today's world, men are leaving families or being left, not caring enough for themselves and their children, misunderstanding their sons' need for their attention, not helping the larger community of men and women to mentor their sons appropriately, and in some cases, doing evil, bad, immoral, or illegal things (the wording can be argued but the outcome is the same no matter what we call their actions, which take them away from family bonds, causing more grief and anguish). Men are also being pushed out of families by their spouses and by the courts, with many judges and parents lacking training in male development, and not realizing the necessity of making sure that adolescent boys, especially, stay close to fathers.

It is extremely difficult for an adolescent boy to become a seeker after purpose and a heroic self if he lacks a father or father figures. He can become a kind of "imposter man" who is constantly unsure of himself and not necessarily a mature man.

The Wisdom of Purpose

THERE IS NO SHORTER ROAD, MY SON

"There is no shorter road, my son," said he, "than really to be wise in those things which you wish to seem to be wise. . . For example, if you wish to seem to be a good farmer when you are not, or a good rider, doctor, flute-player, or anything else that you are not, just think how many schemes you must invent to keep up your pretensions. And even if you should persuade any number of people to praise you, in order to give yourself a reputation, and if you should procure a fine outfit for each of your professions, you would soon be found to have practiced deception; and long after, when you were giving an exhibition of your skill, you would be shown up and convicted, too, as an imposter."

"But how could one become really wise in foreseeing that which will prove to be useful?"

"Obviously, my son," said the father, "by learning from everyone you can all that it is possible to acquire by learning."

—Xenophon, *The Education of Cyrus the Persian*

Focusing on helping boys make purposeful decisions via community involvement will not solve all the problems we face. But it can be an effectively amazing start. Let's explore changes we can all make at the communal level—changes that can practically help boys develop internal and neural "fail-safes" for character development, conscience, and love.

What the Community Can Do for Our Sons

If you saw a boy acting out in a grocery store, what would you do? What if his mother was having trouble controlling him? What if she was obviously distressed? Would you go up to her and say, "Can I help you with your son?"

Most of us would not.

Why not?

Just two generations ago, most community members would help moms (or dads) whose kids needed some extra assistance. In the baby boom generation that I grew up in I was both the object of communal parenting and also part of the transition away from it. In some of the places my family lived (for instance, in India), other parents told me what to do and when to do it. My brother and I were parented "communally." In some places, however (American cities), neighbors kept to themselves—they emerged into my family's life mainly to complain about me (or my brother), which put increased pressure on my parents to do more to parent us, beyond what they were already doing, and without much help.

The Loss of Community Parenting

Professor Stephanie Coontz, who specializes in family studies at Evergreen State College, has recently noted that the shift away from "community-parenting" in America (we are one of the only countries that has shifted significantly away from it) began over a century ago, in the 1830s, as class distinctions emerged.

"Often," she notes, "it wasn't so much 'our family has different rules' as 'our *type* has different rules.'" Different types and classes of people began to separate their children from other classes and types. This became especially true as different immigrant groups flocked to other neighborhoods in cities to work and care for one another. People of one group could co-parent other kids in that group, but not kids outside the group. Different groups didn't trust one another's values.

As Americans moved to the suburbs in the mid-twentieth century, some communal parenting in neighborhoods did emerge again, but soon, changing lifestyles denigrated communal parenting. One family's suspicion regarding another family's values, individualistic attitudes among families and groups, the increase of electronic stimulation, and decrease of time spent with children are all factors that have chipped away at communal parenting.

Adding to these issues were increasing issues of suspiciousness and distrust of boys and men in particular. In the grocery store scenario, if you are the mother or father of the boy having trouble, you might notice that if a woman came to help you, you would feel more comfortable than if a man did. The high level of suspicion of male strangers in our culture today has roots in both the historic changes since the industrial revolution and our present reality—as incarceration rates show us, there are a number of males doing bad things around us, which only increases suspicion about their offers of assistance.

What Some Mothers Want and Need

At the same time, if you are the mother of a ten-year-old boy who is acting out uncontrollably, is it possible that a part of you wishes a strong male would walk down the aisle and help you manage your son? When I bring this up to mothers, many admit that on all fronts that they wish other people, both women and men, would help them more with their sons, both in public situations and in long-term development.

They note needing help in the following ways:

- Keeping the boy safe from society's harms (and his own risky behavior).
- Managing "boy energy," especially regarding discipline and self-discipline.
- Helping him express his feelings in both words and healthy actions.
- Developing good values and character in him, so he becomes a good man.
- Helping him understand how to handle bullies, and how to avoid becoming a bully or high-risk boy himself.
- Teaching him how to become a good male role model to other boys (women inherently sense their sons' needs for communities of men and male role models).
- Helping him set specific success goals for his future. As one single mother told me, "I don't want my son to be aimless. He's twelve now and I know he needs a whole village to help him find his direction in life."

Women sense a deep need for help with their sons. They seek a way to establish safe communal parenting.

Some of the solutions—and the practical way of catalyzing communal parenting in your town—can be found in the very lack of it you might see immediately around you. A mother of two boys under five recounted a recent incident that cried out for community involvement, and from this incident, solutions emerged.

> Some kids had been tagging doorbells on our block since 7 PM. They would ring doorbells, then hide in the bushes. My father-in-law hid on the porch in the dark to see what was going on. He saw seven kids, between eleven and thirteen. When we put our kids to bed at 9:30, it happened again. This time my husband walked up the street to try to put a stop to it. He confronted the boys and many ran, but

two did not, saying they were just having fun. My husband told them to stop doing the tagging. One of the boys laughed and my husband got angry. He grabbed the boy and pushed him and told him to get out of there. My husband tried to scare them into stopping.

A short while later, a bunch of people came to our house to complain. They said the boy was scared now and they were calling the police. The police came and heard both sides of the story. Then they told the group of us that the boys had trespassed and harassed homeowners. They impressed on the boys the problems they could have if they did this again. They also said my husband overreacted and shouldn't have been physical, because if there had been injuries, he could have been charged with assault. Then they told everyone to go home and stay off the streets.

This mother concluded her story by speaking for her husband, too, regarding confusion about what was right in this case. "It seems like such a small incident but we are stumped as to how we should handle similar situations that are sure to arise in the future as our own sons get older. What is right and wrong for a neighborhood to do in this case?"

Ending the Loneliness of Caregivers

A crucial thing to note in this powerful email is the fact that this mother and father felt alone in trying to figure out what to do. The aloneness experienced directly by both the adult male trying to handle the boys without help, and by the adult woman watching, is something we have perhaps all felt at some point. It is a feeling of powerlessness. It shows a lack of communal parenting.

When this mother wrote to me, I asked Kathy Stevens to join me as a male-female team in responding. The following is her very useful part of our response:

The behavior of those boys reminds me of shenanigans that happened when I was young, but now the stakes are higher. In Colorado Springs recently a high school senior, basically a good kid with a temper, was shot by a man (a retired Air Force Officer) on the interstate. The two males were jockeying for position on the highway and then pulled to the side in anger. The officer became scared of the young man and pulled his gun. He killed the teenager but was acquitted because he was, in his words, "afraid for my life."

It is specifically because the world around us is so much more dangerous now that neighborhoods like yours need to have a community conversation. It can happen in a high school or middle school gym. Local organizations that work with nonviolent options can facilitate it. School personnel, legal individuals, and police representatives should be involved. Those thirteen-year-old boys are crying out for communities to help them manage themselves. The "managing" can't just be left to one father who is alone to face the adolescent boys and must become scared for himself, or in your case, for his own family. A man or woman scared for their family can do just about anything. The community needs to bond together so this situation doesn't occur.

THE JOY OF PURPOSE

The Source of Restraint

In caring for others and serving heaven,
There is nothing like using restraint.
Restraint begins with giving up one's own ideas
In favor of ideas on virtue gathered from
the past, and from those who are virtuous.

—Tao Te Ching

Changing Community Perceptions

To move in the direction of these kinds of teams and meetings, we will need to shift some of our social programming away from aloneness and toward revitalization of community spirit. "That's obvious!" one might exclaim. But *how* do we do it? Here is a short list:

1. Make it your personal priority to meet five other neighbors and talk about your children's needs.
2. Bring people together to meet with schools and other agencies to set up town hall and neighborhood meetings.
3. Be the person who asks if the mom in the store needs help, even if she rebuffs you.
4. Become the mom (or dad) who asks for help.
5. Put together a phone list and put it on your wall so that when the boys come by harassing homes, phone calls are made in seconds.
6. Meet with police representatives and gain insight in how to handle high risk behavior in neighborhoods.

As community members who want to move to a greater level of communal parenting, we will need to let go of our personal sense that we must be "perfect parents." We will be more likely to set up or attend neighbor meetings—and thus help create a community of purpose and character development for boys and girls—if we start out from the point of view of "I need these other parents. Needing them is not a deficiency in me, nor in my son (or daughter), but part of human bonding and raising children." To fight through our fears of being viewed as a failure when our child does something wrong is to develop a wonderful community courage. This kind of courage, this breaking down of expectations of child or parental perfection, can ultimately save lives.

Invest in Corporate or Community Mentors

The community meeting and neighborhood alliance option is crucial to providing direction and purpose to our boys. Aligned directly with it is involvement of institutions and businesses.

If you are a man who works hard at your business but you are not mentoring someone else's child (or your own), teaching your vision or your way of success, then you may be missing an opportunity to truly change the world. America's Promise is a powerful organization that helps create mentoring opportunities. 100 Black Men is specifically a business organization set up to help mentor boys of color. Organizations such as these understand that corporate health and community health are intertwined in real life, because corporations need young men to be purposeful, directed, healthy, safe, good people. As a corporate or business leader, or as a successful individual who has found your purpose in life, you can fund and support internships, workplace trainings, neighborhood programs, clubs, workshops, and dialogues, as well as mentor other people's children.

A corporate CEO and mentor told me:

> I am a father of a daughter and do a lot with her and her friends, but I also decided to mentor a boy. As it turned out, both out of friendship with two families and out of my professional commitment to link my success with the success of children, I have mentored two young men (who are now in their twenties). It hasn't been easy. Friendships have gone through hard times because I've been critical of one of the guys for drinking too much. The other guy doesn't return phone calls or show up when he says he will. Sometimes my criticism makes the young man and my friends, the parents, uncomfortable.
>
> But I say, we all belong to the same community. With the boys and their families, I've discussed how important it is that we are supportive in both ways to boys—by giving praise and by taking them to task when they need it.

This mentor and these parents (and the young men themselves) have courageously committed to communal parenting. Perhaps all of us sense what they sense (even through the discomfort): the need inside each young man not just for praise from community members, but also for constructive criticism that leads to purpose development—not nitpicking, but critique that deals with crucial areas of development.

The CEO ended his comments with this success statement: "Each of these young guys has said, in his own way, 'Now that I'm a man, I'm glad you were hard on me.'" What a beautiful illustration of the need boys can sense in themselves to have a community around them that will guide them, even if not with praise.

In my experience, most boys and young men are courageous in that way—their hearts may sting from a critique, but they are brave in their desire to improve themselves. They need each of us to do whatever it takes to help them feel that they are surrounded by people who care, in all the ways that people care, for boys and men.

Forming Purposeful Communities for African American Boys

In few American subcultures is the need to alter community and social perceptions more clear than in the lives of African American boys. The incarceration rate of these youths reflects the deep need for purpose development among these sons of America. Nearly half of black males will come in contact with the judicial system in their lifetime, and the highest population per capita of inmates in our prisons are African American males. The National Urban League's recent "State of Black America Report" notes that black males

- Are twice as likely to be unemployed as white males
- Make 75 percent per year what white males make
- Are nearly seven times more likely to be incarcerated than white males
- Experience, on average, jail sentences ten months longer than white males, for the same offenses
- Have a shorter life span than white males by eight years and, especially in the 15–34 age group, are nine times more likely to die of homicide
- Are seven times as likely to die of AIDS

Suicide rates among black boys have also increased in the last decades. For instance, among the 10–14 age group, suicide rates increased 233 percent in fifteen years. In the 15–19 age group, the increase was 146 percent. Adding to these tragedies is the fact that black males commit suicide at a younger age on average than white males. This is not true among black females. Among all teenagers of all races, black females are the least susceptible to suicide.

The Failure in Education

One of the crucial ways to develop meaning, morality, and success is education. Though there may be disagreements among social thinkers on what to do to help black males, no one contests the importance of education. Unfortunately, the statistics regarding schooling for black males have worsened over the last thirty years while the situation for other groups of males (except Native American) has improved economically. In urban areas, the high school dropout rate of black males has climbed to over 50 percent. Here are some other painful statistics:

- Black males make up 32 percent of school suspensions, and are twice as likely as whites to be suspended.
- Only 41 percent of black males graduate from high school.
- Only 22 percent of black males finish college within six years.

What are the effects of not gaining schooling? In 2000, 65 percent of black male high school dropouts were jobless (unemployed or incarcerated). Within four years, that percentage grew to 72. This compares to 34 percent for white males and 19 percent for Hispanics.

In 1995, 16 percent of black males in their twenties who did not attend college were in jail or prison. In 2004, it had climbed to 21 percent. Among black males who drop out of high school, 60 percent have been in prison by the time they turn thirty-five (if they live that long). Understanding the gravity of this situation is perhaps best accomplished not only by realizing the early death rate for black males, but also by noting that this is the only demographic group in which more individuals are in prison (34 percent) on any given day than are working (30 percent).

The Communal Legacy of Slavery and Discrimination

Robert Mincy, professor of social work at Columbia, has pointed out the growing dichotomy between black males and black females. Although black girls face immense challenges, statistically it is the black boy who is most at risk. Dr. Mincy warns, "We spent $50 billion in efforts that produced the turnaround for poor and black women. We are not even beginning to think about the men's problems on similar orders of magnitude."

When black boys grow into manhood, there are fewer paths to healthy, moral, and successful purpose awaiting them in their communities than there are for all other demographic groups except Native American males. Note these statistics, provided by activist and professor Archie Wortham:

- Fewer than 50 percent of black families own their own homes.
- Among black families with earnings of $100,000 annually, fewer than 30 percent have retirement savings exceeding $5,000.
- Although African Americans make up approximately 12 percent of America's general population, black professionals make up only 3.2 percent of lawyers, 3 percent of doctors, and 1 percent of architects.

The black boy today is often the boy in your community who falls behind nearly every other group. Helping these young males find purpose requires courage and risk taking on all our parts. Although it goes without saying that many young black males are flourishing, African American boys and the American community as a whole still live, even if unconsciously, in the legacy of purposelessness and the resultant dangerous escape behavior that James Baldwin wrote of eloquently in *The Fire Next Time*, as he described for young black people their origins and challenges. We will have to deal with this inner world in the next decade, one community at a time, and in solidarity as a nation, so we don't lose increasing numbers of black boys. Speaking to a young black boy on the one hundredth anniversary of emancipation from slavery, Baldwin wrote:

> We have not stopped trembling . . . this innocent country set you down in a ghetto in which, in fact, it intended you should perish. . . . You were born where you were born and faced the future that you faced because you were black . . . the limits of your ambition were, thus, expected to be set forever. You were born into a society which spelled out with brutal clarity, and in as many ways as possible,

that you were a worthless human being. You were not expected to aspire to excellence: you were expected to make peace with mediocrity. Wherever you turned . . . you have been told where you could go and what you could do (and how you could do it) . . . the details and symbols of your life have been deliberately constructed to make you believe what white people say about you.

When a young male is born into and raised through a legacy of slavery and socially inculcated disrespect for his identity, he is less likely to develop a sense of moral purpose and high character than the young male who is born into and raised in a legacy of respect for his individual potential in his community. White males, should they be betrayed or abandoned by their families, risk losing their inherently worthwhile legacy; they may also act out later for no discernible cause, or simply lose their struggle with their own demons and go astray in their community. For black males, however, the risk is not of losing an inherently worthwhile identity or legacy, but of entering a world in which it feels like your very legacy is inherently worthless to the larger community in which you are supposed to somehow gain respect. This creates a terrible feeling of powerlessness deep within a psyche.

Our children act out our adult sorrows, and few populations more clearly speak the truth in our culture than our young black males, many of whom die before they are twenty-five, having risked everything to find some sort of self-respect in even the slimmest hope of community—through gangs, dealing drugs, and gangsta rap groups. The parents of these young men often cannot help them, for it is the larger society and community that abandoned these boys before birth.

To solve issues of purpose and success for boys in America, we will have to solve issues of purpose and success in black communities. There is no agreement on how to do that. Bill Cosby, for instance, has become a controversial elder in black American life by writing and speaking against gangsta culture. He argues that this culture creates a defiant lack of assimilation into mainstream culture—forcing black males (and females) to gain respect through aberrant behavior, violence, social dysfunction, and black-on-black disparagement. He argues that African Americans are destroying their own chances for future success.

Others in the black community disagree with his approach to the issue, claiming that gangsta culture, baggy pants, rap music, the use of "nigga," "ho," and other similar epithets actually help African Americans develop their own discrete culture, their own self-respect, their own ability to express anger through art, and ultimately, their own form of social expression that can be exported into and exploited for success in mainstream culture.

Whether one agrees with Cosby or a rapper singing "nigga," the common ground of both is the hope that their wisdom and art will bring healthy purpose and community to a relatively purposeless generation of black boys. The polar opposites in their approaches are not opposite in wanting community members to reach out to black youth to try to help them succeed by discovering paths of identity and meaning in the community. One political view prefers mannerly behavior, the other prefers open expression of angry will; both know black boys are desperate to feel respected, not enslaved, in their communities.

The brain-based and biological material in this book becomes crucial information in the discussion of "respect." The importance of respect is amplified in a population of males who are inherently disrespected by the larger community, and thus born without a path to purpose nurtured throughout a three-family system. This population will experience inordinate trauma and stress; they are often raised in poverty, one-down in society, victims of prejudice, and grieving lost parents (mainly lost fathers).

All of these social factors increase cortisol levels in the brain (the stress hormone), affecting development of emotional and cognitive centers in the frontal lobe, making for a "seeker" or even a "hero," but one who destroys rather than creates. Can we avoid any longer looking at how this constantly stressed boy is naturally more likely than the less stressed boy to take extraordinary risks, discover constant danger, seek status-providing groups such as gangs, and *harm others to gain status?* The self-respect brought by group status (the gang) relieves stress for this boy in the short term, though in the long term it only creates more stress for him (early death, prison, injury) and for his group.

Helping Black Boys Gain Respect

My thanks to Robert Haley and Norman Johnson, both of whom are former presidents of 100 Black Men of Atlanta and Gurian Institute advisors, for helping me compile this list of community activism and innovation needed to help our black boys gain respect and purpose. These are innovations that we know are working in communities around the country.

- Single-sex schools and classrooms. Over the last decade, the Gurian Institute and a number of other organizations have helped start single-sex schools and classrooms in inner city environments, and helped train schools that were innovating in this way. We have collected enough success data to show us that this innovation is indeed working for many black boys. Although this innovation will be controversial for years to come, you can find success data to help you support this innovation in your community on www.gurianinstitute.com and in books and articles referenced in the Notes and Resources at the end of this book. One of the reasons we believe the innovation holds a great deal of promise for black boys specifically is that the majority of these boys are raised without significant male presence in the home. The boys-only school or classroom provides healthy male presence.
- Increase the number of black fathers, uncles, grandfathers, and businessmen who volunteer in schools, and teach young black males responsible access to work and economic gain. Privately and publicly, communities need to fund the development of black males in teaching and counseling professions. Older brothers need to guide younger brothers toward paths of purpose. No matter a

man's present state of mind or place in society, or whether a father or grandfather feels inherently hated or unworthy, his own self-respect depends to a great extent on rising beyond circumstance and teaching the young men around him the wisdom of healthy purpose he has gained in his journey.

• Increase participation in clubs and rite-of-passage programs that teach black boys to become leaders (see Chapter Eight for rite-of-passage models). Every black boy can benefit from a Boys' Club or other similar club. Every black family can benefit from the kind of purpose development that a rite of passage affords. Black males are taking their natural need for rites of passage into gangs' initiation rites (beating up another person or being beaten up themselves, even killing someone to gain status and respect), which provide them with a sense of belonging, purpose, and identity. One effective way to help groups of black boys gain respectable manhood outside of gangs is for communities to provide these passages directly to the boys in their particular community.

• Teach black boys their ancestry. DNA ancestry databases such as www.africanancestry.com or www.genomecenter.howard.edu/intro.htm now exist through which you, your family, and your community can help a black boy go back into his past to find some of his purpose and mission. If you can help fund a black boy's discovery of who his ancestors were before slavery and perhaps even those ancestors who fought against slavery, you may be helping him develop a sense of purpose from deep within.

• Teach black boys self-reliance as a marker on the road toward self-respect. Traumatized boys must first be rescued from their trauma, but also, at a certain point of resilience, they may start saying to you or your community, "Okay, now is the moment I want to become a man. Don't give me manhood, stand with me as I find it myself." Helping a black boy in your community may require you to take hold of this moment not by giving a special share or privilege, but by showing him how to work independently.

UNDERSTANDING PURPOSE

Purpose Among Black Boys Is Also an Issue That Goes Beyond Race

Mississippi State football coach Sylvester Croom provides a story that exemplifies how necessary it is both to respect the need for black boys to gain unique ways of purpose development *and* to see beyond race. Coach Croom remembers how much he wanted to play football for Bear Bryant at Alabama nearly forty years ago. Croom's father told Bryant, "Don't give him nothing because he's black. And don't take nothing away from him because he's black." These two men agreed that for this boy to become a man of purpose, he would need to show, regardless of color, his mettle. They also knew: this boy's discovery of male identity and purpose could not succeed without community member Coach Bryant (and other white teachers and coaches) standing ground around this boy as he learned to succeed in gaining self-respect.

- Be clear in your community discussions on the role of a man, a husband, a father. If you are a woman, you play an essential part in helping black males discover a sense of purpose, whether as husbands, lovers, or sons. A thirty-five-year-old black lawyer talked openly to me during a therapy session regarding the immense grief and anger he felt in black women. He said, "Black women are enraged at me and my friends, but I think it's because they feel betrayed by us because we don't know how to love them. They are afraid and sad and decide somewhere along the line to just pretend they don't need us."

If a boy lives in a constant stressed state of vigilance regarding self-respect, purpose, and identity, grows through adolescence in a household that may have had a missing father, enters a society that inherently undervalues whatever self-respect he has achieved, begins love relationships and intimacy from a constant one-down position in his wife's opinion of him, then he and his relationship will most likely fail. He will play his part in the failure—his spouse or partner cannot control that. But she can improve the situation by better understanding this man's battle for self-respect. She can help him feel needed rather than lost. And even if her husband or the father of her child does indeed leave his marriage or relationship, she can still help her son feel needed as a black man.

• Protect black boys from overuse of media. The media provides stereotypically limited, highly sexualized, and highly violent models and images of black masculinity. As much as you can, become a part of communities and neighborhoods that distract young black males from media with "seeking activities"—sports, schools, families, and faith communities—that will fulfill the need for black males to seek and find models for identity and purpose.

• Help professionals understand male biology and black male legacy. In the next section of this chapter, we will focus on the importance of the helping professions, including counseling and therapy, in moving toward a community-based model that understands the specific needs of all boys. Especially in the case of black boys, many people in the helping profession have not been trained in understanding the population. Without deep cognizance of the male culture that they are dealing with (and, even more specifically, the black male culture) they apply general therapeutic techniques that may find little success with black boys.

One approach that is having success with young black males is the modernization of *Nguzo Saba*, an African-based value system that provides meaning and direction through facilitation of seven principles in families and communities: *Umoja* (unity), *Kujichagulia* (self-determination), *Ujima* (cooperative work), *Nia* (purpose), *Kuumba* (creativity), and *Imami* (faith). This model, similar to the HEROIC model we described in Chapter Four, challenges the counselor to be not just a "listener" to a boy's feelings, nor to impose a Western theory of psychology on the young black male, but to work from a toolbox as much informed by ancestral Africa as possible. The counselor becomes a community member who finds resources around the boy that can teach each of these principles.

Our African American sons are calling out to us for help every day, help that involves creative approaches, historical models, communal intensity, and attention to the purpose of each boy. The loneliness, alienation, and frustration of black boys today will haunt all of us until our streets, schools, and homes see it for what it is—boys haunted themselves by their own lack of meaning and purpose in life.

Questions of Purpose

How Can I Help You, Young Man?

- How can I as a community member help you become a good man?
- What are your values as a young man?
- What is your purpose in life?
- What men and women in your ancestry most inspire you?
- What men and women in the media most inspire you?
- What is most stressful or desperate about your life right now? How can I help you solve this problem?
- Will you come to me when you need help? Do you know I am always here for you?
- Will you let me teach you what I know about being good to women?
- Are you being hurt, bullied, or harassed by anyone? Will you let me help you through this?
- In what ways do you think your community needs your talents and gifts?

Many of these questions are those that we imagine parents would ask, but each can be asked just as well by committed members of a communal parenting system.

Changing Helping Professions to
Focus on Boys' Needs

Whether you are concerned about black or white males, or any other population, you may find that a critical resource in building and caring for our communities are the helping professions, especially the therapeutic profession. We must ask: Is this community of assets, this group of professionals, focused well enough on our young males? My experience tells me that over the next decade it needs to become far better aligned with the needs of our sons.

In my own decades as a therapist, I have learned from and taught many therapists who are beginning to look closely at how the caring professions care for boys. My own therapy profession is beginning to admit that it does not protect the purpose of boys as well as it does the empowerment and healing of girls.

This lack of protection of boys is not a sin of commission, but omission. Therapists are mainly trained to talk about feelings, and that works fine for many boys, but much better for many more girls and women. For many boys it is not the best strategy. Part of our evidence that we are not doing well enough is that boys generally engage in counseling as a part of punishment. Men usually choose to avoid the therapy profession altogether, much to the detriment of their health, their marriages, their parenting, and their self-improvement.

As we look at how we care for a boy, it's crucial to remember that in the female brain, verbal expression of feelings signals oxytocin to flow through brain circuits, which helps girls carry their own burdens into bonds with therapists and others. For boys, however, verbal expression of feelings often just increases internal vulnerability, heightening internal stress (thus raising adrenalin and testosterone), and confusing the healing and empowerment of the boy. He often needs to learn how to control his actions, not necessarily talk about what he is feeling.

Of course, in saying this, we have to remember that many boys do need *more* talk time about their feelings. As psychologists Michael Thompson, coauthor of *Raising Cain*, and William Pollack, author of *Real Boys*, have observed, many boys need much more help with emotional literacy than we give them. Many boys do indeed need to talk about feelings and cry more in order to find outlets for their pain.

At the same time, the future of boyhood in communities requires that helping professionals do much more than talk with boys. Talk therapy belongs in the toolbox, but we must also learn to utilize other methodologies appropriate specifically for the male brain. It is my hope that every therapist in the future will be trained not just in "psychother-apy" but in "boys and men." All of us in these professions now can gain immediate insight by looking into the eyes of the boy right in front of us, and asking questions regarding the primary needs of *this* boy. If you are seeking a therapist for your son, and you might ask the therapist if he or she has successfully asked and answered these questions:

- Do I personally have the training to help this and other boys?
- How can I become a part of this boy's three-family system?
- To what extent does this boy need a safe verbal-emotional outlet, that is, does he mainly need to talk about his feelings and cry?
- But also, to what extent are feeling talk and tears going to be not enough for this boy?
- What traumas in this boy's life may have rewired his brain away from empathy and moral conduct?
- How can I help connect this boy with family or community members who can help him learn from male role models how to be empathic and moral?
- Does this boy need character development, and if so, how do I facilitate that, including directing the family toward commu-nity members and faith communities that can help?
- Am I, personally, the right therapist for this boy? Does he need a man (or woman), someone other than me?
- Does he need a group-therapy model, in addition to my (or another therapist's) one-on-one relationship with him?
- Is my office set up for girl talk rather than boy action? If so, how do I change it to incorporate strategies that I inherently know can work, such as video games, play therapy, sand painting, graphics, chess, or other boy-friendly activities that will appeal to this boy?

Tips for Therapists

If you are a therapist or another community member who works with boys, here are some tips for improving care. I have personally instituted these in my practice. If you are a parent searching for a therapist for your son, these tips can serve as landmarks for looking carefully at a potential therapist.

- Seek new insight into the way males think. Even if you have been a therapist for a while, you may need to get male-brain training, especially if you were mainly trained in talk therapy or other verbal-cognitive models.
- Walk with boys, outside, and talk to them while you walk . . . this is Socratic, peripatetic counseling. It gets boys moving, and it allows for shoulder-to-shoulder contact, which is more comfortable, especially for high-testosterone boys.
- In a first or second visit, ask the boy to complete (in writing or verbally on tape) a questionnaire of interests. Provide him with tools for these interests, and ask his parents to bring in these tools next time. If, for instance, he is interested in a particular video game, ask him to bring it to your office next time.
- Talk with the boy while he uses these tools—enjoy his hobbies, games, sports, and so on with him—so that he'll open up to you while "doing" something with his hands and mind.
- Help the boy's "first family" not only with its own family issues, but also by helping them set up a male mentoring system for the boy (especially if he is ten or older), that becomes his second family.

Enjoying Communities of Purpose with Boys

Our sons are meant to be a great source of joy for us. Boys are fun loving, filled with energy, brilliant in their inventiveness, humorous and sly in their talk, and challenging of our authority—but also good-hearted, hopeful, and true seekers after the good.

Our neighborhoods and communities can be joyful places for sons, and thus for ourselves. A friend of mine, therapist Gary Plep, in

Los Gatos, California, who specializes in male development, once used the metaphor of horses, a wide fence, and the far mountains to talk about the joy of males. His family has been involved in working with horses for two decades.

Gary said:

> Horses have a way of showing their joy, both inside the fence and outside. Each young horse can have a mother and father inside the fence, and stands close to them at first (especially the mother), then as the year goes by, the colt expands its circle out among the other horses. He enjoys the testing, the pushing, the grooming, the playing among the others. He may look outside the fence, toward the far mountains, but as he becomes domesticated inside the wide fence, he learns who he is and how he fits, and gets his joy from that.
>
> It's not until after the rancher has trained him and the community of other horses themselves have cared for him that he gets a chance to run outside the fence. That's its own joy, too, for sure, but by then he pretty much knows where home is, and who to trust, and how to be a member of his herd. I've been around horses a long time, and I've seen the joy in the eyes of the ones who know not only how good it feels to run free, but also how good it feels to come back home.

I love this metaphor. Boys are not horses, you might say, and quite rightly. But boys are children and then adults who long for love. They cannot feel the joy both of running free and coming home unless their communities take charge of their energy. They know that the fence of community is not an oppression if it teaches them identity. When they gain their own portion of the wealth of care and respect possible inside the fence, they become joyful, focused, and purposeful, and carry that joy wherever they later wander, however far away they run, and toward the day, at some point in adulthood, when they may choose to return home.

7

Changing Schools Toward Relevance and Purpose for Boys

> The power and quality of education is this: Each of us receives from Nature what is central in ourselves, what indeed makes us truly and individually who we are, but in a rough and unfinished form; it is the function of education to bring this to its highest perfection, and to discover in it the highest purpose for which it is capable.
>
> —ADAPTED FROM *ON THE EDUCATION OF BOYS* BY RENAISSANCE
> PHILOSOPHER JACOPO SADOLETO

A FATHER SENT ME THIS EMAIL:

I am a father of an eight-year-old boy who seems to be having difficulties in school. My son's teacher says that he has trouble concentrating, but when he does focus, he accomplishes the work. Usually when he comes home, he has to finish work that he didn't complete during the day. In the mornings, he often says he hates school and doesn't want to go.

Because he's a year behind in reading and math, we enrolled him in Sylvan Learning Center. A lot of his friends in the school have been told that because they have trouble paying attention, they should go on Ritalin. I believe most of these boys don't have ADD. I think the school isn't helping them the way they need to learn. I am scared that if my son is misdiagnosed this will harm him the rest of his life. I'm writing you wondering if he is just immature and will grow out of this phase, or if he is beginning to become one of those boys who hate school so much he'll fail later.

An email from a mother began this way:

> My son is a lost middle school boy. He is smart but disinterested, falling behind in several subjects, forgetting to complete and/or turn in assignments, etc. He is a pretty sensitive kid, not that interested in sports. He spends hours alone, playing computer games. His disinterest in school and his boredom began in third grade. He hated school and we were told he had ADHD. We got him tested and he didn't really test as deficient but the pediatrician put him on Concerta just in case. After a week of trying to get my son to take the pill and him resisting, we gave it up. I took him to a pediatric neurologist who confirmed he had no brain disorder. The neurologist said we should look at whether he was in the right school for him. I don't really know what that means. What school is right for him? What school will help him feel like education matters to his future?

Research worldwide shows that education is a constant pillar in future success and happiness for both boys and girls. Over the last two decades, this research has also shown that the number of boys "checking out" of school is increasing, and so too is the number of boys "checking out" of fruitful life. Although it is not impossible for a boy to find his purpose in life without being well educated, it is, especially in today's high-stakes world, very difficult. The number of boys who are falling behind in school or "checking out" is epidemic, and this deeply affects their ability to succeed in life.

How Boys Are Struggling for Purpose in School

The Boy's Project, which I mentioned in Chapter One, has been collecting data on what is happening to boys in schools in the United States and abroad. Tom Mortenson of the Pell Institute is a Boy's Project board member and has compiled a wealth of statistics. Some of the most telling regarding the schooling of young boys are these:

- For every 100 girls suspended from public elementary and secondary schools, 250 boys are suspended.
- For every 100 girls expelled from public elementary and secondary schools, 335 boys are expelled.
- For every 100 girls diagnosed with a special education disability, 217 boys are so diagnosed.
- For every 100 girls diagnosed with a learning disability, 276 boys are so diagnosed.
- For every 100 girls diagnosed with emotional disturbance, 324 boys are so diagnosed.
- For every 100 girls diagnosed with multiple disabilities, 189 boys are so diagnosed.

When we look at grades, we find that the majority of Ds and Fs received in schools are received by boys. In many schools with which the Gurian Institute has been called to work, two-thirds of Ds and Fs are received by boys. In the same schools (and statistically nationwide), girls not only tend to avoid Ds and Fs but also receive the majority of As. Over the last couple of decades, some analysts have claimed that boys may fail more than girls, but boys also succeed better than girls in the long run. If that was once true, it is no longer true. On average boys fail in comparison to girls in our contemporary school system. It thus comes as no surprise that boys comprise the vast majority of high school dropouts. When we then look at college applications and retention, we might be shocked to see the following effects in higher education:

- For every 100 women enrolled in college, 77 men are enrolled.
- For every 100 American women who earn an associate's degree, 67 American men earn the same degree.
- For every 100 American women who earn a bachelor's degree, 73 American men earn the same degree.
- For every 100 American women who earn a master's degree, 62 American men earn the same degree.

Boys "turning off" from education is not just an American phenomenon; it is global. According to the 2003 PISA study, which tracks educational progress in fifty-seven countries, boys are behind girls in overall educational markers. There is no industrialized country in the world where boys are ahead of girls in total markers, though in some countries boys may be ahead in a subcategory such as science.

"Boys are in trouble," warns Judith Kleinfeld, director of the Boys Project, "not only boys of color, not only boys of poverty, but boys themselves." Dr. Kleinfeld has pointed to the gender gap in literacy skills as an example of universal boys' issues. Among children of white college-educated parents, for instance, 23 percent score "Below Basic" in twelfth-grade National Assessment of Educational Progress reading tests. These are high school seniors unable to read a newspaper with understanding. The number of sons of educated parents with this deficiency has grown to one-quarter of the population.

Fixing the Mismatch Between Schools and the Purpose of Boys

When a boy is growing up, his sense of purpose is subtly defined by his educational environment. If he feels mismatched for too long, he feels shame. He comes to believe he can't learn. He compares himself to others, both boys and girls, and feels one-down constantly. In this state of mind, he is less likely to feel like the boy who will save the world, nor the young male seeker after the truth. He often becomes unhappy, unable to gain status; he may act out and get in trouble, be put on medication, and withdraw from success models that are available to him through school environments. His trajectory for contextualizing his ultimate purpose in life can become skewed in these ways:

- Whether he can talk about it or not, he is learning that the place that is supposed to prepare him to lead, compete, serve the world, earn a living, and care for a family actually devalues his nature, his mind, his heart, and his soul from early on.
- The people who are supposed to model purposeful learning and action are good people, but they seem to dislike who he is, and so he cannot fully integrate their modeling in order to be a hero—in fact, he sees only rebellion or withdrawal as his possible paths to heroism.

The social paradigms that are supposed to instruct him in how to succeed and become relevant to the future of society become irrelevant to his self-survival. Overall, by middle school he becomes one of those kids who hates education and loses out on the paths of purpose that only education can give him.

Many boys are experiencing these issues and many of the resulting pathologies; much of this situation cannot be sourced to the boy, but rather to the system that educates him. Matching the school's teaching style much better to his brain—thus to his body, heart, and soul—can work wonders. It does not solve family problems or other social ills, but it can lead to great success.

What the Gurian Institute and Its Partners Have Been Doing

The Gurian Institute has been helping redress these issues for the last ten years with an eye to how girls' and boys' brains learn differently. We have observed that when schools address this mismatch, they

- Improve boys' grades
- Improve boys' test scores
- Improve boys' behavior
- Lower the need for medications such as Ritalin
- Improve retention of boys in high school
- Improve male college retention rates

One of the key initiatives that we help put into action is the vision of the school as a learning community, or in our language, "second or third family." We put specific focus on the bonding and attachment of teachers with individual students. We also emphasize connecting teachers with parents, as well as with other classroom volunteers, such as grandparents, in younger grades, and with older siblings or older mentors (from high schools) who become mentors to younger students. Although parents can't lead teachers in curricula issues or objective school learning standards, teachers often feel very grateful for parental involvement; parents can also become immensely powerful advocates and leaders for boys in school.

Overall, as we work toward educational reform, we believe we are proving that if boys can, from preschool through college, be in a school environment of almost familial challenge and gentleness that is a good fit for the male brain, they can find purpose, relevance, and opportunities for skill building that match the way their minds and hearts already exist in real life. From this depth of supportiveness they are more likely to succeed in school and, later in life, as seekers and heroic men.

Making Schools a Better Fit for Boys

These three issues—"matching schools' teaching styles to the male brain," "helping schools to be like third-family members," and "making schools an environment of relevance and purpose for boys and young men"—are intertwined. This chapter will help you marshal forces in your schools and establish home support to make these things happen. If you are a parent who sees your son entering a school that does not utilize any of the boy-friendly and boy-purposeful strategies in this chapter, you may need to become a strong advocate for boys in that school.

UNDERSTANDING PURPOSE

Boys' and Girls' Brains Learn Differently

All of the differences between boys' and girls' brains that we've discussed in previous chapters can apply to learning. It is useful to remember that most teachers are not trained in these differences in graduate school and teacher certification programs, thus, many schools and teachers are not aware of the importance of these differences. Let's review the most important differences here again:

- Boys' brains mature, on average, more slowly than girls' brains in fine motor skills. Many boys cannot initially fulfill a number of the writing and other fine motor tasks of the early grades as well as many girls do. If they are judged as incompetent because of brain growth differences, they can suffer throughout future school years with a self-image of educational failure.

- Boys develop reading and writing skills later than girls, on average, due to
  1. Fewer brain centers devoted in the male brain to word production
  2. Later maturation and growth of these centers

  When boys are judged deficient at five years old if they can't read competitively with girls, many of them decide reading has little or no purpose in their lives. Reading and writing, which are two of the ways humans develop identity and purpose, are negated for such boys.

- Because they mature later and in different ways as compared to girls, boys often need one or more parents and teachers to become close one-on-one mentors for development of skills, especially in the early years. Without these individuals in their corner, boys can often feel lost, and as a result act out, get suspended, fail to learn, and thus not feel connected to education.

- Boys often need, on average, more physical movement in order for their brains to perform on a par with girls in educational environments. Sitting still for fifty minutes is often the wrong way for a boy's brain to work—the male brain often needs to be kept stimulated through physical movement in order to perform cognitive tasks as well as girls do. To neglect this brain fact is often to try to force a boy to learn in a way that runs counter to his nature, which ultimately turns him off to learning, developing in him a sense that education has no purpose for him.

- Because there is less white matter in boys' brains, boys may not concentrate as well as girls on multiple tasks at once. The issue of ADD/ADHD is often a mismatch between the multitasking that schools require of young children and the male brain. The classroom, built around a verbal, multitasking model, may be a mismatch with a male brain that seeks to focus on one learning task at a time. If the educational team allows a boy to focus his brain on one purposeful, skill-building task for a relevant period of time, he is more likely to succeed. If schools don't know this, boys can often appear to be naturally defective, in comparison with girls or with other early maturing boys.

Thankfully, many colleges are beginning to teach these differences, but many teachers, most of whom are women, still walk into classrooms with their own female brain learning model in mind. Although teachers are some of the most professional, caring, and essential people your children will meet in a lifetime, they are hampered in their ability to help boys find knowledge, skill, identity, and purpose when they aren't provided with training in the male brain in their own college coursework. And because they are so busy, and they have not fully understood the individual boy's need for attachment and team learning, they may not realize that bringing a few more people into the mix can immediately affect the boy for the better.

As teachers innovate in these areas, not only can a boy's performance be positively affected, but also *his love of school*. Remember the emails with which we began this chapter—the undercurrent in both was that the boy hates school. From a positive improvement in love of school come a cascade of improvements in male buy-in not only to education, but later on, to successful discovery of a purpose in life.

Innovations from Another Country

In the PISA study mentioned earlier, Finland occupied the number one slot in science test scores, and number two in math and reading out of the fifty-seven countries tested. The United States tested below Finland (also below Canada, Estonia, Japan, Australia, and many others).

Finland's approach to education is worth looking at, for it is more brain-based than ours. For instance, many children don't start school until age seven. Knowing that large parts of a given population of children (mainly males) don't reach equal levels of cognitive brain growth until around seven, Finnish schools begin at a time when there is more equality of growth.

As the test scores show, Finnish children catch up to and pass children in other countries, such as the United States, that pressure young children to read, write, and do other multitasking, fine motor skills, and other cognitive tasks that might not be a fit for millions of young brains in their school system.

Finnish schools don't give a lot of homework. The kind of "busy work" that American schools pile onto kids—which most girls complete every evening but which far more boys rebel against because of its irrelevance to their lives—is not as highly valued in Finnish education. High school students in Finland get approximately one-half hour of homework per day. Very few Finnish boys (or girls) are on Ritalin or similar drugs.

Finnish schools also look to attachment and bonding issues before looking at medication. When a child is failing, attention is first given to situational stressors at home and in the child's community. Medication is a last resort, and very little medication is used, per capita, on Finnish boys.

Should every school in the United States suddenly change to the Finnish model? This would be very difficult, of course, and there are significant cultural differences between countries—for example, the United States is educating far more students than Finland. Furthermore, one could make the argument that though our educational system may not be as strong, we still command a better standard of living and are as a whole more competitive economically in the world than Finland. One could say, "We must be doing something right."

Indeed we are. Statistics and test scores don't tell the whole story. Many things are going well in America. The example of Finland is most valuable, I think, not as a call to alter our whole school system, but as a brain-based myth-buster regarding some of our social and educational assumptions.

Avoiding Myths About School and Learning for Boys

Here are a few myths you and your family team can work to bust, in school and at home:

- Not every boy or girl needs to read by the age of five. If we are reading to him at home and helping him learn his letters, he may well be just fine.
- Not every boy needs to learn computers by age five. In fact, during the toddler and early years of brain growth, most boys

will need far more outdoor and nature learning time, as is emphasized in Finland.

- Not every boy needs to be able to multitask at five to prove he has an attention span. We may need to redefine "attention span" to mean "ability to do the task a brain chooses to do," rather than what we tacitly call it now: "ability at five to do a set of tasks that I want that brain to do."

- Boys who are falling behind may need their parents or other mentors to spend more time with them or pay closer attention to emotional stressors in their lives before looking toward medication as a fix.

Finding Teachers Who Like to Bond with Boys

Lisa Gordon, an early childhood diversity consultant and mother of two sons, has utilized information regarding matching learning styles to male brains in a program she developed called *Promoting the Self-Esteem of Boys of Color*. In our Notes and Resources, you'll see how to access this program. Lisa highlights a teacher who utilizes brain-based information to adapt a classroom to fit boys' natural brain styles, making sure to bond and attach with the boys just as "boys," whether they are black, white, Hispanic, Asian, or Native American. Not surprisingly, this kind of teacher also helps boys develop a sense of purpose in education.

Lisa writes:

> Let me tell you about Mrs. Travis. She is a second-grade teacher doing phenomenal work with boy students. She has integrated principles of male nature into understandings of nurture and culture. My seven-year-old was blessed to be in her class. Other parents have remarked, "She really gets male students," and "My son has never been so on task." Here are two examples of her techniques:
>
> - On her desk is a sign, "Travel with Mrs. Travis Down Language Arts Boulevard." Students physically move and walk between stations of her lesson. She does this also as "Travel with Mrs. Travis Down Social Studies Boulevard."

- Another sign on her desk reads "Travis Automotives: Specializing in Complete Car Care for all Makes and Models." She engages the boys right where they live, with toy cars all around the room. These kinds of things allow her to connect with the boys (and the girls love her too). From this connection, she is able to bring the best out of the boys and really give them a head start in finding out what direction they will want to go in life.

Mrs. Travis is an example of a teacher working from the earliest school years to match a boy's learning and bonding style with his future sense of success, happiness, and purpose. In her classroom, boys become journeyers, travelers, searchers, seekers, explorers, heroes. They learn about interest areas that many of them might already associate with higher self-image. They learn under the wing of a teacher who loves them as boys.

Teachers who bust educational myths and bond "down and dirty" with boys become huge allies for parents who want the best for their sons in school.

Looking to the Past for Solutions to Boys' Issues

Lou Burdick, a parent and professional in Minnesota, wrote me an email that recalled his childhood:

> My own mom raised nine kids on a farm—four of them were boys. And for one year I went to a one room school where boys and girls of all ages spent the entire day in a single room. Both my mom and that teacher had the same solution for restless boys: they would simply order everyone out of the house or school and demand that they run around the building ten times and then come back inside and "settle down and behave themselves." It worked like a charm as all the pent-up energy was discharged. And I suspect it didn't hurt the girls either.

Boys today need as much or more of this kind of attention to their brains and bodies, because those brains and bodies are being brought up, socialized, and nurtured in a culture that does not provide the natural physical movement opportunities of a farm, nor the natural sense of purpose that farm life inculcates from birth.

THE JOY OF PURPOSE

A Boy Goes Off to School

"And now, Tom, my boy," said the Squire, "remember you are going . . . to be chucked into this great school, like a young bear with all your troubles before you—earlier than we should have sent you perhaps. If schools are what they were in my time, you'll see a great many cruel blackguard things done, and hear a deal of foul bad talk. But never fear. You tell the truth, keep a brave and kind heart, and never listen to or say anything you wouldn't have your mother and sister hear, and you'll never feel ashamed to come home, or we to see you."

The allusion to his mother made Tom feel rather chokey, and he would have liked to have hugged his father well . . . as it was, he only squeezed his father's hand, and looked bravely up and said, "I'll try, Father."

"I know you will, my boy," his father said.

—Thomas Hughes, *Tom Brown's Schooldays*

One of the primary innovations used by both parents and teachers is "physical movement during learning." Physical movement can be a "brain break" between learning tasks, where the body moves around, giving the brain a chance to recharge and refocus. Even a boy moving around in a small space (pacing) near the kitchen table where he is doing homework or next to his desk at school is getting a brain break.

The purpose of boys is somewhat locked in—and set free through—the physicality of boys. It is crucial to remember this. Though boys can indeed sit still when needed (as can men), boys and men often need to move around more often than many girls and women—and boys and men often seek "who they are" by moving, pacing, exploring in physical space.

Holding Boys Back in Kindergarten or First Grade

Another way of making sure education fits the purpose of boys is to look carefully at matching the educational system to the boy when he is young, that is, to consider holding him back a year before entering first grade (or having him repeat kindergarten). Kathy Stevens has helped me respond to at least a hundred email questions from parents in just this past year regarding whether to hold a son back, emails similar to these:

"My son's birthday is 7/25. He will be 5 this July and can go to kindergarten. I'm struggling with either sending him or holding him back a year and putting him in a Pre-K class. I can't decide if he will be ready for the stresses of kindergarten."

Or: "My son's birthday is in September. Should I let him develop one more year before he goes to first grade? I'm not sure he's cognitively ready for first grade. His reading is definitely not great. I don't want him to hate school because he fails early."

If you are wondering about what to do with your own son or know another parent who is wondering, the following are research-based questions we hope you'll consider. They are designed to help you discern whether your son is developmentally ready for the grade he is to go into. In pondering these questions, remember always that no expert opinion or study should trump your best instincts.

1. If your son is developing more slowly than girls (or other boys), look at the cost of forcing him into a school environment. If you hold the boy back now, will the extra year actually help him when he's in fifth or ninth or twelfth grade—that is, will he gain a year to catch up developmentally at the outset, when he's five, so that he'll be on a more even playing field later, and thus will like school more, and succeed better when it really counts?

2.   Were any other boys or girls in your family history held back?
     It is possible that late development or "late blooming" is a
     family trait, and this is worth factoring in (it can bring a
     sense of relief, history, and lineage or legacy to your son's
     dilemma).

3.   Most boys who get held back feel a hit to their self-esteem for a
     few weeks (because their friends move up and they don't), but
     two factors lessen the effects of this over a few weeks: (1) it is
     becoming more common for more boys to be held back, so your
     son may not be alone, and (2) after a few weeks, your son will
     probably make other friends in other communities. Most sons
     are not emotionally scarred by being held back.

4.   Does your son have significant behavioral, anger management,
     or other emotional issues? If so, consult with the potential
     school principal or teacher to determine if he would have
     trouble in that school setting. These factors might be good
     reasons to let him mature another year. To throw him into an
     environment that is not yet a good fit with his developmental
     identity could hurt him later.

5.   Does your son have significant separation anxiety when he
     leaves you now? If so, factor this into your decision. It may
     (though it also may not) indicate later maturing. Right now, the
     three-family member your son may need help from the most
     might be you.

6.   Get a list of expectations from the kindergarten or first-grade
     teachers and see how many your son does not fit. Some of these
     can be as obvious as "Can he dress himself?" and some more
     subtle such as, "Does he like to pick up a book and look at it?"
     or something purely academic like "Does he recognize letters
     and write his own name?" If your son isn't ready for kindergar-
     ten, you or another three-family member can work with him
     during the year on all the developmental tasks, and master
     them at home or in child care.

7.   Ask your son what he wants to do. Does he want to go to kin-
     dergarten or repeat it? He might hold the key to your answer in

his own thinking. He might have a deep, unconscious sense of where, right now, he wants to take the next step in developing his own sense of purpose in life.

8. Does your son have any special needs? Has he been diagnosed with a learning disorder or disability? If so, this can factor into your discussions with prospective schools or teachers. If your son has special needs, remember that much of his life journey, his heroism, and his sense of purpose will be discovered through his disability.

Does anyone hold the "final word" on holding back boys? No, but one thing research does indicate is this: if you can't decide what to do, it may be best to err on the side of caution and hold a boy back. The present educational system is hard on boys; especially those we suspect aren't ready for it. If you are questioning entrance into kindergarten, remember that now is the best and safest time to make such a change. If you wait till a later grade, such as third or fourth, to hold a boy back, damage to self-esteem, identity, and purpose development can be more severe.

Two good Web sites for further reviews of research are:

www.kidsource.com/kidsource/content5/kindergarten.entrance.html
www.isteve.com/2002_Redshirting-A_Kindergarten_Arms_Race.htm

Helping Elementary School Boys

Susan Horn in St. Louis, Missouri, a Boys Project board member and education specialist who utilizes brain-based information to train teachers in how to help boys succeed, has provided this report of what works best with boys. Many thanks to Susan for these innovations, which she originally provided to the Boys Project. I have adapted them into a list format here that I hope helps you serve the little boys in your care. If you are a parent looking at a school for your son, you can use this as a checklist. Does the school understand these principles and innovations? If it does not, it may not be good for your son.

As a teacher, administrator and now as an inclusion consultant, I see on a daily basis how teachers do not appreciate boys for being boys. Things we have to watch for:

- First of all, the schedules are not always boy-friendly. For example, many times a circle time follows story time and the children may end up in the same spot for over thirty minutes. This amount of sitting time is too long for any child, much less a boy.
- And often, circle times come before outdoor time. I have made suggestions to many educators to have the boys run and play outside before the children gather in a circle time.
- Also, visual schedules are very helpful for boys. (They are less bored by them than written ones.) The more teachers use these, the more success they have with boys.
- Another note on schedules: often, they don't allow for a long time for the children to be outside. Because many educators don't like being outside themselves, they shorten outside time. Many educators particularly do not like being outside when it is cold so they really shorten this time and the boys are inside for the bulk of the day and cannot expend their energy. Few schools have appropriate indoor gross motor areas, which only complicates the problem.
- Educators are not always cognizant of wait time. Too many times, educators have all twenty children line up for bathroom time, going outside, and so on. This wait time increases negative behavior. An easy solution is to have the class broken down into two groups of ten.
- Room arrangement is another concern for boys. The block and science areas are rarely large enough; however, the dramatic play area is usually very large! This is usually a pretty easy fix and when educators change their rooms, they are amazed that negative behaviors are diminished.
- Also, few classrooms have good cozy areas. Classrooms need more of them. Not only can boys go there to be calm, but they can also be a great place to let off steam.
- Little boys tend not to gravitate towards writing centers, so I encourage educators to take writing utensils and paper to the block area. Drawing maps and writing signs are good literacy skills. Usually "Do not touch" is the first sign made.

- I also encourage educators to read boy-friendly stories with lots of visuals. Because boys do not on average hear as well as girls, boys often need to be positioned closer to the educator. Oftentimes they are put in the back of the reading space, which only encourages them to do what they do best . . . fidget with their neighbor!
- It has been my experience that educators often try to squelch rough and tumble play. I have encouraged educators to really look at their own circumstances and to reflect on different times of the day and whether or not to just let some things go! I remind them that our goal is not to make little boys into little girls!

Susan concluded, "My ultimate message is: hold boys to high standards just like we hold girls, but let them reach them in their own way." This is a crucial point, and one that each of us as parents and teachers needs to look at in our own way. Sometimes, the message that schools need to cater better to boys' minds and hearts will be taken as "excuse making," or lead to the question, "Wait a minute, why wouldn't we hold boys to the same standards we hold girls to?" In fact, boys should be held to very high standards, but subjecting every child to the same learning style is not a standard. Boys and girls can all reach the highest of goals, in their own ways.

The Value of Debating

Carl Strom, a sixth-grade teacher in Kentucky, wrote me regarding this very point. He said, "I hold my boys to the same high standards as girls, but teach so that they can meet the standards." Carl told me he hands this quote from Michel de Montaigne's sixteenth-century essay, "Educating Boys," to his students and their parents, hoping to enlist parents in teaching boys with him, or, in other words, to build a three-family system for educating boys.

"Let the boy's conscience and his virtue shine forth in his speech, and be guided by reason. Make him understand that to confess the error he discovers in his own reasoning is a mark of judgment and honesty, which are the chief qualities he aims at; that obstinacy and contention are vulgar qualities, most apparent in the basest minds; that to correct oneself and change one's mind, and in the heat of ardor to abandon a weak position, is a sign of strong, rare, and philosophical qualities." Carl discusses these values and asks parents to pursue them at home as he is doing at school.

A NOTE ON USING DEBATES   Carl pointed out another innovation for boys, one that can work as well at dinner tables as at schools:

> Developing purpose in boys is all about 'mastery' to me, and I preach that. In my Language Arts class, we debate EVERYTHING. The debates help both the boys and girls discover high standards. In all my classes, I find that the girls tend to be more nose-to-the-grindstone no matter how I teach them. With the boys, I have to show them boy-specific ways, like honing their positions in debates, to get them to be as attentive as the girls, and reach the high standards Montaigne wanted everyone to reach.

Elementary schoolchildren are not too young to be compelled to care about what they learn by having to support their positions argumentatively. By fourth grade, children can pick positions that mean something to them, and prove those positions. The brain is ready, and many male brains need this kind of focus-mechanism for energy, acumen, and learning. Debates such as those in Carl's classroom, or those you can have at the dinner table at least one night a week at home, can form memories of relevance and success in children. These memories are resources that they can mine later, as they develop a longing to be more concretely purposeful during adolescence and adulthood.

Questions of Purpose

Son, How Do You Like School?

Before your sons leave elementary school, it is crucial to ascertain how they feel about school. These questions can be asked of older boys, but I hope you'll also consider asking them, if possible, before your young sons leave elementary school. If the answers sadden you or give you cause for alarm, I hope you'll look closely at other schooling options for your son.

- What do you love about going to school? Which parts don't you like? Which parts do you like?
- Which class is your favorite? Why?
- Which teacher is your favorite? Why?
- How do other kids treat you? Are you being bullied (or are you a witness to bullying or a bully)?
- What would make your classes better?
- Do you get to move around enough at school? Do you get enough recess?
- Which tests do you like? Which tests don't you like?
- Do any of your teachers think you're a failure? Which teacher?
- Do you finish and hand in your homework? If not, why not?
- Have you heard from your friends about another school or a different kind of school that you might like better than the school you're in now?
- Would you tell me if you hated school?

Helping Boys in Secondary School

The Gurian Institute uses four further guiding principles for secondary level educators:

1. Every middle or high school teacher should consider making a commitment to **mentoring** at least one boy (and girl). If possible, a male teacher should mentor a boy. Mentors can be assigned at the beginning of the year, and a system often needs to be in place so that one teacher doesn't end up being asked by twenty boys to be their mentor. It is crucial to remember that more than half of the boys who are failing in secondary school are being raised without a father—male mentors can help fill this void of male role modeling.

2. **If it helps boys, it can help girls**, and vice versa. Any strategy that works for boys can help girls. In fact, in the schools we've worked with, when boys' test scores go up, so do girls' scores. When adolescent boys find education to be purposeful and relevant, they are less defiant and more willing to learn, which frees girls up from having to deal with hours and days of behavioral problems around them.

3. Secondary teachers, especially in high school, sometimes think of themselves as "**content experts**" and devalue "teaching strategies." They just want to lecture about their content. We must all encourage them to realize that *how* they teach in high school matters as much as *what* they teach. One teacher who shows specific and strategic attention to boys can increase a boy's chances of finishing high school. If every teacher makes learning strategically relevant to real life, more boys stay in school. It's as simple as that.

4. Most boy-friendly innovations take five minutes, not the whole hour—**we *do* have time for them**—and they don't derail or hamper our state-required or school-required curricula.

Strategies That Help Boys Learn Successfully

Our Model Schools use these strategies and they show strong quantitative and qualitative success data in all kinds of school environments, from urban to rural, low socioeconomic to high.

1. Allow **movement** or use **squeeze balls**, even during quizzes and tests. Try having reluctant learners or fidgeting boys move around in a small space near their desk while they are tested (and monitor, of course, for cheating off another student's test) or let these boys hold a soft squeeze ball in their nonwriting hand. These activities keep the brain more active and awake. The boys get better grades, do better on tests, write better papers, and like learning more.

2. Make lessons, lesson plans, homework, reading material **more relevant**. Boys (and girls) need to read information that feeds

their sense of seeking a purposeful life. Adolescence is the developmental time when directing boys toward purpose through education is crucial. If high school does not feel relevant to future success, many boys will drop out.

3. Utilize **project-driven** curricula. Help the students do one project, in all sensorial media possible, for one to two weeks at a time. Filling out lots of worksheets is a turnoff, and boys (and girls) don't retain much from them anyway. If a science, math, language arts, or other class can do a group or long-term individual project that teaches the same material, boys are more likely to retain the material, and keep learning.

4. Wrap lessons around **identity development** that expresses "here is how this lesson can help you discover who you are." Here is one strategic way to do this. Ask students to provide **introduction speeches**. Give students time to think about what they could tell the class about themselves for one minute. Make a list of information they could provide: where they live, description of their family, hobbies, things they can do well, favorite color, favorite meal, television shows they like, what they want to be when they grow up, what values they care most about, and so on. Display the list of potential subjects on the overhead projector or board, or at the back of the room for them to look at if needed while delivering their speeches. In commenting on their speeches, concentrate on delivery more than content of speech.

5. Help boys **debate** as much as you can—teach them the difference between **theory, fact**, and **opinion**. Carry on a five-minute debate about something every day, even in a math or science class. One way to bring this into the teaching day is **The Silent Debate**, which was designed by Russell White, a teacher at Crespi Carmelite High School. "Introduce the debate to the students as an idea that espouses a philosophy relative to current content—it could be 'How do we fix the welfare system?' Divide the students into pairs, then give each pair a topic . . . either a side of an argument, or they

get a philosopher/person to represent. They debate by writing on and passing a piece of paper back and forth for 10–12 minutes, with no talking during that time." When the debriefing time comes, Russell notices playfulness such as, "Your philosophy sucks" and "No, yours does," but eventually, Russell says, the boys get down to good content. After the time is up, the pairs present their results to the class.

6. Use **graphics** such as **comic books** and **storyboards** if needed in language arts. Michael Blitz, founder of the Columbia University Teachers College Book Project, recently said, "Educators are increasingly looking toward comic books to encourage children's literacy and English-language skills. Teachers are looking for ways to engage their children, and they're finding some of that in comic books." The Comic Book Project has expanded in six years to 860 U.S. schools. Blitz notes, "For kids who may be struggling and for kids who may be new to the English language, **that visual sequence is a very powerful tool**."

7. Use **DVDs** and **movies** whenever appropriate. These, too, are visual, and stimulate the male brain's very active visual-graphic centers. Steve Hadaway, who teaches at Riverside Military Academy for Boys in Gainesville, Georgia, teaches math and ethics. In his ethics class, he explores such themes as the death penalty, core values, suicide, decision making, racial tension, and prejudice, and he utilizes a movie or story to focus the debate. This has improved student performance. He used the movie *Men of Honor* in his math class because the protagonist, Carl Brashear, a Navy deep-sea diver, initially struggled with his math abilities in dive school. By contextualizing even math lessons in stories of men finding their purpose in life, Steve is helping his students identify their own talents (and even possible failures) with male role models who persevered.

8. Teach **brain development and gender differences**, get students talking about them, in science as well as in language arts, social studies, and history. Read aloud some of the brain

differences in this book and let the young people in the class talk about how they have or have not noticed these in boys and girls, and women and men.

9. Teach **parents** how to help adolescents with **homework**. Sometimes, teachers need to coach parents to make sure video games are a privilege or reward and not a right. ("Homework first, video games second.") At times we parents also need to sit with our high school student at the kitchen table for an hour to supervise homework, check his folder or backpack, complete a "checklist" each evening to make sure the young man has turned in his homework. Many boys fail in school because of homework issues—they don't turn in homework (though they say they do) or they don't do homework (but go to their rooms and play with electronics). Often, the three-family unit needs to solve this in communication with one another. Sometimes, for a few months at least—until the young man gains his own homework skills and motivation—parents and extended family must supervise him. This does not mean doing the homework for him—it means watching over him until he "becomes a man" who follows through himself.

The Wisdom of Purpose

SCHOOLS TEACH JUSTICE, TOO

During the boyhood years until sixteen or seventeen, boys are kept occupied with duties, for this time of life demands the most watchful care. . . . The boys go to school and spend their time in learning justice as well as reading and writing . . . and the teachers teach the boys self-control and self-restraint by lessons of law, debate, and duty, and by themselves, as elders, acting temperately.

—Xenophon, *The Education of Cyrus the Persian*

Investing in Schools of Purpose

Boys' learning should be filled with wonder, for it is a boy's purpose, especially when he is young, to live in wonder, and engage in whatever joyful and confusing results emerge from that sense of wonder. A tree, a light bulb, a friend, a challenge, a vision of outer space . . . a book he reads, a conversation, a prayer, a disagreement, a pattern he sees, a scientific inquiry . . . a moral challenge, a physical failure, a teacher's words, an image from the past to which he aspires . . . anything and everything that enters his mind and heart will have its moment there, and some things will remain in him as founding parts of his identity and purpose in life.

Schools that attend to the inherent nature of children are schools whose lessons will endure in the boy well into his adulthood, and help define his heroic service to himself, his family, and his world. Schools and teachers that do not attempt to match learning with the already self-defining impulses in the boy himself so disrespect his nature that their life work and teaching can become reasons for grief and failure, not successful lessons that help the boy make the world a better place. And as educational failure statistics are showing us, when boys' brains are not matched by their schools' teaching style, and parents and schools are isolated from one another, boys often fall behind. When the school and family become a learning community that takes into consideration the minds and hearts of boys, boys do better.

As we save our sons one boy at a time by advocating for schooling that is purposeful and relevant to young males, we will not only create a more successful generation of male learners, but we will also create a happier, more successful, and more purposeful generation of men. Teaching boys should be a joyful profession, for boys themselves are so filled with joy and wonder. As we reform our educational system to become a boy-friendly learning community—family oriented and professionally inspired—we will create a world of wonder for boys, and revive in our culture a love of learning in males.

8

Creating and Providing Rites of Passage for Your Son

> If we do not initiate our sons into manhood, they will burn the village down.
>
> —AFRICAN PROVERB

BRET STEPHENSON IS A SOCIAL WORKER in Lake Tahoe, California, who specializes in helping adolescent boys. Part of his sense of purpose in doing this work grows from his own boyhood. In his book, *From Boys to Men*, he begins his story this way:

> I was a great thief when I was a teen. I was successful in my illicit endeavors for several reasons. I was smart and patient. I was a wholesome local boy, a sports star whom everyone thought of as a good kid. But what really made me a good thief was that I enjoyed the risk factor, the exhilaration that made the fear of being caught acceptable.

Bret recalls how he decided one day to steal one thing from every shop in the mall in a neighboring town. He continues:

> I proceeded to carry out this plan, even stealing from the stores that held no purpose in my young boy's life, such as the women's lingerie store. Slowly, relentlessly, I meandered throughout the mall, completing my task.

When I was finished, rather than basking in my success,
I felt empty, dissatisfied. Was this not challenging enough?
Was I so good I needed to move on to bigger and better projects?
The answer came in a flash: put it all back! That would be the
ultimate challenge. . . . So I proceeded to risk being caught a
second time, not to increase my bounty but to rid myself of it.
When I'd finished, [I could see] the actual merchandise and my
sense of entitlement were just a means to justify the ends: risk and
challenge.

Bret goes on to talk about the hundreds of boys he has worked
with, each of whom was struggling to define himself through risk, challenge, and the development of a sense of purpose. As he discusses all
this, Bret writes, "It's amazing to me that with adolescence such a powerful and influencing dynamic in our lives, one that every adult human
on earth has been through, we treat it like an illness to be cured of."

That comment cuts to the heart, doesn't it? We wish we could cure
kids of adolescence. Perhaps we can go even deeper into this and ask,
"Why do we treat it like a disease? Why do we want a cure for it?" And,
"Are we perhaps afraid of it?"

Indeed, whether we are a child going through adolescence, or
a parent dealing with an adolescent, there is fear in us. Adolescence
can be a tough time. It always has been. Every culture before us and
around us has felt the fears of highly aggressive and very sensitive adolescent males. Each society has seen the risks these boys take. Ours is
no different. We are called to move through the fear and turn it into
courage—we are called to develop practical activities and structures,
rites of passage into manhood that serve not only the young men but
the needs of the culture as well.

Guiding a Son Through Male Adolescence

This chapter is about how to lead and supervise boys into healthy male
adulthood through organized physical and spiritual actions of risk
and challenge. I hope you'll enjoy delivering rites of passage in your

families, communities, and schools. The rite of passage is a culminating project that the three-family system gives to a young man—it is a powerful and true delivery system for questions and answers between boy and society that end with, "Now I know myself as a seeker after truth and respect in my community, and understand my own purpose more deeply."

To begin the delivery of this gift, take a moment to look at the ways in which adolescent boys call out for the delivery of this ritual. Look at the adolescent boys around you—their clothes, their games, their conversations with peers. Watch their body language, their rituals of greeting. What are they trying to accomplish, and how do you feel about these adolescent boys?

Remember a time when you were walking down the street and a pack of four or more adolescent boys was walking toward you. What did you do? Did you cross the street? Did you wrestle inside yourself with how to confront their energy? Did you turn back and walk the other way? Did you push forward, but with your heart nervously beating faster than it had before?

Remember your own adolescence. Men, think about the adolescent boy you were and others you knew; women, think about the adolescent boys you knew. When did you worry about an adolescent boy? When he drank, when he did drugs, when he got into the wrong crowd, when he drove a car? If you encounter, in your memories and observations, groups of adolescent males, you'll see that there is an "edge" to them.

In Chapter Three, we discussed the constant journey happening inside boys, through which they need to transform boyhood into an adult purpose. We looked at how they try to become seekers who can discover maps for the very human and uniquely male search for maturation. Boys like Bret Stephenson and your son, too, know there is great potential for risk taking inside them. They sense that this risk taking is good for them and the world, but they also sense that it needs direction and guidance—it needs passage from "boy energy" to "manhood." Adolescent boys are trying to make this passage every day as they try to direct their risk taking on their own. They know unconsciously that becoming a man is very risky, so they take their chances with their masks, their actions, their posturing, their dreaming.

Often they will succeed, but often they wind up hurting themselves or others. And not every boy takes on risks the same way. Some boys go inward and isolate themselves from their parents, directing their risks into computers, video games, even porn. Some go outward, forming violent gangs in which to meet the challenge of simply staying alive. Whether isolated or becoming physically dangerous, even the most hardened young man began his adolescence as a young boy who yearned, because of his own internal nature, for his family, community, and society to provide him with safe risks, important challenges, and deeply felt rites of passage to purposeful manhood.

UNDERSTANDING PURPOSE

Young Males Have a Natural Need for Rites of Passage

We mentioned earlier that during puberty (and beyond) boys get between five and seven spikes of testosterone per day through their bloodstream and brain. The testes release the chemical at the insistence of the brain's hypothalamus gland. The brain asks for the release of chemicals to augment male growth hormones. In other words, the testosterone is needed for growth of the boy, so it would be detrimental to try to stop the testosterone.

What the brain does not do is direct this aggression and risk-taking hormone toward health, purpose, and character. It just releases the chemical, creating a risk-taking, searching young man. Family and society need to provide direction, maps, and goals for the chemical's expression. Family and society can create milestones of growth and challenge by which the seeker will understand how to use his energy toward purposeful manhood.

And hormones are not the only biological reason an adolescent boy needs and wants purposeful rites of passage.

- In your adolescent son, the emotional centers (limbic system) of the brain are in hyperdrive, so the boy is likely to feel gut reactions—bursts of anger, fear, and elation—every day. He yearns for people and activities to help him direct these instinctive reactions toward civilized and successful behavior patterns.

- The frontal cortex (the CEO of the brain mentioned in previous chapters), is one of the last parts of the brain to mature and is more asleep than awake during various times of adolescent development—it is especially more asleep than the brain's limbic centers and hormones. The executive decision-making part of the brain needs to be awakened through challenging processes of growth. Without rites of passage, it may awaken toward survival, and it may even become quite competent at certain skills, such as stealing one item from every store, but it may not fully awaken to a life purpose.

- Dopamine is a powerful neurotransmitter, or brain chemical, involved in producing a positive mood or feelings of pleasure. Dopamine rises when males take risks, thus males keep trying to take more risks. Dopamine also rises when males do the kinds of established rite-of-passage activities that we'll explore in this chapter. These rites of passage direct and challenge this chemical to become active in positive rather than negative ways.

- Serotonin, the neurotransmitter that induces relaxation, regulates mood, and helps human beings deliver good social skills and moral behavior, is often higher among girls than boys. Boys sometimes become desperate for activities and coming-of-age experiences that instill greater amounts of this chemical, especially as a compensator to testosterone and dopamine.

Very recently, scientists have discovered that children with ADD/ADHD, most of whom are male, can be up to three years behind in development of the brain areas that handle attention and concentration in both the limbic system and frontal cortex. Watching one of these boys, you can see an almost extreme version of male psychobiology, as well as its drive for rites of passage to achieve clear and successful manhood. Hyperactive boys can often feel "outside" of mainstream activities—these boys are described as "hard to handle," "undirected," "unfocused." Rite-of-passage programs are just one of the social activities that can help direct and focus these boys who, like every boy in his own way, are asking all of us to please help them carry their powerful boy energy through a well-crafted adolescence and into a purposeful adulthood.

Developing Your Own Rite-of-Passage Programs

Before considering a rite of passage you can adapt and use right now in your family and community, let's review current other rites of passage that exist around you already (through your son's everyday growth events), and specific pieces of rite of passage that boys need in order to feel they have moved from boyhood to manhood with a sense of purpose.

Rite-of-Passage Possibilities We Have Right Now

Like Bret Stephenson's mastery of theft, boys already have ways of passage in our culture. In your own community, you should be able to find some or all of the following rites of passage. Looking at them briefly can be the best starting place for making your own judgments about how much more rite of passage your son may need between the age of ten (when prepuberty starts) and the age of twenty or so (when he is becoming independent of you).

1. Athletics and sports (coaches can lead boys through some passages)
2. School (schools and colleges can help with rites of passage if they understand boys and young men)
3. Religious ceremonies (such as bar mitzvah in Judaism, confirmation in Catholicism, two-year mission in the Mormon faith)
4. Extracurricular activities (such as debate team, chess team, chemistry club, Boy Scouts, a rock band, city orchestra, any

structured process in which tasks are laid out for the gradual
development of a young man's gifts and character)

5. Crisis intervention (drug and alcohol rehab, juvenile justice system, Big Brothers programs for boys raised by single moms . . .
   all of these can inculcate rites of passage)

6. Paid work, possibly at a parent's workplace, or volunteer work,
   in which boys learn as early as possible what is expected of
   them if they are to "earn it" in life can be a rite of passage

7. Random risk taking among boys, like Bret Stephenson's stealing, is unstructured by society, and often rebellious toward it,
   but provides rites of passage

8. The military, later in adolescence

And of course, along with these formal rites, sexual courting and
early sexual experiences can be a rite of passage, as can be a simple
thing like driving for the first time. Nearly any risky act can become a
developmental rite of passage for the boy.

All of these possibilities are available, all of them can help a boy
direct his energy, and all can help each of us feel that our sons are learning to direct their risk taking toward the greater good. But are these
options enough? Generally, they can use augmentation in order to
make sure a boy gets the full developmental completion of passage into
manhood. Often, none of the above are a complete substitute for one
or more rite-of-passage activities.

As you appraise the rite-of-passage activities around you right
now, look at this checklist of specifics. It includes fundamental elements of successful rites of passage from around the world. Check
off in the margin which ones you feel are being successfully applied
in the rite-of-passage experiences your son is naturally and socially
involved in right now; and see where there are gaps in his developmental opportunities.

In rites of passage throughout the world:

1. A boy is provided with (and chooses) a number of successful
   and powerful mentors. Early on, some of these may be women;
   as adolescence continues, most of these will be men. These men
   become partly responsible for his character development (thus,

his understanding of HEROIC manhood: honor, enterprise, responsibility, originality, intimacy, creativity).

2.   The boy is provided with (and chooses) ongoing challenges; through these, he meets obstacles, gains tools for embracing failure, becomes involved in opportunities to succeed. Throughout this adventure, there is always built-in time for solitude and reflection.

3.   The boy is placed in emotion-laden situations, over a period of years, wherein he feels life's fears, pain, grief, empathy, love, valor, courage, honor, sacrifice, and peace. He is guided through life experience, everyday actions, and self-questioning processes, to know the wide range of feeling inside the human soul, and especially, the man.

4.   The boy discovers a set of individuals with whom he can ask any question, feel any fear, find any support he needs—this structured rite-of-passage community feels emotionally and spiritually safe to him because it goes through challenges together with him.

5.   Important family, community, religious, and other traditions are passed down from the elder generations to the boy. He spends time learning what these traditions are, deciding which ones to take on for himself, and then making moral and social promises to his family and community.

6.   The boy is given or decides on a new name—either literally, such as "Dad (or Mom), stop calling me Mikey, I'm Mike now," or in his role association, such as "I'm a letterman now," or "I'm a Marine," or in his internal sense that "I am now a man, not a boy, so don't call me 'boy' anymore."

7.   The boy earns emblems, badges, or other physical expressions of his successes, and may keep a record in a scrapbook or develop a "box" of souvenirs. In Boy Scouts, the emblems are literally badges; in a bar mitzvah ceremony, the "badge" could be a "tallith" (a prayer shawl); in a summer workplace, they could be raises in pay. These will be important enough that twenty years down the road, the man will take the "badges,"

literally or figuratively, out of a box, and look at them and remember what his hopes and dreams had been when he was a boy.

8. In a community ceremony, the boy is judged and encouraged by his parents and mentors, who speak directly to him about what they hope his purpose in life will bring to community and the world.

9. The young man speaks aloud, in a prepared speech at a ceremony, or at a number of times during his adolescence in social groups, about his heroes, what he will do with his life, what sacrifices he wants to make, what he is seeking, what he wants to improve upon in himself, the man he wants to become.

10. When the rite of passage is done, it is done. The boy leaves the mentors and marks the end of his adolescence and the beginning of manhood by often moving out of his parents' house or earning, completely, his own living. A rite of passage is not complete until the boy becomes a man, but once he does, he moves on. A boy who stays in a rite of passage for too long remains always a boy.

As you ponder these ten elements, look at your son carefully and talk to others about your son. If your son is old enough, talk to him yourself about these elements. Ultimately, you are looking to see whether your son is getting what he needs right now from the structures in which the three-family system currently has him enrolled.

If he is ten or eleven, he might just be enrolling in some of these structures. He might just be bonding with a coach, teacher, or other mentor.

If he is twelve or thirteen, he will probably be hungry for formalized rites of passage. If you have Jewish friends, go to a bar or bat mitzvah. You can model a rite of passage after that if you wish. You can also find reference to similar rites of passage in this book's Resources and Appendix.

If your son is in his middle teens, he needs to be involved in one or more powerful rites of passage. This is a pivotal time, and one quite suitable for the "Here I Am" rite of passage that we'll discuss in a moment.

If your son is in his late teens or early twenties (or grown), see what you think of his life—is he becoming the man you know he can be? At this age, you can talk to him about nearly anything, even though he will not always listen to you. And, especially, if he is not flourishing as a man, mentors will be crucial to his rite of passage.

Questions of Purpose
Son, Who Are You?

Here is a group of questions that helps you determine just how much your son needs a rite-of-passage structure—and if he already is in one, whether he is developing well within it. If your son can't answer any of these questions with texture, substance, humor, or a modicum of self-understanding (this is true even if he is only ten years old), you might want to put more energy into helping develop a rite of passage for him.

- Son, who are you? (When asking this question, you will probably need to model an appropriate answer, something like, "I am Michael Gurian, a writer and teacher, a husband and father, son of Jack and Julia Gurian . . .")
- What makes you different from your friends? In what ways are you the same as your friends? (If you are asking this of a younger boy, you may need to model an answer.)
- What do you learn from your friends about being a man? (This is a good time to explore with your son what masculine and male models he is learning.)
- Where do you think you fit in best? In school? In athletics? In band? Reading a book? (You may need to fill in the question with these sorts of individualized prompts because this is a "niche" question—gaining answers to it can help you

determine what area of life already motivates your son, and might be the right place to look for or create new rites of passage, and find new mentors.)

- Where are you going in your life? (This is a question about what his future might look like, and what kind of future he is seeking. Watch for pride and self-esteem in your son's eyes as he answers, but also for anxiety and sadness—your son may have no sense of where he's going, and this might be a call to action for you, a reason to create a new rite-of-passage structure for him.)
- Son, what gives you the most joy in life?

The "Here I Am" Rite-of-Passage Program

Depending on the age of your son right now, you might want to check out three developmental rites of passage referred to in the Notes and Resources. One is for ten-year-old boys and their families, another for twelve- to thirteen-year-olds, another for eighteen-year-olds. Also, in Appendix, you will learn about other rite-of-passage programs.

The Here I Am model in this chapter is for the age group right in the middle of those, fourteen to fifteen, though you can modify it for use with boys anywhere during adolescence, between ten and twenty. The Here I Am model helps a young seeker find maps for his search, celebrates where he is right now in his maturation, and emphasizes the strengths and goals that will be the foundation of his adult life of purpose as a man.

I had important help developing this model. Social worker Adie Goldberg and I worked together to create this program for Temple Beth Shalom, where she was religious education director. The program was actually given its name by Rabbi Jacob Izakson, who got the idea for the name from the section of the Torah (Jewish bible) in which Abraham calls out, "Here I am" (Hineni) when God calls out to him. Abraham is not only calling attention to himself, but also to his readiness for whatever lies ahead.

Since the program's inception at Temple Beth Shalom, the Gurian Institute team has been working to expand the Here I Am model for use in any community structure, no matter the religion, and even outside a religious context. It is the adapted version I provide here for your use in any family and institutional system. You should find this version of the model specific enough and yet universal enough that you can alter it to fit your life and environment.

As I present the specifics of the model, I'll speak directly to each participant in the program, beginning with parents.

Rationale for the Program: A Brief for Parents

Your son is now fourteen to fifteen years old, a boy in middle adolescence, with four psychosocial themes essential to him: Identity, Autonomy, Morality, and Intimacy.

- He wonders who he is and will become (including wondering what parts of you, his parents, he has absorbed).
- He wonders when he can get free of the strictures of his upbringing (but he's not ready yet to be fully independent).
- He wonders if he is doing the right thing (or wrong thing), and explores, deep within himself, feelings of moral joy and shame.
- He wonders what love really is, and whether he will ever fully experience it.
- Your son is no longer a boy, but he still falls back into boyhood easily, as if gravity still holds him; your son is not yet a man, but he leaps upward into manhood in sudden bursts that he hopes he'll soon learn how to sustain. Your son, we assume, is seeking a heroic path (as we defined these elements in Part One). He needs a rite of passage to make this path very clear.
- By now he knows what honor is, even when he doesn't quite live up to it all the time.
- He has discovered some talents he's comfortable in, and is ideally developing a sense of enterprise around them, doing his athletics or academics diligently, succeeding in band or a club or debate, working on his interests and hobbies.

- He knows what responsibility is (even when he does not live up to what he knows), and does his chores (mostly!) and understands why he is disciplined when he does not fulfill a responsibility.
- He has a budding sense of himself not only as a searcher after social status and respect, self-confidence and moments of joy, but also how he is an original being, a young man who can start thinking about his own uniqueness in the team of men.
- He has experienced new and confusing feelings around intimacy, not just with girls, but also with changing roles and emotions regarding parents, siblings, and other friends. He has reached a point in life when he needs elders to set aside specific time to hear some of his joys and confusions.
- He has a sense of himself as a creative person who, no matter what happens in his life, can persevere toward the good and the exciting, the fresh and the new; but in this, as in every other aspect of his sense of his own seeking and his own heroic potential, he needs specific time and energy from elders that is devoted completely to focusing on solidifying his feelings into a core of manhood.

The Talmud says of this time in a boy's life, "He doesn't have to know the whole truth yet, but he should know the people of truth, and learn from them." You and the three mentors you will pick for this program are your son's "people of truth." This Here I Am program involves a year of mentoring and challenge which your family team facilitates with your son, culminating in a rite-of-passage weekend you cosponsor with and for your son. Through this sometimes serious and sometimes just plain fun rite of passage in this crucial middle adolescent year, you and your community help your son bring greater depth to his search for truth, and greater maturity to his sense of purpose.

Your Responsibilities as Parents

Your first job as you begin this Here I Am program is to help your son reach out to three men (one of whom can be a "peer mentor," college age or late teenager). These men will become your son's mentors for the year, representatives of a three-family system in which he can be safe.

STEP 1. Sit with your son one evening at the dinner table and make a list of about five to ten men he might enjoy working with over a one-year period. In making this list, think aloud with your son about:

- What man or men in the immediate family would be good mentors? Perhaps dad's brother, mom's father, or a male cousin who is just home from college and working in town . . . any man in the family might be a good mentor. You and your son will feel instinctively whom he might like to get to know better and get help from in this pivotal adolescent year.

- What are his favorite activities right now? Make sure at least one of the men is involved in a similar activity, so he could relate to your son via that activity. For instance, if your son loves debating, think about a lawyer you and your son get along with (or just want to get to know better). If your son loves a certain sport, think about a man who might also love that sport. Middle adolescent boys tend to relate to men more through doing activities together than through a lot of sitting and talking. Activities and interests of mutual value are often essential.

- What kind of man does your son need right now in his life? Let's say your son is pretty rebellious right now—he may need a male mentor who holds his authority well, is not a pushover, and will challenge him in ways mom or dad can't right now. As you look at possible men to mentor your son this year, think about what parts of HEROIC he may need extra help with. Look for at least one mentor of the three who could directly serve one or more of your son's areas of need.

Once you have made a list, talked as a family, and decided on these mentors, have your son write all five to ten names in order of preference, with the three preferred mentors at the top. If one or more of the three mentors are not available, you can go to the fourth, the fifth, and so on.

STEP 2. Now, reach out to the mentors. In some cases, your son will want to do it himself. In others, you might do the reaching out. Of course, the two of you might do this together. If you need help reaching out, go to religious communities, schools, athletics programs . . . indeed, any available resource. Don't give up! Sometimes single moms especially will say, "There aren't any men around to help my son!" It can feel this way, and it can be true, for sure; at the same time, you may have to alter a life choice in order to be creative. Perhaps, for instance, you have turned away from a religious or social community—maybe now is the time to reengage in that community for the sake of your son.

One single mother told me, "I really liked the idea of three mentors, but I didn't think I could find three men who would fit. It took me six months! We ended up with granddad, a teacher, and my older son. Just trying to find and then get the mentors all in one place (granddad had to fly in from Phoenix to Seattle five times a year) brought my son and me closer together. It was a big part of the whole exercise for us."

STEP 3. Once you have gotten commitment from the three mentors, keep communication lines open, set a meeting time for parents, mentors, and son to get together, and create a loose plan for:

1. How often the three mentors will each meet with your son
    during the year. Each mentor will probably meet separately
    with your son, but some activities can be done with parents,
    mentors, and boy together. Each mentor needs to commit to
    meet with the son at least five times in a year.
2. Logistics of how and when meetings and activities will occur,
    expectations of mentors and sons, expectations of parents.
    Review any details you think you'll need to look at now, and
    be open to phone calls and emails during the year as logistics
    change. (You'll get more logistical help with some of this later
    in this chapter.)
3. Psychosocial boundaries. Let your son put down some
    boundaries about what he does or does not think he needs.
    His language will probably be "I want . . ." or "I don't want . . ."

Although some of his wants will change over the year (and it's not worth arguing with him now), it is important to hear what he senses that his needs are as he enters the Here I Am program.

After this meeting, your responsibilities are to be present, active, and adaptive to the flow of the rite-of-passage adventures during the next year.

You will also need to help do logistics and provide resources for the rite-of-passage weekend (discussed later in the chapter).

To help your son understand the need for this rite of passage, you might want to give him sections of this book to read. It can also be helpful to ask him what he has noticed about rites of passage in the movies he sees (such as the movies we discussed in Chapter Three that come out every year) about younger searchers and seekers. If your son is a reader, you might want to introduce him to such books as Hermann Hesse's *Siddhartha* and *Narcissus and Goldmund*, Mark Helprin's *A Soldier of the Great War*, Robert Heinlein's *Stranger in a Strange Land*, Chaim Potok's *The Chosen*, or any other books that involve adolescent boys and young men growing up through challenges, mentoring, and discovering maps for the male search.

As you explore this rite of passage with your son, it can also be helpful to show him the next section, in which I address him directly. Of course, you will become me in this piece of the process, altering my words to fit your dynamic with your son.

Your Son's Responsibilities

Son, as a boy who is becoming a man, you are responsible for helping us choose who your three mentors will be.

You are responsible for being a part of the process. If you are just going to resist it, you may end up hating it and giving up. I hope, even if you are resistant, that you and we will keep trying this for a few months, just to see whether you finally see some worth in it.

You are responsible for treating your parents and mentors with respect.

You are responsible for growing up as much as you can in a year, under the guidance (and in the affection and safety) of parents and three men who care about you.

If things ever feel uncomfortable for you during the rite-of-passage adventure, make sure to talk to us or your mentors. We love you and are here for you.

The Mentors' Responsibilities

Now I will address the mentors. If you are reading this as a parent, I hope you will show this section to the men who have been chosen for the honor of mentoring your son into deeper identity and life purpose.

Mentoring of young men is a sacred trust. Mentoring is also fun, and you don't need a college degree to do it well. Mostly, you have to follow your instincts, let yourself care about a young person, and give time and attention to a growing soul in the ways you needed that time and attention when you were his age.

Although not the boy's parent or teacher, a mentor is some of both. A parent is ultimately responsible for the boy's day-to-day doings, but a mentor is not; a teacher is responsible for instructing the young man in what he needs to know about the workings of the world, but a mentor is not. However, a mentor is responsible for both guiding and teaching the young seeker. A young man may turn to you for help that his parents can't quite give him, because he is separating from them and trying to be independent. A young man may turn to you for wisdom, lessons, and skills training that only you can provide—via your professional training or your innate talents and skills.

Your job entails meeting with the boy's family, the other mentors, and your mentee. Make sure to stay in touch with everyone over the course of the year. Set up specific meeting times. Do sports or other activities with your mentee, and just go get some food and talk. Take part in communal activities with the boy and his father and mother, and other mentors, too.

Teach this young man what you can, through your own solo efforts with him, and alongside the community of men you find and form for this year. You don't need to go into this mentoring year with a huge lesson plan in mind—just be open to what you discover that your mentee needs.

As you mentor this boy, keep referring back to the list of rite-of-passage elements that I presented earlier in this chapter. See which of the following points you can and are helping with.

- Are you presenting the boy with challenges?
- Are you listening to him?
- Are you teaching him the tools of work and life that you know?
- Are you letting him feel, at times, that he's teaching you as much as you are teaching him?
- Are you helping him understand what real power is?
- Are you helping him face failure successfully?
- Are you doing fun activities with him, and working substance and conversation into them?
- Are you asking him questions about who he is?
- Are you helping him understand how a man handles emotions?
- Are you helping him, by good example, understand how to treat girls and women?

These are just a few questions you can reflect on. You have a year to try to accomplish parts of these goals. Your mentee will thank you, even if not until he is your age and remembers you fondly.

 The Wisdom of Purpose

THE POWER WHICH RESIDES IN A MAN

There is a time in every man's education when he arrives at the conviction that envy is ignorance; that imitation is suicide; that he must take himself for better or worse as his portion; that though the wide universe is full of good, no kernel of nourishing corn can come to him but through his toil bestowed on that plot of ground which is given to him to till. The power which resides in him is new in nature and none but he knows what that is which he can do, nor does he know until he has tried.

—Ralph Waldo Emerson

The Rite-of-Passage Weekend

The Here I Am program builds toward a rite-of-passage weekend that will transpire during spring or summer (assuming that you began your Here I Am year the previous spring or summer). I have personally been involved, as a mentor, in various forms of this weekend. There is no single "best" place or way to do it.

It can transpire

- At a cabin owned by your family or a mentor's family
- A retreat house owned by a faith community
- A rafting trip or other adventure weekend, organized by a vendor, and reserved just for your group
- Any place in nature where you can pitch tents and have some privacy as a group

Even if you cannot get out of the city and into a natural place, you can still modify this model to fit your surroundings. It can take place in a home or apartment, or in the backyard, as long as the group has the privacy to be fully focused on the experiences the boy needs.

Because so many of these weekend rites of passage take place outdoors (and because of the inherent advantages to boys in finding an outdoor location), I'll provide a layout for the weekend with an outdoor locale in mind.

Organizational Logistics, Writing Letters Beforehand, Bringing Photographs

Someone will need to take on the jobs of logistics and organization. If mom decides to email everyone, plan schedules, reserve rooms, make checklists for what to bring, and takes care of other preparatory details, it is crucial that the men and her son help her, and that they honor her in some clear way, perhaps with a dinner out on the weekend before. She won't be going on the retreat, but she is a crucial presence in the boy's rite of passage.

And even if mom plays no organizational part, there must still be a way of honoring her. She brought this boy into the world and has in large part raised him, and the men will want to honor her for it.

Two kinds of letters need to be written before the retreat occurs (these can be emails, poems, or even drawings with captions). These letters will not be read until during the retreat.

1.   The mentors and parents should make sure that each adult has written a letter to the boy, letting him know what is admirable about him, including anecdotal stories from the past year (or, if the relationship predates it, from anytime in the past). Even though mom isn't going on this men's retreat, it is essential that she write a letter to him. He will read it during the retreat. If a mentor or parent is having any trouble with what to write, go to page 184 and look at the list of ten elements of rites of passage. Each one provides grist for the mill. Perhaps you can write about what traditions you hope your son takes forward. You could write about his risk taking, or how he has met challenges.

2.   Your son needs to write letters (even if only short ones) to mom, dad, the mentors, and any others who are important to him, have taught him wisely, and have touched his heart. It is often important to focus him on these letters at least a month in advance of the retreat. He may need a great deal of time to write these five or more letters to his satisfaction. Just like the letters written to him, his letters will be most moving if they are focused on what he admires in his mentors and parents, on giving thanks to them for what gifts they have handed him, on telling anecdotes and stories, and even on asking tough questions, the kinds of questions to which a young man needs answers.

Each person (including mom, the son, and the mentors) ought to bring (or, in mom's case, send) photographs of the boy—from childhood, more recently during activities or sports, and during interactions with the mentors. Any photograph you feel could stimulate dialogue is probably a good photograph to bring. They may not all be used, but they can really help men and boys talk and grow together.

It is also important that each mentor and the boy bring objects they consider "sacred" or "important." Each mentor should bring one or more objects he wants to present to the boy. The boy should bring gifts for the mentors.

During the Retreat

Everyone likes to spend a weekend their own way, so this section does not need to be prescriptive about exact schedules. The men (mentors, father, and son) can get together a month or two in advance of the retreat and create a rough schedule. In this meeting, the pecking order of the retreat can be established. This is not a competition but more like voting for delegates and alternate delegates.

Men generally work best when they have leaders and are organized, so your team of men needs to make decisions about who will lead which parts of the retreat. Each man will feel good at various tasks; all the men need to agree to let the boy lead the last event of the retreat. The following is a sample scenario that has been used successfully, on which you can model your own variation of the weekend.

Friday: Arrive at location, get settled, prepare and eat a meal. Toast the occasion and remind everyone why we are here, and what the Here I Am year has been about: helping this young searcher become a man of mature and joyful purpose.

Opening Activity: Clean up after dinner then create a talking circle in a safe, comfortable place, perhaps around a small fire. Laugh, tell jokes, walk around, do whatever is needed to transition from dinner. Meanwhile, have the boy search around the grounds of the natural setting for a stick or branch which can be a "talking stick." Throughout the weekend, this object will be passed to each man when he wants to speak. This tends to curb interruptions.

Now it is time to hear from everyone at least once. Go around in a circle and talk about what the year has been like. This is a form of "checking in." What activities has each man enjoyed the most with his mentee? Don't start with the young man; end with him. Ask him what he remembers fondly from his time with each man.

Remember that my instructions are just suggestions. If this evening dialogue goes in other directions, that's great. There is no single right way to do any rite of passage activity, per se.

After the men and the mentee have shared stories, ask each man a clear Here I Am question: *What is your purpose in life?* As each man talks, challenge him as a group to stay focused on what *his* purpose is, how *he* is living out his manhood. Avoid broad political discussions. Whenever you feel the dialogue straying, come back to the deep-seated joys we all seek, questions such as:

- What am I searching for?
- What gives me the most hope?
- When did I know I was becoming a mature man?
- How am I trying to help other people?
- What helps me the most when I get tired or overworked or become angry?
- When I am on my deathbed looking back on my life, what will I remember as the most important people and moments?

Here are some actual answers that have been given on retreats to the question, "What is my purpose in life?" Following are two answers men gave who felt safety in a small group on a retreat weekend, and spoke their truth for the sake of the growth of a young man they loved:

> My purpose is many purposes of course, like being a good dad and a good husband, and a good mentor, and working hard. I'm kind of a workaholic, right? So part of my purpose is to really listen and watch when I see that Sara and the kids are lonely for me. I'm also pretty shy. I always have been. I'm forty-six but I'm still trying to become better at speaking in front of people. That's a big part of my purpose now.

> My purpose is to teach. I'm a teacher and I know the kids call me Mr. Mucho and make fun of me for how I keep trying to learn Spanish (this man, of Mexican descent on his mother's side, uses the word "mucho" in his speaking instead of "very" or "much"), but I know the kids learn from me, and I never had kids, so this is

what I'm about. Being Tim's mentor has been like helping to raise the son I never had, and I really thank you, Tim, for letting me be a part of your search and your journey.

After the men have spoken, ask the boy, "Okay, now it's your turn, so, who are you? What is your purpose in life? You can't know everything about yourself yet, but do you have some insights, some hopes?" Prompt him with as many questions of this sort as needed. His ability to respond will depend on how verbal he is, how comfortable he feels in this setting, and how much he has previously reflected on these issues with his parents or mentors.

THE JOY OF PURPOSE

Boldness Has Genius

Until one is committed, there is hesitancy, the chance to draw back, always ineffectiveness. Concerning all acts of initiative and creation there is one elementary truth: that the moment one definitely commits oneself, Providence moves too. All sorts of things occur to help one that would never otherwise have occurred. A whole stream of events issues from the decision, raising in one's favor all manner of unforeseen incidents and meetings and material assistance, which no man could have dreamed would come his way.

Whatever you can do, or dream you can do, begin it.
Boldness has genius, power and magic in it.

—Goethe

Saturday and Sunday: Depending on your location, you can best decide how and when to provide activities that fulfill the actions I will present here.

1. Set aside one or more times to read aloud the mentor letters (the mentee's letter will be read last, at the end of the retreat).

2. When the mentor letters are being read, ask the mentee what important insights he is learning from each about honor, enterprise, responsibility, originality, intimacy, and creativity. Have a discussion about each of these as necessary. Answer his questions. If he has none, ask him questions. Use photographs in this and other rituals as much as needed to stimulate dialogue and camaraderie.

3. Provide some kind of challenge on this retreat—some action! Perhaps you can do a ropes course during the retreat, or go rafting or fishing, or go on tiring hikes. Exhaust this boy with activity, then admire in the evening how well he has met challenges.

4. Give yourself and the boy time for solitude and reflection. Let the young man be bored, if needed. Don't worry if you are bored, or if there are silent moments in conversations. Send the young man off somewhere to be alone for a while.

5. Make sure that at least one talking circle is about emotions. Fifteen-year-old boys are still boys when it comes to emotionality. They need to know from you that crying is okay. They need to hear you talk about what you think are appropriate emotional boundaries. They need to hear your stories of feelings that overwhelmed you, whether with other men or with women. They need to hear stories about your adolescence.

6. Somewhere in this challenging and loving weekend, there will be moments where it is just right to ask the young man, "What are you most afraid of?" If you don't see such a moment by Sunday morning, make sure to have a talking circle that morning in which each man answers this question, after which the boy answers. During this time, have each person write on a slip of paper what he most fears. Light a fire in the fireplace or in the woods or somewhere safe and burn each piece of paper. This is an effective and memorable form of "giving away" the fear. Let this be a prayerful or peaceful time of silence and

ritual. Many boys and men have found it powerful to write down their deepest fear(s), such as "fear of inadequacy," "fear of commitment," "fear of loneliness," "fear of bullies," "fear of dying," then watch the fears turn to ash and dust.

7. Pass on important objects, traditions, and "badges" to the boy. If the young man's father is on the retreat, he will need to make sure to create an activity in which he passes on important family objects to his son. This should be handled similarly with a grandfather or other family member. If the retreat is done in a religious context, perhaps a family Bible will now get passed on. If the retreat is not religious, the sacred objects and traditions will be heirlooms, perhaps. Make sure the young man makes a "public" (surrounded by these men) moral and social promise to honor the family or spiritual tradition. Make sure the young man understands the story behind the object you are gifting to him, so he will honor that object with his life energy later on.

8. Somewhere during the time of the retreat, set aside a talking circle for the boy to be given or to decide on a new "name." I've seen this done many ways, everything from animal associations (Hawk, Eagle), as native Americans do, or religious traditions (a Hebrew or Christian name that is now better understood as purposeful) or a mentee deciding he likes his middle name better, or even a humorous interchange in which the mentee defers to the men, with each man "bestowing" a funny but touching name on the young man. Even if the young man does not leave the retreat with a guiding new name, he will have experienced the ancient process of "renaming" and he will remember it, perhaps not getting actually renamed until he goes to college and joins a fraternity, or goes into the military, or takes on a job and is called "manager," or gets married and has children and is renamed "husband" and "father."

9. As much as possible, let the young man lead the final activity. This is the time for him to read his letters to mentors and family members aloud. Perhaps he has been changing the letters a bit here and there as the days in the company of these

men have progressed. After he finishes each letter, thank him, admire him, and, if needed, ask questions of him. Try to sense what sacrifices he wants to make in order to become a good man, what parts of himself he wants to improve, who he wants to become. Support his insights and his awkward attempts at humor and wisdom.

10. As the final ritual ends, pass the talking stick around and "check in" again, as you did on the first evening. This time, verbalize final thoughts, and pass on final gifts to the young man. A year of mentoring has passed; so has a weekend of closeness and vitality. What needs to be said before this moment in the young man's life is gone? Say it, and let the young man say what is left for him to say. When all this is done, it is fair to suggest to this men's circle, "One at a time, let's call out one word that captures how each of us feels right now." Generally, words like "excited," "moved," "happy," "ready for anything" are verbalized.

As this weekend rite-of-passage ceremony ends, you will have completed an important part of a young man's life journey. He will see better than before how to exist with emotional depth in the big world. Whatever inner fire is in him will be all the more passionate now. His questions will not all be answered, but he will now have seen new ways to ask his life questions. The bonding and camaraderie of the male-on-male time will open the young man up to an internal dialogue of male purpose in empowering ways as he moves through middle adolescence. This experience will continue to guide him as he ratchets up his search for truth and purpose on his own, very soon, as his own man.

In twenty years of leading rite-of-passage weekends of this kind, I have rarely if ever heard significant negative comments from any boy, man, or mother to whom the boy returned. Mothers themselves, who often do a lot of logistical work (both to help find mentors and to help set up the weekend), do so in a kind of leap of faith that the Here I Am male-oriented program will help their son. I've found that they end up being glad the boy became a young man during the last year.

This son mom sent away often comes back to her more respectful of her gifts (and her flaws), better at being her son but also his own man, better at doing his chores, more invested in homework, less distractible, more motivated to be a good man. He is still a boy in many ways, but he is also something of a man in ways that can fill her with the kind of pride and love that only a mother can feel for the man she has so graciously and hopefully raised.

The Power of Purposeful Men

When Bret Stephenson directed himself to go out and steal and then return one item from every store, he was a boy asking the world to direct him. "I'm a boy ready to risk it all," his psyche was saying. "What do you want to do with me, world? I challenge you to be as smart as me. I challenge you to take me on. Will you meet the challenge?"

Will we meet the challenge our boys put to us? A rite-of-passage year and ceremony do a great deal to meet the challenge. In order to put our love and power fully behind this kind of program, we have to believe in the inherent and beautiful power of purposeful men. Women have to believe in it, and men have to believe in it. Single mothers have to push hard to find communities and programs in which men are available to their sons. Men have to sign up to do the mentoring that boys in these programs need. Fathers need to become active in adolescent boys' lives, providing not only fathering, but access to mentors. And every man, whether he has children or not, must listen to the song of his own male soul. It is whispering, "Boys need men to lead them through rites of passage." It is singing, "Here I am I am on a journey, constantly searching for help. Right now, I am searching for you. Will you help me?"

EPILOGUE: COMING TOGETHER TO ADVOCATE FOR BOYS

The future belongs to those who believe in the beauty of their dreams.

—ELEANOR ROOSEVELT

DO YOU REMEMBER THE MOMENT when you first held your son in your arms? There was so much joy, so much anticipation, so much to do. This young life needed you in ways you had not been needed before. Feelings, deep and immeasurable, touched you and those around you, and resources appeared that perhaps you didn't know you or others possessed. If you had not been a dreamer before, you were a dreamer now. If you had not felt you were living an exciting adventure before, you sensed it coming now.

And as your son grows, how are your dreams doing? What are your son's dreams now? Is he on an adventure? The complex and real world is measuring him every day. Does he feel, among all his activites, wonderful moments of pride in how he measures up? Does he see yet what you know: how each of us becomes a little smaller than we thought we were, chiseled down by the beautiful and difficult jobs of life?

Nothing chisels us down to our own essence like raising a child. Raising a child can refine us and smooth out our surfaces until we feel our own core selves in touch with whatever is our small but significant place in the world.

I hope this book has helped you raise your son joyfully. I hope it has given you a deeper understanding of your son and of the full, loving family he needs. I hope you have found in it a map that can help your son past obstacles. You can probably tell from my words that I believe every boy is a hero, every boy deserves love and success, and every boy needs to be understood by his culture, better than this culture understands boys today. You can probably also tell that I, as a father of daughters, do not see advocacy for boys as harmful to girls. I think girls need us to care for boys as much as for girls. Boys are the men of my daughters' futures.

As you return to the complexities of your life with your son, I hope you'll look into your community and do some rabble-rousing on behalf of boys. I hope you'll convince your community that every boy deserves to become a man who can make a meaningful contribution to this world—nothing will ultimately feel more heroic to our sons than to look back, when they are old, like Grandpa Dean, or Private Ryan, or another elderly man you may know who can say, "I have done it, I have been a good man."

As you work to give every boy the chance to live this good life, this life of dreams and maps and journeys and truth, I hope you'll advocate for a world where your son can both obviously succeed and successfully fail, so that he can learn to pick himself up again. I hope you'll teach him to be both tough and tender. I hope you'll help him understand that a man not only bests his opponents, but just as often wanders into a garden inside his own heart, where there are no opponents at all.

And if ever you feel alone in caring or advocating for your son, go onto the Internet and check out resources and organizations that are emerging every day, many of which you'll find in the Notes and Resources section. Each is, in its way, developing ever-widening circles of a three-family system for boys. Each is becoming a community of assistance, and all care deeply about helping boys find meaning and purpose. I have interacted with most of them, and even though there are political and personal differences between some, all agree that it is time for a "boys' movement" in our culture, a grassroots movement that is propelled mainly by individuals like you, who love our boys, and who will tend their fire without cultural or personal fear of that fire.

The time has come to reinvent boyhood in our culture, and to celebrate manhood as a servant of the greater good of our new millennium. I hope you will look into boys' eyes from now on and see in them the best part of yourself, a spirit that is ready, eager, and loving. Most of all, I hope your own courage to change the world will be inspired by the boys themselves who call out to us, even in their silences, "Please help me know who to be, please point the way, please make sure this world celebrates the purpose of boys."

NOTES AND RESOURCES

INTRODUCTION: WHAT DO YOU WANT TO BE, SON?

WHAT IS THE PURPOSE OF BOYS?

Warren, Rick. *The Purpose Driven Life*. New York: Zondervan, 2007.
Tolle, Eckhart. *A New Earth: Awakening to Your Life's Purpose*. New York: Penguin, 2008.
Keleman, Lawrence. *To Kindle a Soul*. Southfield, Mich.: Targum Press, 2001.
Damon, William. *The Path to Purpose*. New York: Free Press, 2008.
The Core Model (Compassion, Honor, Responsibility, Enterprise), and the Ten Integrities Teaching Tool can be found in *A Fine Young Man* (1998).
I first introduced the Three Families Paradigm in *The Wonder of Boys* (1996).
My colleagues and I first introduced the Boys and Girls Learn Differently curriculum in the book of the same title (2001). The Gurian Institute team, under the direction of Kathy Stevens, constantly expands and adapt these programs.
For ongoing data, see www.gurianinstitute.com (Success).

PART ONE
THE PURPOSE OF BOYS

I THE LOSS OF PURPOSE IN AMERICAN BOYHOOD

WHY PARENTS WANT TO PROVIDE PURPOSE FOR BOYS

Dr. Tom Mortenson's statistical research and analysis are carried on an ongoing basis on the www.boysproject.net Web site. Dr. Judith Kleinfeld is the director of the Boys Project. Both Tom and Judy can be contacted through the Web site, and Tom can also be contacted through www.postsecondary.org.
Please see also Tom's "The State of American Manhood" report, which you can access through www.postsecondary.org. It was published in the *Postsecondary Education Opportunity Journal*, in Sept. 2006.

Conlin, Marie. "The New Gender Gap." *Business Week Online*, May 26, 2003, available from www.businessweek.com. Jacqueline King is quoted in Richard Whitmire's editorial in *USA Today*, Dec. 27, 2005. Vickers, Melana Zyla. "Where the Boys Aren't." *The Weekly Standard*, Jan. 2, 2006, 16.

Hunt, Kasie. "Record Seven Million in Criminal Justice System." *Associated Press*. Nov. 30, 2006.

Noguera, Pedro A. "The Trouble with Black Boys: The Role and Influence of Environmental Factors on the Academic Performance of African American Males: Part 3." In *Motion Magazine*, May 13, 2002.

Teacher and public school administrator Cynthia Martone has written an important book in this area—*Loving Through Bars: Children with Parents in Prison* (Santa Monica Press, 2005). There are 2.3 million children with a parent in prison.

Media statistics from the Media and Policy Institute appear in interviews on *Journeyman*. See www.mirrormanfilms.com.

"Why Are We Drugging Our Children?" *Education Week*, Sept. 27, 2006.

Tanner, Lindsey. "Study Links Third of ADHD to Smoking, Lead." *Associated Press*. Sept. 19, 2006.

Organization for Economic Cooperation and Development. The PISA Assessment Framework. (2003). This study provides data on the situation boys face in all the industrialized countries. For more specific data on England, see www.statistics .gov.uk; Australia, see *Boys in Schools*, edited by Rollo Browne and Richard Fletcher (Lane Cove, Australia: Finch Publishing, 1995) and Steve Biddulph's *Raising Boys: Why Boys Are Different—And How to Help Them Become Happy and Well-Balanced Men* (Berkeley: Celestial Arts, 1996); Canada, www.statcan.ca. Bruce Ivany, assistant superintendent of Abbotsford, B.C. (Canada) school district, provided reporters with this summary of the issues his district faces: "Provincial test results and statistics over the past few years suggest girls do significantly better than boys in school, and are more likely to graduate." CBC news further reports, "In Quebec, three out of five boys still do not have a high school diploma" (CBC's The Current, Jan. 26, 2003). See also the School Achievement Indicator Program. Canada, 2002; the Commonwealth of Australia House of Representatives. *Boys: Getting It Right*. 2002; Mike Baker, BBS Education Correspondent. Feb. 28, 2004. See http://news .bbc.co.uk.

Further regarding the loss of purpose of our sons in the educational system, it is useful to note that when the new U.S. Department of Education's Study on Gender Gaps in Educational Achievement came out in Nov. 2004, U.S. Secretary of Education Rod Paige wrote, "It is clear that girls are taking education very seriously and that they have made tremendous strides. The issue now is that boys seem to be falling behind." Indeed, the National Assessment of Educational Progress showed boys behind in most categories.

According to researcher Judith Kleinfeld, "From grade school through college, females receive higher grades and obtain higher class ranks. They also receive more honors in every field except science and sports."

When specific schools, school districts, and states are looked at statistically, the gender gap in grades and ability testing clarifies even more specifically. The following are some examples from specific regions:

In literacy scores, the Michigan Gender Equity Team reports that in statewide 2001 testing (MEAP), girls got 67 percent of the highest scores (Level 1) while boys got 67 percent of the lowest scores (Level 4).

USA Today reported on Dec. 22, 2003, about a Greensboro, North Carolina, school (High Point Central High School) in which "412 boys got unsatisfactory grades, compared to 303 girls."

Anderson, Curt. "Homeless Beatings Seen as Trend." *Associated Press,* Jan. 20, 2006.

Regarding college statistics see: O'Brien, C. Pell Institute for Study of Opportunities in Higher Education, at www.pellinstitute.org.

Center for Labor Market Studies. *The Growing Gender Gap in College Enrollment and Degree Attainment in the U.S. and Their Potential Economic and Social Consequences.* May 2003. Boston: Northeastern University.

Gayle, M., and Osborn, H. "Commentary: Let's Get Rid of Learning Factories; In the Age of High Tech, a New Model Must Be Found for Schools." *Los Angeles Times,* May 27, 2004.

MOVING FORWARD WITH NEW VISION

Sommers, Christina Hoff. *The War Against Boys.* New York: Simon & Schuster, 2000.

Lewin, Tamar. "How Boys Lost Out to Girl Power." *New York Times,* Dec. 12, 1998.

2   HOW LITTLE BOYS DEVELOP THEIR SENSE OF PURPOSE

Harmon, Kitty. (Ed.) *Up to No Good.* San Francisco: Chronicle Books, 2000.

THE EMPATHY OF BOYS

Thompson, Michael, and Barker, Teresa. *It's a Boy!* New York: Ballantine, 2008.

BRAIN DIFFERENCES BETWEEN BOYS AND GIRLS

Applying brain differences to the understanding of the lives of boys and girls is something we do carefully. The basics of gender biology don't change over the decades, but not every study agrees completely with every other. It is important to go into this field, especially the applications process with which this book is mainly concerned, in a state of openness to change and adaptation.

If you are a fellow professional or a concerned parent who wonders, "Should we trust brain sciences? Aren't brain facts changing every day? Can we really say we know enough about the male and female brain?" And further: "What if a professional, like yourself, or a parent, gets a brain fact wrong—will that then lead to significant trouble for a boy (or girl)?" I ask you not to worry, so long as you are being careful.

The new gender sciences are trustworthy. Simultaneously, we do not need perfection of research or application to do good for children. Every parent and every professional "gets something wrong" many times in a life, but we still do best when we make sure to utilize the new sciences of human nature to their fullest potential, for the good of our children and their families.

Most of the sex and gender differences noted in this chapter are corroborated in this recent and very detailed study: Halpern, D. F., Benbow, C. P., Geary, D. C., Gur, R. C.,

Shibley Hyde, J., and Gernsbacher, M. A. "The Science of Sex Differences in Science and Mathematics." *Psychological Science in the Public Interest,* Aug. 2007, 8 (1). This study comprises this whole special edition issue of *Psychological Science.*

Rhoads, Steven E. *Taking Sex Differences Seriously.* San Francisco: Encounter Books, 2004.

Carmichael, Mary. "The New War on Pain." *Newsweek,* June 4, 2007. Cover story regarding nerve fibers and much more.

Cordero, Maria Elena, Valenzuela, Carlos, Torres, Rafael, and Rodriguez, Angel. "Sexual Dimorphism in Number and Proportion of Neurons in the Human Median Raphe Nucleus." *Developmental Brain Research,* 2000, *124,* 43–52.

Onion, Amanda. "Sex in the Brain: Research Showing Men and Women Differ in More Than One Area." ABC News, Sept. 21, 2004.

Amen, Daniel. Personal interview with Michael Gurian, July 2004.

Carter, Rita. *Mapping the Mind.* Berkeley: University of California Press, 1998.

Blum, Deborah. *Sex on the Brain.* New York: Viking, 1997.

Baron-Cohen, Simon. *The Essential Difference.* New York: Basic Books, 2003.

Diamond, Marian. "Male and Female Brains." Lecture for Women's Forum West Annual Meeting, San Francisco, CA, 2003.

Caviness, V. S., and Kennedy, D. N., et al. "The Human Brain Age 7–11 Years: A Volumetric Analysis Based on Magnetic Resonance Differences." *Cerebral Cortex,* 1996, *6,* 726–736.

Moir, Anne, and Jessel, David. *Brain Sex.* New York: Dell, 1989.

Marano, Hara Estroff. "The Opposite Sex: The New Sex Scorecard." *Psychology Today,* July-Aug. 2003, pp. 38–44.

Gur, Ruben. *CNN Saturday Morning News-Weekend House Call,* Dec. 6, 2003. (Transcripts available: www.fdch.com.)

Dewing, Phoebe, Shi, Tao, Horvath, Steve, and Vilain, Eric. "Sexually Dimorphic Gene Expression in Mouse Brain Precedes Gonadal Differentiation." *Molecular Brain Research,* Oct. 21, 2003, *118*(1–2), 82–90.

Biochemical and neurochemical research appears in the following books. Each one is a wonderful read, and will deepen any parent's understanding of both the neurochemistry of boys and girls (as well as women and men!).

Amen, Daniel. *Sex on the Brain.* New York: Harmony, 2007.

Brizendine, Louann. *The Female Brain.* New York: Broadway Books, 2006.

Taylor, Shelley. *The Tending Instinct.* New York: Times Books, 2002.

See also:

Roberts, B. W., Kuncel, N. R., Shiner, R., Caspi, A., and Goldberg, L. "The Power of Personality: The Comparative Validity of Personality Traits, Socioeconomic Status, and Cognitive Ability for Predicting Important Life Outcomes." *Perspectives on Psychological Science,* Dec. 2007, 2(4).

Achiron, Reuwen, Lipitz, Shlomo, and Achiron, Anat. "Sex-Related Differences in the Development of the Human Fetal Corpus Callosum: In Utero Ultrasonographic Study." *Prenatal Diagnosis,* 2001, pp. 116–120.

Iacono, Robert P. *The Nervous System: The Blood-Brain Barrier.* Available from www.pallidotomy.com/index.html.

VanScoy, Holly. "Hot Headed Guys? It's All in the Brain." *HealthScoutNews,* Oct. 11, 2002.

3   **HOW ADOLESCENT BOYS SEEK THEIR PURPOSE IN LIFE**

How Adolescent Boys and Girls Seek and Develop Purpose Differently

Dr. Varmuza made the statement on TVO's *Big Ideas* in Dec. 2007. See also the very powerful book by paleontologist Frans De Waals called *Our Inner Ape* (Berkley Books, 2005), as well as Dr. De Waals's 1984 article, "Sex-Differences in the Formation of Coalitions Among Chimpanzees." *Ethology & Sociobiology*, 1984, 5, 239-255.

I am including here a number of primary research studies that confirm the brain differences in other chapters, and also provide a powerful foundation for the thesis that boys and girls develop their sense of life's purpose, motivation, self, and character differently. There is hardly a time when this is more true than adolescence.

The following studies come not only from the United States but from all over the world, increasing the power of the idea behind this book, that primal differences between males and females are not just cultural (though include culture) but are, at the biological level, worldwide phenomena.

1. Spatial-Mechanical and Verbal-Emotive Processing Differences

Eals, M., and Silverman, I. "The Hunter-Gatherer Theory of Spatial Sex Differences: Proximate Factors Mediating the Female Advantage in Recall of Object Arrays." *Ethology and Sociobiology*, 1994, 15, 95-105.

Frederikse, M., Lu, A., Aylward, E., Barta, P., and Pearlson, G. "Sex Differences in the Inferior Parietal Lobule." *Cerebral Cortex*, 1999, 9, 896-901.

Gryn, G., Wunderlich, A., Spitzer, M., Reinhard, T., and Riepe, M. "Brain Activation During Human Navigation: Gender-Different Neural Networks as Substrate of Performance." *Nature Neuroscience*, Apr. 2000, 3(4), 404-408.

Gur, Ruben, et al. "An fMRI Study of Sex Differences in Regional Activation to a Verbal and Spatial Task." *Brain and Language Journal*, 2000, p. 74.

Sandstrom, N., Kaufman, J., and Huettel, S. A. "Males and Females Use Different Distal Cues in a Virtual Environment Navigation Task." *Brain Research: Cognitive Brain Research*, 1998, 6, 351-360.

Saucier, Deborah, et al. "Are Sex Differences in Navigation Caused by Sexually Dimorphic Strategies or by Differences in the Ability to Use the Strategies?" *Behavioral Neuroscience*, 2002, 116, 403-410.

Silverman, I., and Eals, M. "Sex Differences in Spatial Abilities: Evolutionary Theory and Data." In J. Barkow, L. Cosmides, and J. Tooby (Eds.), *The Adapted Mind: Evolutionary Psychology and the Generation of Culture* (487-503). New York: Oxford University Press, 1992.

2. Gray and White Matter Processing Differences

Cordero, M. E., Valenzuela, C., Torres, R., and Rodriguez, A. "Sexual Dimorphism in Number and Proportion of Neurons in the Human Median Raphe Nucleus." *Developmental Brain Research*, 2000, 124, 43-52.

Diamond, Marion. "Male and Female Brains." Lecture for Women's Forum West Annual Meeting, San Francisco, Calif., 2003.

Gur, Ruben, et al. "Sex Differences in Brain Gray and White Matter in Healthy Young Adults." *Journal of Neuroscience,* 1999, *19.*

Gur, Ruben, et al. "Sex Differences Found in Proportions of Gray and White Matter in the Brain: Links to Differences in Cognitive Performance Seen." Study, University of Pennsylvania Medical Center, May 18, 1999. Available from www.sciencedaily.com/releases/1999/05/990518072823.htm.

3. Differing Structures in the Brain

De Lacoste, M., Holloway, R., and Woodward, D. "Sex Differences in the Fetal Human Corpus Callosum." *Human Neurobiology,* 1986, *5*(2), 93–96.

Hamann, S., et al. "Men and Women Differ in Amygdala Response to Visual Sexual Stimuli." *Nature Neuroscience,* 2004, *4.*

Joseph, R. *Neuropsychiatry, Neuropsychology, and Clinical Neuroscience.* (3rd ed.) New York: Academic Press, 2000.

Killgore, W. D., Oki, M., and Yurgelun-Todd, D. A. "Sex-Specific Developmental Changes in Amygdala Responses to Affective Faces." *NeuroReport,* 2001, *12,* 427–433.

Killgore, W. D., and Yurgelun-Todd, D. A. "Sex-Related Developmental Differences in the Lateralized Activation of the Prefrontalcortex and Amygdala During Perception of Facial Effect." *Perceptual and Motor Skills Journal,* 2004, p. 99.

Kilpatrick, L. A., Zald, D. H., Pardo, J. V., and Cahill, L. F. "Sex-Related Differences in Amygdala Functional Connectivity During Resting Conditions." *NeuroImage,* Apr. 1, 2006, *30*(2), 452–461. Available from http://today.uci.edu/news/release_detail.asp?key=1458.

4. Brain Chemistry, Neurochemicals, and Hormones

Albers, H. E., Huhman, K. L., and Meisel, R. L. "Hormonal Basis of Social Conflict and Communication." In D. W. Pfaff, A. P. Arnold, A. M. Etgen, S. E. Fahrbach, and R. T. Rubin (Eds.), *Hormones, Brain, and Behavior,* Vol. 1 (393–433). New York: Academic Press, 2002.

Christiansen, K. "Behavioral Effects of Androgen in Men and Women," *Journal of Endocrinology,* 2001, *1,* 170.

Compaan, J. C., et al. "Vasopressin and the Individual Differentiation in Aggression in Male House Mice." *Annals of the New York Academy of Sciences,* June 1992, *652,* 458.

Liu, L. "Keep Testosterone in Balance: The Positive and Negative Effects of the Male Hormone." *WebMD,* Jan. 2005.

5. Different Reactions to Stress

Carletti, R., Benelli, A. and Bertolini, A. "Oxytocin Involvement in Male and Female Sexual Behavior." *Annals of the New York Academy of Sciences,* 1992, *652*(1), 180–193.

Shors, Tracey J. "Stress and Sex Effects on Associative Learning: For Better or for Worse." *The Neuroscientist,* 2001, *4,* 353–364.

Shors, T. J., and Miesegaes, G. "Testosterone in Utero and at Birth Dictates How Stressful Experience Will Affect Learning in Adulthood." *Proceedings of the National Academy of Sciences,* Oct. 15, 2002, *99,* 13955–13960.

Weiss, L. A., Abney, M., Cook, E. H., and Ober, C. "Sex-Specific Genetic Architecture of Whole Blood Serotonin Levels." *The American Journal of Human Genetics,* 2005, *76,* 33–41.

Wood, G., and Shors, T. J. "Stress Facilitates Classical Conditioning in Males, But Impairs Classical Conditioning in Females Through Activational Effects of Ovarian Hormones." *Proceedings of the National Academy of Sciences,* 1998, *95,* 4066–4071.

Gibbs, Nancy. "A Nobel Warrior." *Time,* Oct. 22, 2007, p. 90.

Dobnik, Verena. "Two Teens Arrested in Violent School Plot." *Associated Press,* July 14, 2007.

Geary, David, et. al. "An Evolutionary Analysis." *Developmental Review,* 2004.

For the elephants research, see "Elephants." *60 Minutes.* This episode can be acquired via contacting CBS television at www.cbsnews.com or by going directly to www.gurianinstitute.com.

What Motivates Different Boys

Peter Eriksson's work appears in "When Does Your Brain Stop Making New Neurons?" *Newsweek,* July 2, 2007, p. 64.

Studies regarding male-female brain difference in memory are quite fascinating. See:

Casiere, D. A., and Ashton, N. L. "Eyewitness Accuracy and Gender." *Perceptual and Motor Skills,* 1996, *83,* 914–914.

Davis, P. J. "Gender Differences in Autobiographical Memory for Childhood Emotional Experiences." *Journal of Personality and Social Psychology,* 1999, *76,* 498–510.

Doherty, R. W. "The Emotional Contagion Scale: A Measure of Individual Differences." *Journal of Nonverbal Behavior,* 1997, *21,* 131–154.

Horgan, T. G., et al. "Gender Differences in Memory for the Appearance of Others." *Personality and Social Psychology Bulletin,* 2004, *30*(2), 185–196.

Herlitz, A., Nilsson, L. G., and Backman, L. "Gender Differences in Episodic Memory." *Memory and Cognition,* 1997, *25,* 801–811.

Herrmann, D. J., Crawford, M., and Holdsworth, M. "Gender Linked Differences in Everyday Memory Performance." *British Journal of Psychology,* 1992, *83,* 221–231.

Schlaepfer, T. E., Harris, G. J., Tien, A. Y., Peng, L., Seog, L., and Pearlson, G. D. "Structural Differences in the Cerebral Cortex of Healthy Female and Male Subjects: A Magnetic Resonance Imaging Study." *Psychiatry Research: Neuroimaging,* Sept. 29, 1995, *61*(3), 129–135.

Shors, Tracey J. "Significant Life Events and the Shape of Memories to Come: A Hypothesis." *Neurobiology of Learning And Memory,* 2006, *85,* 103–115. Available at www.rci.rutgers.edu/~shors/pdf/Significant%20life%20events%202006%20Shors%20article.pdf.

4   SON, YOU ARE MY HERO

The Heroic Son

Campbell, Joseph. *Hero with a Thousand Faces.* New York: New World Library, 1972.

The Story of Joseph

I have used two translations of the Joseph story: the King James Bible, which was not translated directly from the Hebrew-Aramaic, and the Etz Hayim Torah (Five Books of Moses), which is a direct translation. For general development of the heroic journey of Joseph, the two versions are actually similar. There are subtleties on which they disagree, but the seven stages appear in both.

The Story Ends, for Now

If you have time, look at the rest of the Joseph story in whatever Bible is close to you, and notice how he continues his heroic journey, well into manhood (and even as he nears his death). He continues to grow and mature (and even make mistakes), as we all do!

PART TWO

HELPING OUR SONS FIND THEIR PURPOSE IN LIFE

5   CREATING FAMILIES OF PURPOSE FOR BOYS

Creating a Three-Family System: The Parent-Led Team

The child psychiatrist Arthur Kornhaber has written, "In the child's mind, each unit (in the family) has its own place, is unique in its functions, possesses its own privileges and responsibilities, and occupies its own dimensions of time (age)." In his very powerful book, *The Grandparent Solution,* Kornhaber provides parents and grandparents with practical ways to connect with one another and their children so that the developing physical, social, emotional, spiritual, and practical intelligence of the child is best protected and best nurtured.

Kornhaber is one of many child development experts today whose life work in studying children has led to the conclusion that children grow with natural needs for not only soil but also sun and rain, not only these emotional and social nutrients, but also pruners and shapers. In this bio-anthropological view, your son is so internally wired for complex development that you alone are not enough. Knowing this as a parent is not knowing a defect—it is a liberation. It leads to a restudying of parenthood, and for many parents, a sense of relief.

The Development of a Boy's Sense of Destiny in the Family System

Some, Malidoma. *Of Water and the Spirit: Ritual, Magic and Initiation in the Life of an African Shaman.* New York: Arkana, 1994, p. 1.

The Ten Values Tool

In order to learn more about how to discover your son's inborn assets, you might enjoy the book *Nurture the Nature: Understanding and Supporting Your Child's Core Nature.* It gives you tools for understanding your son's "hardwired" personality and talent set, from birth through early adulthood.

See also:

Kluger, Jeffrey. "The Secrets of Birth Order." *Time,* Oct. 29, 2007.
Wallis, Claudia. "Is This Disorder for Real?" *Time,* Dec. 10, 2007.
Burt, S. Alexandra. "Genes and Popularity." *Psychological Science,* 2008, *19*(2).
Weiss, Alexander, Bates, Timothy C., and Luciano, Michelle. "Happiness Is a Personality Thing." *Psychological Science,* 2008, *19*(3).
Alonso-Zaldivar. "ADHD Drugs Risky, FDA Panel Says." *Los Angeles Times,* Feb. 10, 2006.

THE VALUE OF TEACHING SEXUAL PURPOSE

To learn more about the effects of oxytocin and other brain chemicals, see these very good books:

Amen, Daniel. *Sex on the Brain.* New York: Harmony, 2007.

Brizendine, Louann. *The Female Brain.* New York: Broadway Books, 2006.

Fisher, Helen. *The Anatomy of Love.* New York: Ballantine, 1994.

Taylor, Shelley. *The Tending Instinct.* New York: Times Books, 2002.

See also Arletti, R., Benelli, A., and Bertolini, A. "Oxytocin Involvement in Male and Female Sexual Behavior." *Annals of the New York Academy of Sciences,* 1992, 652 (1), 180–193.

Seth Borenstein, the AP science writer, has written a fascinating article called "Sex and Financial Risk Linked in the Brain." *Associated Press,* Apr. 7, 2008.

HELPING OUR SONS FIND PURPOSEFUL WORK

Conversation with Dan Labell, Mar. 2008.

Further information about the Washington State student-trades program can be found in the *Seattle Times,* Apr. 3, 2008, and also by visiting www.washington.gov.

HELPING BOYS FIND PURPOSE IN THEIR MEDIA USE

Personal correspondence with David Bartholomew, May 2005.

Brock, Barbara. *Living Outside the Box.* Cheney: Eastern Washington University Press, 2007.

Nyhan, Paul. "40 Percent of Babies Watch TV, UW Study Finds." *Seattle Post-Intelligencer,* May 8, 2007.

Gensheimer, Jolene. "How Technology Has Changed Childhood." *ParentMap Magazine,* May 2005.

Gleiter, Sue. "Electronic Devices Disrupt Children's Sleep Patterns." *Newhouse News Service,* Feb. 11, 2008.

Ghassemi, Jeffrey. "Brain Drain." *Washington Post,* Sept. 18, 2006.

Johnson, Carla K. "School-Night TV Slows Learning, Study Finds." *Associated Press,* Oct. 2, 2006.

Kuchment, Anna, and Gillham, Christina. "Kids: To TV or Not TV." *Newsweek,* Feb. 18, 2008.

Opdyke, Jeff. "Does a Ten Year Old Need a Cell Phone?" *Wall Street Journal,* Dec. 3, 2006.

See also www.parentschoice.org and www.commonsensemedia.org.

Boodman, Sandra G. "Young Who See More Television Less Attentive." *Spokesman-Review,* Sept. 24, 2007.

"Teen TV Buffs Prone to Learning Problems." *HealthyDay News,* posted May 7, 2007.

Gwinn, Eric. "Narcissism on the Internet Comes with Its Share of Risks." *Chicago Tribune,* Mar. 20, 2007.

See also:

Got Game by Adam Carstens of the North Star Leadership group (www.nslg.net), which argues that children who grow up with video games are different from those who don't.

Green, C. S., and Bavelier, D. "Action-Video-Game Experience Alters the Spatial Resolution of Vision." *Psychological Science,* Jan. 2007, p. 88.

Springen, Karen. "This Is Your Brain on Alien Killer Pimps of Nazi Doom." *Newsweek,* Dec. 11, 2006, p. 48.

Shrieves, Linda. "AMA Doctors to Assess Video Game Addiction." *Orlando Sentinel,* June 22, 2007.

Carnagey, Nicholas, Anderson, Craig, and Bartholow, Bruce. "Media Violence and Social Neuroscience." *Current Directions in Psychological Science,* 2007, *16*(14), 178.

6   CREATING COMMUNITIES OF PURPOSE FOR BOYS

Kluger, Jeffrey. "What Makes Us Moral." *Time,* Dec. 3, 2007, p. 54.

Agee, James. *A Death in the Family.* New York: Vintage, 2007. (Originally published 1957.)

THE LOSS OF COMMUNITIES OF PURPOSE FOR BOYS

Crary, David. "One in 99 Adults in Jail." *Associated Press,* Feb. 29, 2008.

Becker, Paula. "Parenting Solo." *ParentMap Magazine,* Mar. 2006, p. 47. Also visit www.parentmap.com/singleparenting.

Stephanie Coontz is quoted in "Your Child Was Out of Line," by Kathleen Deveny. *Newsweek,* Oct. 22, 2007, p. 65.

"Teen Boys' Anger Tied to Brain Development." *Reuters,* Feb. 25, 2008.

FORMING PURPOSEFUL COMMUNITIES FOR AFRICAN AMERICAN BOYS

The National Urban League Report, "State of Black America," was released on Apr. 17, 2007, by NUL president, Marc. H. Morial.

Educator and columnist Archie Wortham's statistics appeared in his "Men 2 Fathers" column, on Jan. 17, 2008. He can be reached at archie@flash.net.

Day-Vines, Norma L. "The Escalating Incidence of Suicide Among African Americans." *Journal of Counseling and Development,* Summer 2007, p. 370.

Robert Mincy is quoted in Eckholm, Eric. "Plight Deepens for Black Men, Studies Warn." *New York Times,* Mar. 20, 2006.

Matus, Ron. "Black Male Teachers Needed." *St. Petersburg Times,* June 3, 2005.

Baldwin, James. *The Fire Next Time.* New York: Delta/Dell, 1964.

My thanks to Robert Haley and Norman Johnson of 100 Black Men of Atlanta for helping me and other Gurian Institute staff to better understand the needs and solutions regarding black boys. Thanks also to Ron Walker and the many other mentors, advocates, and community members that 100 Black Men of America enlists on behalf of our children.

Briggs, Jonathon. "School Gives Boys the Key to Becoming Real Men." *Chicago Tribune,* May 27, 2007.

Gewertz, Catherine. "Black Boys' Educational Plight Spurs Single-Gender Schools." *Education Week,* June 20, 2007.

Gurian, Michael, Stevens, Kathy, and Daniels, Peggy. *Successful Single-Sex Classrooms: A Practical Guide to Teaching Boys and Girls Separately.* San Francisco: Jossey-Bass, 2009.

Spielhagen, Frances. *Debating Single-Sex Education.* Lanham, Md.: Rowman & Littlefield, 2007.

The School Administrator Journal of Jan. 2005 includes a number of very powerful and practical articles under its cover story, "Saving Black Boys."

The story of Sylvester Croom appears in Chris Talbott's "In the Shadow of 'Bama, the Bear," *Associated Press,* Dec. 24, 2007.

The magazine *Black Family Today* is a wonderful resource for parents raising and educating black children.
See also:
Baggerly, Jennifer, and Parker, Max. "Child-Centered Group Play Therapy with African American Boys at the Elementary Level." *Journal of Counseling & Development,* Fall 2005, p. 387.
Texeira, Erin. "CSI Actor Offers Guidance to Black Youngsters in New Book." *Associated Press,* May 14, 2006.

CHANGING HELPING PROFESSIONS TO FOCUS ON BOYS' NEEDS

Kindlon, Dan, and Thompson, Michael. *Raising Cain.* New York: Ballantine, 2000.
Pollack, William. *Real Boys.* New York: Henry Holt, 1998.

ENJOYING COMMUNITIES OF PURPOSE WITH BOYS

Gary Plep's work can be found on www.mensgroups.com or at camensctr@aol.com.

7 CHANGING SCHOOLS TOWARD RELEVANCE AND PURPOSE FOR BOYS

HOW BOYS ARE STRUGGLING FOR PURPOSE IN SCHOOL

See Tom Mortenson's statistics on www.boysproject.net.
Gurian, Michael, and Stevens, Kathy. *The Minds of Boys.* San Francisco: Jossey-Bass, 2005.
For a large archive of articles on this issue, see www.gurianinstitute.com's Articles page. We update that page with new articles on a monthly basis.
Male-female brain differences discussed in this chapter are cited above in Notes for previous chapters.
Full reference for the PISA study appears in the endnotes for Chapter One.
Conversation with Judith Kleinfeld, 2007.
See also Barthlow, Michelle. "Reversal of the Gender Gap in Science." Etowah High School, Science Department. Georgia. Michelle.barthlow@cherokee.k12.ga.us.

FIXING THE MISMATCH BETWEEN SCHOOLS AND THE PURPOSE OF BOYS

To contact Lisa Gordon, write ltgordon1@verizon.net.
Gamerman, Ellen. "What Makes Finnish Kids So Smart?" *Wall Street Journal,* Feb. 29, 2008, p. W1.
My thanks to Kathy Stevens, Kelley King, and our Gurian Institute Certified Trainers for helping me develop practical strategies.
In *The Minds of Boys* and on www.gurianinstitute.com, we feature schools that have had positive results.
For issues regarding holding boys back, see www.kidsource.com/kidsource/content5/kindergarten.entrance.html and www.isteve.com/2002_Redshirting-A_Kindergarten_Arms_Race.htm
In *Strategies for Teaching Boys and Girls: Elementary Level and Secondary Level,* coauthored with Kathy Stevens and Kelley King, you'll find hundreds of in-class strategies and innovations.
Many thanks to Susan Horn for sharing her suggestions with me via email and with the Boys Project via the listserv at www.boysproject.net.

The *New York Times* (Dec. 26, 2007) reference to comic books reads, "Educators are increasingly looking toward comic books to encourage children's literacy and English-language skills. Teachers are looking for ways to engage their children, and they're finding some of that in comic books," said Michael Bitz, who founded the Columbia University Teachers College Comic Book Project, which in six years has expanded to 860 U.S. schools. "For kids who may be struggling and for kids who may be new to the English language, *that visual sequence is a very powerful tool.*" Quoted from ASCD SmartBrief, Dec. 16, 2007.

If you are a teacher or parent who wants to increase your use of books and movies that teach honor and character to boys, you might enjoy *What Stories Does My Son Need?*, which I co-wrote with young adult author Terry Trueman (New York: Tarcher, 2001). It includes one hundred books and movies that build character in boys.

8 CREATING AND PROVIDING RITES OF PASSAGE FOR YOUR SON

Stephenson, Bret. *From Boys to Men*. Rochester, Vt.: Park Street Press, 2004.

Brain facts presented in this chapter have been noted in chapters above and appear in the Notes for those chapters.

See also the interesting online article "ADHD Kids' Brains Mature More Slowly," available at www.msnbc.msn.com/id/21757514/.

A wonderful video, recently released by Mirror Man films, out of Minneapolis, Minnesota, is *Journeyman*. You can learn more on www.mirrormanfilms.org.

Rite-of-passage and mentoring programs have been emerging all over the country (and indeed the world) for over a decade. Some include:

Stan Crow's longtime program, www.icajourneys.org.

The Boys to Men Network, www.boystomen.org.

The National Mentoring Partnership, www.mentoring.org.

The Minnesota Mentoring Partnership, www.mentoringworks.org.

The MATT-COA program, at the Washington Ethical Society. If you go onto the Internet and search for Washington Ethical Society, you will find a number of useful references.

Young Men's Ultimate Weekend, in partnership with the Headwaters Outdoor School, www.ymuw.org.

The Colorado program called Training Ground, www.trainingground.com.

The international organization, Global Passageways, at www.globalpassageways.com.

The Odyssey Program in Australia, created by educator Jane Higgins (authenticity.counselling@hotmail.com).

To reach the Boys and Girls Clubs of America, see www.bgca.org.

To reach the Boy Scouts, see www.scouting.org.

To reach Big Brothers and Big Sisters of America, see www.bbbs.org.

DEVELOPING YOUR OWN RITE-OF-PASSAGE PROGRAMS

Depending on the age of your son right now, you might want to check out three developmental models I presented in *A Fine Young Man*. They appear in Part Two of that book. One is for ten-year-old boys and their families, another for twelve- to thirteen-year-olds, another for eighteen-year-olds. The "Here I Am" model in this chapter is for the age group right in the middle of those, fourteen to fifteen, though it can be modified by you for use with boys anywhere during adolescence (between ten and twenty or so).

To learn more about your roles during boys' rites of passage, whether as parents or mentors, you might enjoy reading *A Fine Young Man* or viewing the *Journeyman* documentary.

BIBLIOGRAPHY

Amen, Daniel. (1999). *Change Your Brain, Change Your Life*. New York: Random House.

Amen, Daniel. (2001). *Healing ADD*. New York: Putnam.

Amen, Daniel. (2005). *Sex on the Brain*. New York: Bantam.

Arnot, Robert. (2001). *The Biology of Success*. Boston: Little Brown.

Baron-Cohen, Simon. (2003). *The Essential Difference: The Truth About the Male and Female Brain*. New York: Basic Books.

Bear, Mark, Barry Connors, and Michael Paradiso. (1996). *Neuroscience: Exploring the Brain*. Baltimore: Williams and Wilkins.

Bernstein, Neil. (2008). *There When He Needs You*. New York: Free Press.

Bernstein, Neil. (2001). *How to Keep Your Teenager Out of Trouble, and What to Do If You Can't*. New York: Workman.

Blum, Deborah. (1998). *Sex on the Brain: The Biological Differences Between Men and Women*. New York: Penguin Books.

Borba, Michelle. (2002). *Building Moral Intelligence*. San Francisco: Jossey-Bass.

Borba, Michelle. (2003). *No More Misbehavin'*. San Francisco: Jossey-Bass.

Brooks, Cleanth, R.W.B. Lewis, and Robert Penn Warren. (1973). *American Literature*. New York: St. Martins Press.

Browne, Rollo, and Fletcher, Richard. (1995). *Boys in Schools*. Sydney: Finch.

Carr-Morse, Robin, and Meredith S. Wiley. (1998). *Ghosts from the Nursery: Tracing the Roots of Violence*. New York: Atlantic Monthly Press.

Carter, Rita. (1998). *Mapping the Mind*. Berkeley: University of California Press.

Damon, William. (2008). *The Path to Purpose*. New York: Free Press.

De Waal, Frans. (2005). *Our Inner Ape*. New York: Riverhead Books.

Dobson, James. (2001). *Bringing Up Boys*. Wheaton, Ill.: Tyndale House.

Evans, Robert. (1996). *The Human Side of School Change: Reform, Resistance, and the Real-Life Problems of Innovation*. San Francisco: Jossey-Bass.

Farrell, Warren. (1993). *The Myth of Male Power*. New York: Simon & Schuster.

Flinders, Carol. (2002). *The Values of Belonging*. San Francisco: HarperOne.

Fogarty, Robin. (1997). *Brain Compatible Classrooms*. Arlington Heights, Ill.: Skylight Professional Development.

Garbarino, James. (1999). *Lost Boys*. New York: Free Press.

Gilmore, David. (1990). *Manhood in the Making*. New Haven, Conn.: Yale University Press.

Goleman, Daniel. (1995). *Emotional Intelligence*. New York: Bantam.

Gurian, Jay P., and Julia Gurian. (1983). *The Dependency Tendency: Returning to Each Other in Modern America*. Lanham, Md.: Rowman and Littlefield.

Gurian, Michael. (1997). *The Wonder of Boys: What Parents, Mentors and Educators Can Do to Shape Boys into Exceptional Men*. New York: Tarcher-Putnam.

Gurian, Michael. (1998). *A Fine Young Man*. New York: Tarcher-Putnam.

Gurian, Michael. (2002). *The Wonder of Girls: Understanding the Hidden Nature of Our Daughters*. New York: Pocket Books.

Gurian, Michael, with Patricia Henley and Terry Trueman. (2001). *Boys and Girls Learn Differently! A Guide for Teachers and Parents*. San Francisco: Jossey-Bass.

Gurian, Michael, with Kathy Stevens. (2005). *The Minds of Boys*. San Francisco: Jossey-Bass.

Hallowell, Edward, and John Ratey. (1994). *Driven to Distraction*. New York: Touchstone.

Haltzman, Scott. (2005). *Secrets of Happily Married Men*. San Francisco: Jossey-Bass.

Harris, Judith R. (1998). *The Nurture Assumption*. New York: Free Press.

Iggulden, Conn, and Hal Iggulden. (2007). *The Dangerous Book for Boys*. New York: HarperCollins.

Jensen, Eric. (2000). *Brain-Based Learning*. San Diego, Calif.: Brain Store.

Jessel, David, and Anne Moir. (1989). *Brain Sex: The Real Difference Between Men & Women*. New York: Dell.

Johnson, Steven. (2004). *Mind Wide Open*. New York: Scribner.

Kandel, Eric, James Schwartz, and Thomas Jessell. (1995). *Essentials of Neural Science and Behavior*. Norwalk, Conn.: Appleton & Lange.

Karges-Bone, Linda. (1998). *More Than Pink & Blue: How Gender Can Shape Your Curriculum*. Carthage, Ill.: Teaching and Learning Company.

Kelemen, Lawrence. (2001). *To Kindle a Soul*. Southfield, Mich.: Targum Press.

Kipnis, Aaron. (1999). *Angry Young Men: How Parents, Teachers and Counselors Can Help "Bad Boys" Become Good Men*. San Francisco: Jossey-Bass.

Kindlon, Dan, and Michael Thompson. (2000). *Raising Cain: Protecting the Emotional Life of Boys*. New York: Ballantine.

Koplewicz, Harold. (2002). *More Than Moody*. New York: Perigee.

Kornhaber, Arthur. (2004). *The Grandparent Solution*. San Francisco: Jossey-Bass.

Ladner, Joyce. (2003). *Launching Our Black Children for Success*. San Francisco: Jossey-Bass.

Levine, Mel. (2002). *A Mind at a Time*. New York: Simon & Schuster.

Levkoff, Logan. (2008). *Third Base Ain't What It Used to Be*. New York: New American Library.

Moir, Anne, and Bill Moir. (1999). *Why Men Don't Iron*. New York: Citadel.

Moir, Anne, and David Jessel. (1990). *Brain Sex*. New York: Laurel.

Moore, Robert, and Douglas Gillette. (1990). *King, Warrior, Magician, Lover*. New York: HarperCollins.

Murphy, Shane. (1999). *The Cheers and the Tears: A Healthy Alternative to the Dark Side of Youth Sports Today*. San Francisco: Jossey-Bass.

Newell, Waller R. (2000). *What Is a Man?* New York: Regan Books.

Nylund, David. (2000). *Treating Huckleberry Finn: A New Narrative Approach to Working with Kids Diagnosed ADD/ADHD*. San Francisco: Jossey-Bass.

Payne, Ruby. (2000). *A Framework for Understanding Poverty*. Highlands, Tex.: aha! Process.

Pease, Barbara, and Allan Pease. (1999). *Why Men Don't Listen, and Women Can't Read Maps*. New York: Broadway Books.

Pollack, William. (1998). *Real Boys: Rescuing Our Sons from the Myth of Boyhood*. New York: Henry Holt.

Ravitch, Diane. (2003). *The Language Police: How Pressure Groups Restrict What Children Learn*. New York: Knopf.

Renzulli, Joseph, and Sally Reis. (2008). *Light Up Your Child's Mind*. New York: Little Brown.

Rhoads, Steven E. (2004). *Taking Sex Differences Seriously*. San Francisco: Encounter Books.

Riera, Michael, and Joseph Di Prisco. (2002). *Right from Wrong*. Cambridge, Mass.: Perseus.

Salomone, Rosemary C. (2003). *Same, Different, Equal: Rethinking Single-Sex Schooling*. New Haven, Conn.: Yale University Press.

Siegel, Daniel J. (1999). *The Developing Mind*. New York: Guilford Press.

Slocumb, Paul. (2004). *Boys in Crisis*. Highlands, Tex.: aha! Process.

Smith, Michael W., and Jeffrey D. Wilhelm. (2002). *"Reading Don't Fix No Chevy's": Literacy in the Lives of Young Men*. Portsmouth, N.H.: Heinenmann.

Some, Malidoma. (1994). *Of Water and the Spirit: Ritual, Magic and Initiation in the Life of an African Shaman*. New York: Arkana/Penguin.

Sommers, Christina Hoff. (2000). *The War Against Boys: How Misguided Feminism Is Harming Our Young Men*. New York: Touchstone.

Sousa, David A. (2001). *How the Brain Learns*. (2nd ed.) Thousand Oaks, Calif.: Corwin Press.

Sprenger, Marilee. (2002). *Becoming a "Wiz" at Brain-Based Teaching: How to Make Every Year Your Best Year*. Thousand Oaks, Calif.: Corwin Press.

Stein, David B. (1999). *Ritalin Is Not the Answer: A Drug-Free, Practical Program for Children Diagnosed with ADD or ADHD*. San Francisco: Jossey-Bass.

Stephenson, Bret. (2004). *Slaying the Dragon*. Available from www.adolescentmind.com.

Sykes, Bryan. (2003). *Adam's Curse*. New York: Norton.

Taylor, Shelley E. (2002). *The Tending Instinct*. New York: Times Books.

Thompson, Michael, and Teresa Barker. (2008). *It's a Boy!* New York: Ballantine.

Wiesel, Elie. (1972). *Souls on Fire*. New York: Touchstone.

Wolfe, Patricia. (2001). *Brain Matters: Translating Research into Classroom Practice*. Alexandria, Va.: Association for Supervision and Curriculum Development.

Woody, Jane DiVita. (2002). *How Can We Talk About That? Overcoming Personal Hang-Ups So We Can Teach Kids About Sex and Morality*. San Francisco: Jossey-Bass.

Young-Eisendrath, Polly. (2008). *The Self-Esteem Trap*. New York: Little Brown.

APPENDIX: RITE-OF-PASSAGE PROGRAMS

Over the last twenty years, there has been a growing emphasis at a grassroots level on developing visionary and effective rite-of-passage programs for both boys and girls. Here are five programs that approach rites of passage in their own individual ways. It is my hope that by sharing some of these contacts with you here, I'll encourage you to join in this grassroots movement, as well as potentially utilize a program in your son's purpose development. I am including reports from these leaders in their own words.

There are many more programs active in North America today (some of which appear in the Notes and Resources). You can also Google "rites of passage for boys," or other key words in that vein, and learn of still others. The few I feature here are by no means an exhaustive list. Each program, however, potentially provides what the writer Van Gennes thought of as the three pillars of a rite of passage: "a time of separation from the world, activities that lead to penetration of the self to some deep source of power, and then a life-enhancing return to the world."

> I'm the director of Rites of Passage, a non-profit that offers programs for both youth and adults to mark life passages, including the transition from childhood to adulthood. Our website is www.ritesofpassagevisionquest.org. One of our main programs is the Vision Quest, which we offer as a 9-day event with three days of solo time and careful attention to preparation and to the incorporation process of returning home. We can work with

community organizations, churches, and schools to present the Vision Quest program for boys (and girls). It's appropriate for young people over the age of 16.

We also offer a weekend program, which can be presented separately for boys and girls, called Earth Walk. This program, in the form of a day alone in nature or a 24-hour solo, works as a rite of passage ceremony for younger teens. It can be undertaken within a local community at a park or nature preserve.

—Mike Bodkin, Northern California
mikeb@ritesofpassagevisionquest.org

Cornerstones Community Foundation's programs work with the distinction between purpose based in personal survival and purpose which is inherent in each of us. In the Cornerstones work we call that Soul Calling. In our work with participants, both in the programs and in the community, is the notion that as we, step by step, more fully trust and surrender to our soul calling (our purpose), we will be able to create acts of service that are more aligned with our fundamental or intrinsic values.

What this means is that we prepare people, through trainings and support groups, to find their unique expression of service while staying oriented on their internal call. Expressions of someone's soul calling might be men's or women's work, work with youth and rites of passage, vision quest offerings, work with inner city schools with teen leadership, etc. Currently we are active in all the aforementioned areas to varying degrees. The foundation supports individuals and groups with infrastructure, guidance and resources along with other organizations that appear to be founded in the same principles as CCF such as the Young Men's Ultimate Weekend which we promote.

—David Rubine, Northern California
david@thecornerstonespath.com

We provide summer camps, Rite of Passage journeys, and Family Retreats. Please read a recent article about our work:

• www.idahostatesman.com/life/story/427365.html

We host a family Retreat and Ropes course, Boys Raft-Ropes
Course Overnighter, a Camp and BOYS in the FIRE journey.
In September, 2008, we start our BOYS Adventure and Mentoring
groups . . . Coyote Boys, Boys in the Fire and WILD Boys.

—Forrest Melton, of YES! Youth Empowerment Services
and ALIVE Adventures
www.aliveadventures.co

Cascade Leadership Challenge is a nonprofit in Kent, WA working
to address issues of racism and teen alienation in high schools.
We work in high schools with broad racial and ethnic diversity
where everyone is a minority. In this environment alliance and
cooperation are necessary for anything worthwhile to happen . . . a
perfect learning environment for future community leaders of every
background.

CLC teaches awareness, adaptation and self-organization
to teens. We do this through adventure travel. From igloo
building to whitewater rafting, university tours to roller coasters,
getting there and coming back alive to tell the tale engages any teen
from any culture. With technical and adaptive leadership training,
skill development and constant novelty, our teenagers get the
support and experiences they need to engage the other, the new,
the different.

Successfully coping with difference is the essential competency to
living a good life in a diverse and changing society. Travel challenges
our preconceptions and opens our eyes. We want meaningful travel to
be available to every teenager. What kids learn on the road, they bring
back home. CLC helps kids deal with diversity by connecting them to
the larger world and showing them their important place in it.

—Mark Steelquist
mark@steelquist.net

There is nothing new in the notion of the Men of the Village
taking the young men of the village, out into the wilderness in
their teenage years, some folks have called it Rites of Passage or
Initiations, Vision Quests, all to present the young man with an
opportunity to discover some of his inherent skills, talents, abilities,

potential that will serve him better in adult world. It is a time of preparation, arming him with some of the skills that will help him survive and prevail in the next 30–50 years.

On the man's side, there is no higher place for a man to stand than as provider and protector of his community, and part of that is caring for the next generation of men, who will then provide for and protect the village, the community, his family.

On the young man's side, it is an opening or a discovery of that which he has felt brewing and boiling inside himself over the last few years, and he sees a clear way to understand and use all of his bursting, explosive potential in a good way. It is no mistake that the young man sits in a volcanic cocktail of boiling emotions, testosterone, ego, drives, vision, passion/rage, all seeking an outlet or a direction that can avoid the minefields of anti-social behavior on one side and total suppression on the other.

Lately there has been a disconnect in this process. Men in our community have moved away from knowing that this is one of their fundamental roles in society, there are precious few role models and precedents for this occupation. More often the young men are the ones at a loss, falling through the cracks or distorting their energies into some less than best scenario.

At the Vancouver, BC, Canada-based Young Men's Adventure Weekend we have addressed this for almost 20 years. We take 50–100, 12–17 year old young men and 40–50 men out into the wilderness for 3 days. The men go out early on the Friday to set up camp, build the cookshack, arrange the firecircle and firepit, string tarps, dig latrines: this is wilderness camping, and yes, we leave the place better than we found it.

In the evening the young men catch a bus in the City and drive for 2–3 hours into the "Where the Hell are we going?" Wilderness. An hour down a logging road the bus is flagged down and stops, a group of gruff men, the Enforcer's Gang, orders the young men to "Grab your gear. Get off the bus, follow me, no talking." Then they hike for half an hour through the "Where the Hell are we going?" Forest.

This hike is 90% of the value of the weekend event, the young men are away from their computers and TV's and cars and concrete and they are walking through a forest, they are breathing Green Air, this alone will get them into their bodies, out of their computer brains.

Being a little scared also heightens their faculties, the fact that they are in a pack of 50–100 of them offers some reassurance.

Once they arrive in the camp, they . . . Well that would be telling too much! Let me say that in years past we have had a variety of themes:

- On the shores of Harrison Lake we (all) built a 9 foot high Inukshuk.
- Another year we explored indigenous culture and built 2 sweat lodges.
- This year we looked at "Where will you be leaving your footprint?" by looking at the balancing act/battle between two of our inner parts—the Natural Man, the Green Man, the Be All That You Can Be Man, and the man who accommodates society, the consumer man, the man-made man, the business suit man.

We do not teach them any particular opinion; instead, we create challenges or scenarios for them to discover aspects of themselves. When we hear the feedback and look at the results, they are often beyond anything that we could have imagined weaving into the program.

We run this thing on a break even basis, just to cover the costs of 700–900 meals prepared in the wilderness, buses, souvenir T-shirts, etc. All the men are volunteers and pay the same $125 that the young men pay, all the men do criminal records checks.

The young men are encouraged to earn their registration fee themselves. We say to them, "Consider it your homework, preparation for manhood, pay your way kinda thing."

—Brad Leslie, of Young Men's Adventure Weekend
www.ymaw.com

THE GURIAN INSTITUTE

If you would like to help your community better meet the educational needs of children, please contact the Gurian Institute. The Institute works with parents, schools, school districts, corporations, the legal system, medical and mental health professionals, and others who serve children. We have trainers throughout the world who can help your community.

We provide DVDs, books, parent trainings, monthly newsletters, and a parent-friendly Web site.

For schools, we provide training in (1) the purpose of boys, (2) how boys and girls learn differently, (3) raising and educating boys, and (4) raising and educating girls. The Gurian Institute staff of certified trainers is committed to not only training professionals and parents but also to making participant school districts, corporations, and agencies self-sufficient in their ability to provide ongoing training to their own staff.

Your school can also contact the Gurian Institute to find out how to become a Model School.

We also provide corporate training in gender and training for government and social service agencies. This work has inspired the book *Leadership and the Sexes*, which looks at both women and men in our workforce from the perspective of gender science.

For information on our school and community work, please visit us at www.gurianinstitute.com. For more information on our corporate work, please visit www.genderleadership.com.

THE AUTHOR

Michael Gurian is a social philosopher, family therapist, and the *New York Times* best-selling author of twenty-five books published in twenty-one languages. The Gurian Institute, which he cofounded, conducts research internationally, launches pilot programs, and trains professionals. Michael has been called "the people's philosopher" for his ability to bring together people's ordinary lives and scientific ideas.

Michael has pioneered efforts to bring neurobiology and brain research into homes, workplaces, schools, and public policy. A number of his groundbreaking books in psychology and child development, including *The Wonder of Boys, A Fine Young Man, Boys and Girls Learn Differently!, The Wonder of Girls,* and *Nurture the Nature,* have sparked national debate.

Michael has served as a consultant to families, corporations, therapists, physicians, school districts, community agencies, churches, criminal justice personnel and other professionals, traveling to approximately twenty cities a year to keynote at conferences. His book for corporate leaders, *Leadership and the Sexes,* is used in corporations around the world. His training videos for parents and volunteers are used by Big Brother and Big Sister agencies in the United States and Canada.

As an educator, Michael has spoken at Johns Hopkins University, University of Missouri-Kansas City, Gonzaga University, Eastern Washington University, Ankara University, and UCLA. His philosophy reflects the diverse cultures (European, Asian, Middle Eastern, and American) in which he has lived, worked, and studied.

Michael's work has been featured in various media, including the *New York Times*, the *Washington Post, USA Today, Newsweek, Time,* the *Wall Street Journal, Parenting, Good Housekeeping, Redbook,* and on the *Today Show, Good Morning America,* CNN, PBS, and National Public Radio.

Michael lives in Spokane, Washington, with his wife, Gail, and their daughters, Gabrielle and Davita.

Michael can be reached on the World Wide Web at www.gurianinstitute.com.

INDEX

Muslim boys, 28–29
Mythology, 67
Myths, avoiding, about school and learning, 163–164

N

Names: getting new, during rites of passage, 186, 203; value of, helping boys understand the, 100–101
Narcissus and Goldmund (Hesse), 194
National Assessment of Educational Progress (NAEP), 158
National Urban League, 141
Native American culture, 66, 67, 203
Native American males: and community purpose, 143; and schooling, 142
Natural talents, developing, 40
Nature time, 164
New Earth, A: Awakening to Your Life's Purpose (Tolle), 6
Nguzo Saba, modernization of, 149
Ninja Assassin, 36
No Man is Happy If He Does Not Work (Roosevelt), 22
"No work" trend, changing the, 116
Nonviolent options, facilitating, need for, 138
Nuclear family, the, 92, 93, 94, 95, 132

O

Obesity rates, 21
Obsession, 55, 79
Of Water and the Spirit: Ritual, Magic and Initiation in the Life of an African Shaman (Some), 96
On the Education of Boys (Sadoleto), 155
100 Black Men, 139–140, 146
Originality: meaning of, 65; sense of, gaining a, 84, 191. *See also* HEROIC model
Outdoor time, 164, 170, 197
Overweight boys, 21

P

Parental rite-of-passage responsibilities, 191–194, 198
Parenting, communal, 134–141
Parent-led team: creating a, 91–95; and teaching sexual purpose, 111–115; using

values in a, 99–108. *See also* Three-family system
ParentMap, 132
Path to Purpose, The (Damon), 6
Peers, and the progress of intimacy, 75
Pell Institute, 16, 156
Peripatetic counseling, 153
Pharaoh, 73, 79, 82–83
Photographs, using, for rite-of-passage retreats, 198, 202
Physical movement, during learning, 164, 165–167, 174
PISA study, 157–158, 162
Play time, 128
Plep, G., 153–154
Pollack, W., 151–152
Post-secondary education: and black males, 142; gender differences in, 16, 17, 20, 157
Post-traumatic stress, 68
Potiphar, 71, 73, 74
Potok, C., 194
Power development: in the adolescent seeker, 55; and rites of passage, 196, 205; stage involving, 77–80
Price, C., 59–60
Price, R., 59–60
Prisoner regrets, 131–132
Project-driven curricula, use if, 175
Promoting the Self-Esteem of Boys of Color (Gordon), 164
Psychosocial drivers, described, 29–30. *See also* Adolescent seeker; Heroic adult; Magical boy
Puberty, impact of, 44–45, 60, 182. *See also* Adolescence
Punishment, issue of, 106
Purpose: in an African-based value system, 149; asking the question of, and seeking to address, 4–9; clear questions of, asking, during retreats, 200–201; contextualizing, skewed trajectory for, 158–159; defined, xi; joy of, 18, 35, 47, 77, 86, 101, 138, 166, 201; learning, from without, 34–36; loss of, in American boyhood, 13–24; loss of, within communities, 132–134; meaning of, agreeing on the, 8; needing, gender

MORE RESOURCES FROM MICHAEL GURIAN

THE MINDS OF BOYS
Saving Our Sons from Falling Behind in School and Life

Michael Gurian and Kathy Stevens

ISBN: 978-0-7879-9528-7 | Paperback

"Michael Gurian and Kathy Stevens pull the pieces together in The Minds of Boys, *including the social, emotional, physical, and cognitive needs of boys. This is a must-read for educators from preschool through young adulthood and for any parent or grandparent who is raising a boy. This book is well researched, offering concrete ways to help our boys develop and flourish in and out of school."*
—Dr. Paul D. Slocumb, author, *Hear Our Cry: Boys in Crisis*

In *The Minds of Boys*, Michael Gurian shows parents and teachers how to help boys overcome their current classroom obstacles by helping to create the proper learning environment, understand how to help boys work with their unique natural gifts, nurture and expand every bit of their potential, and enable them to succeed in life.

Gurian presents a whole new way of solving the "boy's crisis" based on the success of his program in schools across the country, the latest research, and application of neurobiological research on how boys' brains actually work and how they can learn very well when they're properly taught.

Anyone who cares about the future of our boys must read this book.

BOYS AND GIRLS LEARN DIFFERENTLY!
A Guide for Teachers and Parents

Michael Gurian

ISBN: 978-0-7879-6117-6 | Paperback

"The insights and innovations in Boys and Girls Learn Differently! *have been applied in our classrooms with phenomenal success, leading to better academic performance and better behavior. I highly recommend this book to all parents, teachers, and school administrators."*

—Dan Colgan, superintendent of schools, St. Joseph, Missouri

"Boys and Girls Learn Differently! *offers valuable and much-needed tools to provide boys and girls with true equal educational opportunities. The new techniques Michael Gurian presents here will transform our classrooms and the way parents teach their children in very positive ways."*

—John Gray, author, *Children Are from Heaven* and *Men Are from Mars, Women Are from Venus*

In this profoundly significant book, author Michael Gurian synthesizes the current scientific evidence and clearly demonstrates how the distinction in hard-wiring and socialized gender differences affects how boys and girls learn. Gurian presents a new way to educate our children based on brain science, neurological development, and chemical and hormonal disparities. The innovations presented in this book were applied in the classroom and proven successful, with dramatic improvements in test scores, during a two-year study that Gurian and his colleagues conducted in six Missouri school districts.

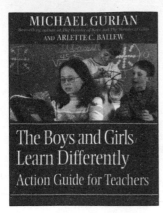

THE BOYS AND GIRLS LEARN DIFFERENTLY ACTION GUIDE FOR TEACHERS

Michael Gurian and Arlette C. Ballew

ISBN: 978-0-7879-6485-6 | Paperback

"Guidance on how to create 'ultimate classrooms' at all grade levels."
—Chicago Tribune

The landmark book *Boys and Girls Learn Differently!* outlines the brain-based educational theories and techniques that can be used to transform classrooms and help children learn better. Now *The Boys and Girls Learn Differently Action Guide for Teachers* presents experiential learning techniques that teachers can use to create an environment and enriched curriculum that take into account the needs of the developing child's brain and allow both boys and girls to gain maximum learning opportunities.

This important and easy-to-use guide offers information on what all children need to be able to learn effectively, based on the latest scientific scholarship on the differences between boy's and girl's brains, neurological development, hormonal effects, behavior, and learning needs. Michael Gurian and his colleagues applied these recent discoveries in the field during a two-year Gurian Institute pilot program in Missouri that led to measurably better academic performance and improved behavior.

NURTURE THE NATURE
Understanding and Supporting Your Child's
Unique Core Personality

Michael Gurian

Now in Paperback!
ISBN: 978-0-470-32252-9

"As scientifically sound as it is humane."
> —Harold S. Koplewicz, M.D., chairman, Department of Child and Adolescent Psychiatry, New York University School of Medicine; founder and director, New York University Child Study Center

"Nurture the Nature should be mandatory reading for parents who want their children to mature into happy, healthy human beings— which is of course all of us!"
> —Dr. Tracey J. Shors, Department of Psychology, Center for Collaborative Neuroscience, Rutgers University

Based on the most recent brain research, *Nurture the Nature* features the Ten Tips for Nurturing the Nature of Your Baby, self-tests, checklists, and many other tools for you to help your kids get exactly the kind of support they need, from infants to adolescents.

While offering positive ideas for nurturing your child, Gurian also shows how to avoid the stress, pressures, and excessive competition of what he identifies as social trends parenting. Most parents know instinctively that their child is unique and has special potential, weaknesses, and strengths. No child is a blank slate. Gurian calls on parents to turn away from one-size-fits-all approaches and instead support the individual core nature of a child with effective and customized loving care.